Xx

JOIN THE  Y!

"I have just finished accompanyi[illegible]g Mathilda [illegible] her [illegible] ng and dramatic journey through the twentieth century. For a time in which 'family' is under heavy assault in our society, the author has created a living portrait of a family as a true community, interactive and mutually supportive in times of stress . . . For the many outside her own family who touched or were touched by this intrepid woman during her long journey, it will stir many a rich recollection . . . A TRULY UNIQUE ACHIEVEMENT!"

— Richard W. Solberg, Historian
author, *God and Caesar*

"'*No One Cried at Her Funeral*'—Bob Lee tells us early on about the last event centering on his mother which drew together her far-spread clan. By the end of her story I could understand why. *MATHILDA'S JOURNEY* is about a life to be celebrated. Reading it, I became an absorbed traveling companion. I watched this indomitable woman of faith plant roots, establish community, survive the Great Depression and support her family and country through two world wars. I entered into her life's celebration . . . and cried a little too."

— Naomi Fro[illegible]
author, *Golden Visions, B[illegible]*

"What a wonderful job—a full and rich portrait . . . I can see my own mother in much of what is written about Mathilda, and I'm sure many other readers will make the same kind of identification. She is representative of Norwegian Lutheran women of her era: devoted to family, church, country. What a gift . . . It will be a treasure for years to come!"

— Paul Enger, New York
TV and Radio Writer, for CBS News

MATHILDA'S JOURNEY

The Life of Clara Mathilda Glasrud Lee

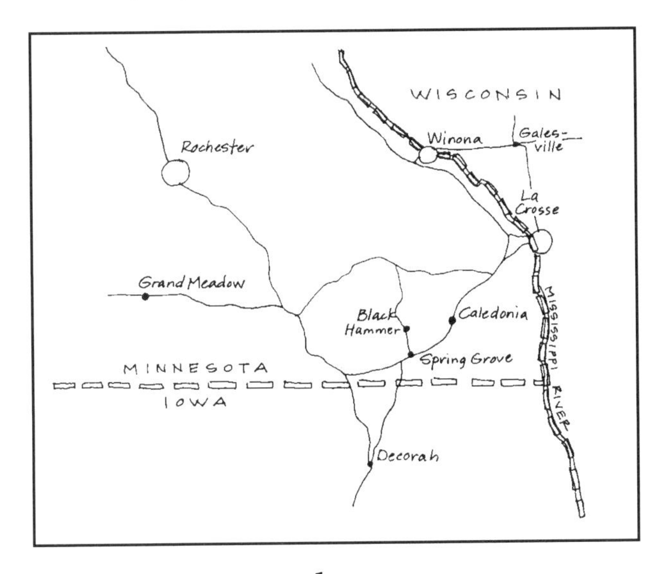

by

Robert E. A. Lee

Illustrations by Margaret Lee Yu

REALWorld Communications
Baldwin, New York

Mathilda's Journey: The Life of Clara Mathilda Glasrud Lee
by Robert E. A. Lee

For additional copies of this book, please send $16.95 plus $1.55 shipping and handling for each copy to the publisher:

REALWorld Communications
766 Lakeside Drive
Baldwin, New York 11510-3509
E-mail: Rlee391325@aol.com
Fax: 516-868-7662

Book design, production, and cover art by:
The Floating Gallery
331 W. 57th St, #465, New York, NY 10019

PRINTED IN THE UNITED STATES OF AMERICA

Lee, Robert E. A.,
Mathilda's Journey: The Life of Clara Mathilda Glasrud Lee
1. Title 2. Author 3. Biography 4. Inspiration

Library of Congress Catalog Card Number 99-76009
ISBN 0-9675900-0-0 Softcover

Dedicated to my four sisters
Barbara, Juliet, Margaret, Naomi
and to the memory of Sylvia and Bill

CONTENTS

ACKNOWLEDGEMENTS

A tape recorder is a marvelous tool. I am grateful for its indispensable help in generously capturing memories of my mother, Mathilda. I was relentless in bothering her and her other children (and several of her grandchildren) with my microphone and my questions. Mother herself, though often reluctant, sat for me and for my even more assertive brother Knute (Bill). Her oral history actually prompted me to write her story. Thanks go to each of my siblings for submitting to my questioning. Their voices, often peppered with effervescent outbursts, provided much of the narrative, which I was honored to edit.

Fortunately a trove of letters to and from Mother was available. Oral memory is very often flawed but dated correspondence is more nearly accurate; it is the precious documentation any biographer needs. Because my brother, like me, saved almost everything, his input into this project was enormous. When he sensed that his memory was failing (from Alzheimer's disease that led to his death in 1999) he sent all his old letters to me. I am sad that he could not savor the results of his collaboration.

Images of Mathilda, both candid and posed, came from the photograph collections of various relatives. A special word of thanks to sisters Naomi Hysell and Juliet Seim, to brother-in-law Paul Thies and cousin Borghild Knutson. We didn't have to rely only on snapshots. Our ancestors took pride in going to Frank Joerg's or Palen's studios where the local photographer would patiently pose his subjects in front of the big plate camera, disappearing at intervals to hide under the black hood in order to adjust the focus.

I am grateful to have had access to local newspapers, especially the *Spring Grove Herald* whose files were made available to me on microfilm through the courtesy of the Minnesota Historical Society and the Baldwin Public Library. Staff at Preus Library at Luther College found clippings and other references from Mathilda's days in Decorah in the 1890s.

My wife, Elaine, and my immediate family have been patient, encouraging, and editorially helpful throughout the years of preparation and writing. I thank them for prodding me and having faith that this biography would some day be fully realized. A special "thank you" to my team of editors—daughters Sylvia and Barbara—who worked through drafts with me and saved me from many goofs and redundancies and to daughter Peg, who invested her artistic talent in photo selection and original illustrations.

Finally, thanks to God for giving us Mathilda, our mother—an individualist very much worth writing about and, we pray, reading about.

Soli Deo Gloria!

Robert E. A. Lee
Baldwin, New York

PREFACE

Some souls seem bigger than life. They're the ones about whom you hear, "I was always in awe of her." Their persona has an aura of dignity and distinction that makes them memorable. Sometimes they are loved—or feared—in a special way. Their legend lives on long after them.

Such a soul was Mathilda. To me she has always qualified as an awesome, dignified and distinguished personage. But then, she was my mother. After I had decided to write her story, I discovered during my research, especially through interviewing so many who knew her, that I certainly was not alone in my estimation of her.

This biography has the goal of laying out the facts of who she was and what she did—how and when and why and where. But it also seeks to reveal her character, a product of a pioneer Minnesota farm family of Lutherans with roots in Norway. Mathilda's stalwart character was molded by her strong-willed widowed mother who had managed a farm for and with her large family of seven sons and two daughters.

The drama of this documentary story carries Mathilda from farm girl into womanhood as a teen-age teacher, a young bride of an enterprising horseman (her emotional opposite), a mother of five daughters and two sons, an activist in educational, church and community affairs in small-town America, a brave battler against the Great Depression's assault on human dignity, and a worried mom during World War II with part of her family actively engaging the enemy. We find Mathilda accepting new challenges in the post-war era—opportunities where she was needed and where she could make a difference. And, as the years pulled her into temporary and transient grandmother-in-residence roles in the homes of her children, she flew around the country from north to south and from east to west. Stories about her accumulated wherever she landed. Because she was also a writer—of articles, histories, newspaper reports and lots of personal letters—much of her story is told in her own words.

I had known for years that some day I would have to tell her story. This is it.

My hope is that *Mathilda's Journey* will speak to many beyond those who may have known her or felt family connections. If tomorrow's generation—those growing up in the 21st Century—can also vicariously share in some of her experiences during her life's journey, this labor of love will have been more than worthwhile.

MATHILDA'S JOURNEY

The Life of Clara Mathilda Glasrud Lee

by

Robert E. A. Lee

Illustrations by Margaret Lee Yu

CHAPTER ONE

No One Cried at Her Funeral

At first it was something of a shock. In arriving at the funeral of my mother, Mathilda, I was prepared for the kind of somber silence and dour expressions on mourners' faces that fit the definition of funereal. I was greeted instead by a loud and happy—really noisy—chatter of several hundred relatives and close family friends.

They had all gathered in the church basement before the ceremony so we could form a procession down the aisle following the casket. The talk and laughter was as joyful as at any family reunion. And, whatever else this was, it was a reunion, a rare gathering of the clan. A party.

It was a Saturday in the summer of 1978. My wife Elaine and I had flown in the day before from New York. My sisters met us at the airport in soggy, flooded Rochester, Minnesota. We drove together down the 70 or so miles to our hometown of Spring Grove, in the corner county of Minnesota with Wisconsin 30 miles east and Iowa 10 miles south.

My mother, Clara Mathilda Glasrud Lee, had died on Wednesday, July 5, in St. Mary's Hospital in Rochester, just 15 days before her 95th birthday. At the time I was working on the finishing touches of the film for PBS that would cap my career for Lutheran Film Associates. The actor who played Johann Sebastian Bach in *The Joy of Bach*, Brian Blessed, had flown over from London to record narration for us. He and my production colleagues were aware that Mother was in critical condition after an earlier fall down a flight of stairs. They were wonderfully supportive and solicitous. When my sister Naomi phoned with the news, we made immediate plans to fly "home."

The word of her death came more as a sigh of relief and resignation than as a crushing blow. For an anxious week we had been apprised daily of her condition by our sisters who had been keeping vigil at the hospital. By telephone they had rehearsed over and over with us the grim details of her accident: she had taken the wrong door at night as she left the bathroom and fallen down the basement stairs. Her neck was broken. She could not accept nourishment. The bruises, including a fractured shoulder, caused swelling and pain. We heard what they said but we couldn't really fathom it all from afar. I remember only that I mentally formulated a prayer of thanks that the moment of death, for which she had been living for almost a century, had at long last arrived.

Among our relatives there was only one Mathilda. She never used her first name, Clara. The legends about this remarkable woman started long before she died. On the ride down to the funeral I heard one of the final anecdotes from her last days in the hospital that typified the special pungency of Mathilda's personality.

Mother had a visitor one day when no one from our family was present. A young intern-pastor from her home church came on a pastoral visit. He took his role very seriously, according to her roommate at St. Mary's Hospital who later shared the story of what happened. The young seminarian spoke to Mathilda and asked if she would like some scripture read. "That would be nice," she said. So he read. Then he asked if she would want him to pray. "Yes, that would be nice, too." He prayed. Then he asked if she had any further questions. He really didn't know our mother very well, if at all. And she was perhaps seeing him for the first time.

She hadn't lost her sense of humor, apparently, for she faced him with a real question: "What's it all about?" We don't know his answer. Perhaps he's still thinking it over. But we think she knew the answer for herself.

Seeing the open casket at the funeral home late that Friday afternoon did not particularly bother me. I understood the tradition but, if there has to be a casket at all, I would normally prefer it to be closed. I have been conditioned by my Christian training to feel that the dead body is no longer the person. What I saw might just as well have been a wax figure. An embalmed body looks rather waxy, anyway, doesn't it? But to me it was not Mathilda, my mother. I did observe the familiar Glasrud family profile that I and some of my own children shared. I saw the lovely pink gown she had worn at her 90th birthday celebration. On her finger was the lovely ring my sister Naomi had given her. I winced a bit when I saw that her spectacles were covering her closed eyes. The logic of that strange symbolism escaped me. The corpse was at peace, certainly, but I felt a strange reflection of swollen suffering from her face.

In New York we would call this a wake. Lutherans in the Midwest don't have a good name for it. "Visitation" is the best we could come up with. But it really was a wake in the sense that it was "a party watching over the dead, sometimes accompanied by festivities." All of Mathilda's living children were there, most with spouses. There were grandchildren and great grandchildren and nieces and nephews and cousins—once, twice and thrice removed—and neighbors and friends. We of the immediate family were engulfed with love and concern. We chatted and recollected and inquired and reported. The legend of Mathilda was rehearsed. It was exhausting but also restorative.

The next day the 2 p.m. funeral service at Trinity Lutheran Church came almost too quickly. The basement parlors, where the aroma of brewing coffee had been clinging to my memory from childhood, were almost full of un-mournful mourners. Lively chatter filled the room. Then, as if someone had turned down the volume control, the buzzing suddenly stopped. Someone must have spotted the pastor coming. The silence was unreal, a loud reminder that we were there, after all, for a sacred duty and ritual.

The Rev. Kenneth Knutson was one of those soft-faced, friendly clergy whose smile seemed to precede his entry into a room. We all looked at him as he spoke simply and beautifully. Then he prayed in words of clear affirmation, reassurance and thanksgiving. He had set the tone for the worship service ahead of us. We followed him up the stairs to the large sanctuary—the same vaulted auditorium where we all, Mathilda's children, had been baptized and confirmed, where we had sung in the choir and been nurtured in the 1920s and 1930s by pastors Alfred Johnson and Oscar Mikkelson.

Music is such a powerful vehicle for communicating emotional and spiritual feeling and we knew it belonged in any celebration of our mother's life. This was to be a service of thanksgiving, praise and hope, not a gloomy droning of dirges. So we picked celebratory hymns: *Praise to the Lord, The Almighty* and *Now Thank We All Our God.* These would underscore the spirit we wanted the service to have.

I had agreed to sing Mother's favorite song, *The Holy City.* I knew it would be difficult to do this, but I wanted to, nevertheless. She had always asked for it when we were making music at home. And when I had sung it, surely dozens of times, she had hummed along and nodded in recognition of the words. Certainly the eschatological meaning of the words, based on the heavenly vision from the Bible's last book, *Revelation*, was just right for her final rites.

Elaine had agreed to play the organ for me and we had checked out the instrument the night before in a brief rehearsal. It was a good thing we did because we found several keys that emitted no sound. (The old organ was later to be replaced by a marvelous new tracker-action instrument.) Elaine knew how to compensate by avoiding the mute notes. She needed no music (she had accompanied my singing for almost four decades) and we determined she would play it in the key of A flat.

Probably no one in the packed church knew the score well enough to discern what happened when Elaine went to the organ and I stood by her in the choir area. She momentarily forgot that we had settled on A flat and automatically started in B flat. After a couple of bars she remembered, and deftly modulated into the lower key while still in the introduction.

My voice was a little more pinched from emotion than I would have liked, but I was able to control it adequately. I concentrated on interpreting the text that I had studied afresh to restore the memorization that had begun over forty years earlier. I had to watch myself carefully to maintain composure. Where does one look when singing in homage to one's mother at her funeral—

at the altar, the casket, the family, the congregation, the stained glass windows? The answer: all of the above. It helped me to focus on the thought that this was my offering, my tribute, and I wanted to share it.

I suppose my older brother, Bill, a pastor himself, felt the same way as he got up to express in spoken words the appreciation of our family. (He was known to most persons outside our family by our father's name, Knute.) He spoke warmly of the Gospel that was Mother's hope and also ours.

Pastor Knutson said in his sermon that a few weeks before, Mathilda had talked to him as she was leaving the Sunday morning church service. She approached him at the door where he was greeting the departing worshipers. She stopped to tell him that something in his sermon had prompted her to think about and anticipate death. Then, as they stood there, she recited for him the entire final stanza of William Cullen Bryant's poem, *Thanatopsis*:

> *So live that when thy summons comes to join*
> *The innumerable caravan that moves*
> *To that mysterious realm, where each shall take*
> *His chamber in the silent halls of death,*
> *Thou go not, like the quarry-slave at night,*
> *Scourged to his dungeon, but, sustained and soothed*
> *By an unfaltering trust, approach thy grave*
> *Like one who wraps the drapery of his couch*
> *About him, and lies down to pleasant dreams.*

And those words became a part of his funeral sermon for her.

It wasn't the music or the perfectly personalized sermon that brought a constriction to my throat. Surprisingly to me, it was *The Lord's Prayer*. I suddenly remembered that time when I was a small child—it is actually the earliest memory I hold—when Mother taught me that prayer along with others. I know where the bed was and in which room I was when it was time for "Now I Lay Me Down to Sleep."

The cemetery in Spring Grove is a half-mile west of the small town. I had marched there playing trumpet in the high school band on many a Memorial Day. This time a caravan of us followed the hearse there. The committal ceremony was somber, but the weather smiled on us. It was a glorious day. We, the children of Mathilda and her husband, Knute, were remembering him too as we stood at his grave, next to hers, and read the dates on his marker: 1879-1939. After the simple service, someone mentioned that when

Mother visited the plot a month or so previously, she had remarked that she would soon be there, too.

In Spring Grove after funerals, there is always the ritual of coffee and sandwiches for everyone. So we went back to the church basement hall. Again, it had the feel of a reunion party. I enjoyed table-hopping, chatting with relatives and Mother's friends and neighbors. Having been living away from my hometown for 40 years, I knew more faces than names. One woman kindly told me that she was present at my birth, helping with the domestic work of a household that, with my arrival, had seven children. Another woman said Mathilda had taught her to knit. Several mentioned how she had actively participated in Bible study discussions when their circle met.

Bill wanted to act out the biblical tradition of children burying their parents. My brother as a pastor had officiated at many funerals himself. He had urged me to bring dungarees along when I flew out for the funeral. Now he got me aside and suggested we drive out to the cemetery again, alone, and fill in the grave. He had already checked with the gravediggers and had paid them their normal wages in order to be sure they wouldn't misunderstand our motives.

We changed clothes and took the shovels that had been set out for us to use. After a brief prayer at the open grave, we went to work. The damp clay was heavy so it took us about a half-hour. For us both it was a new experience. It seemed somehow to seal our physical attendance at her burial and it made these last rites more real and earthy.

After the relatives, neighbors and friends drifted away, there we were—the four daughters and two sons of Mathilda and Knute. It was picture-taking time for the six of us siblings alone and with our spouses. (Our oldest sister, Sylvia, had died in 1965 at the age of 57.)

That evening and the next day, we siblings had a conference while we sorted through Mother's effects in her Spring Grove apartment. She owned the house where we had lived as a family since 1912. Over the years after the end of World War II, she had rented out the downstairs for the meager income it produced and had renovated the upstairs as her own apartment.

Many families have trouble at this point. We had none. We agreed that Barbara and Juliet would handle the estate. And we had a memorable time together, discovering old papers, pictures, letters. What should be saved? What could be tossed out? We had fun comparing finds: a laugh over a picture, a guessing game as to who this or that ancestor on the picture was, the excitement of finding a book or a piece of jewelry that one of us had given Mother once upon a time.

"I have a copy of this picture, so why don't you take it?" was heard many times. Clothes, dishes, furniture, silver—memorabilia of a lifetime. Mathilda's spirit certainly pervaded the exploration into her history. Her daughters remained to complete the task while her sons with their wives returned to the west and east coasts.

Just before we departed on Monday noon, we had a little devotional time together. Feelings flowed to the surface in the prayers we struggled to share. And then we strained our way through the Doxology: *Praise God From Whom All Blessings Flow*.

I have said that no one cried at her funeral. That's true. But tears, at least for me, finally came. It was time. The saved-up emotions of that unforgettable weekend found their release, once I was in the car, about to drive away from Spring Grove.

The experience was etched deeply on my soul. It was one of those memorable crossroads of life. Somehow, we define ourselves, who we are and what we are about in this life, by the self-reflections that come with the death of a loved one—a parent, particularly; a mother, especially. That mysterious bond of belonging is severed and it inevitably induces a sense of loneliness.

Mathilda's surviving children: (L-R) Knute (Bill), Naomi, Margaret, Juliet, Barbara and Robert (Bob) shown together after her 1978 funeral.

With Mathilda's death, an era had ended. This remarkable matriarch was gone. The house that had been our home would soon be emptied of the memories we would now have to store elsewhere. But much remained.

Hope remained. We had affirmed it in the funeral service in the words from the creed we all had spoken in unison: "I believe . . . in the resurrection of the body and the life everlasting."

Most of those who knew our mother saw her as special. They saw her as someone with a kind of peppery personality—an individualist. But who was she, really? What was driving her life? I now look back a century and more as I begin exploring the 95-year-long life journey of Mathilda.

CHAPTER TWO

At Home in Black Hammer

Mathilda's children always felt a strong link to the Glasrud farm in Black Hammer. I vividly remember countless rides over the five hilly miles between Spring Grove and that community of farms in the next township to the northwest. Both our mother's and our father's families had lived there.

As a hamlet, Black Hammer was merely an intersection of county roads, only a stop sign between a brick church with its cemetery and a small country store. The surrounding area, a township of about 23,000 acres, carried the hamlet's name and contained a hilly array of small farms. Most of them, like the Glasrud place, had been grubbed out of woods and prairie.

"So many people, even members of my family, have wondered how Black Hammer got its name," my mother wrote in 1955:

> Black Hammer is a most admirable name because there is none other like it in America, nor will there be, unless some resident moving farther west shall carry the name with him. This is the way the township finally got its name:
>
> Knud Olsen Bergo, who was living just across the town line in Spring Grove, noticed one morning upon arising that a fire had swept over the prairie in the south part of the town, including a bluff which formed a part of sections 27, 28 and 34. Its charred appearance at once suggested to his mind a certain bluff located in Slidre Valders, Norway, which was Mr. Bergo's birthplace. He exclaimed (in Norwegian), "Sort Hammer," which signifies "Black Bluff," and the people have had the good sense to retain the name to this day, which is composed of an English and a Norwegian word.

That combination of the two languages was certainly echoed in the speech of the farm families located there; most had emigrated from Norway, especially from the area around the picturesque Sognefjord. They were often known as Sognings. A number of family names in Black Hammer can be found on the map of the towns, communities and large farms bordering that most glorious of Norway's fjords.

It was into this setting that Clara Mathilda Glasrud was born in Black Hammer on July 20, 1883.

A log house was her birthplace. But that was her home for only a year. Her father, with the help of his sons and neighbors, had built a new home for his growing family. It was ready in 1884.

> The earliest recollection I have—I don't know if it is a true one or just a fancy—I was one year old, they said, when we moved into the house they had built. We had been about a quarter of a mile up in the field in a large log house. This was moved down to where they built the new house and they used it there as a granary.
>
> I have a vague recollection of people coming in the evening. It must have been a housewarming or a little

> surprise. Because I can remember having gone to bed and waking up and I can remember my father picking me up in his arms. I can remember that. So I think it must be true, not just fantasy.

Peter Anton Glasrud, my mother's father, had bought land less than a mile west of the church with money earned working in lumbering in northern Wisconsin just prior to his marriage. His boyhood home had been in a similar farm community, Wilmington Township, on the opposite side of Spring Grove, about 10 miles away. Peter had been born in Toten, Norway, and was seven years old when his parents, Christian and Berthe Maria Halvorsdatter Haukaas, emigrated. They came first to Wisconsin and then to Iowa before settling in Houston County in Minnesota. When he was 15 years old, he and his older brother, John, were mainly responsible for the farm work because their father, famous as an adventurous soul, had joined the Union army to fight in the Civil War.

Peter met his future bride, Sigrid Qualey, in his Wilmington home community. She was one of 12 children of Per and Gitlaug Qualey (sometimes spelled Quale). In 1852 they had come from the Sogndal area of Norway to Koshkonong, a Norwegian settlement near Madison, Wisconsin, where Sigrid was born in 1853. At that time Koshkonong was becoming crowded, and with word that promised farms would be available farther west, many, including several families of Qualeys, moved on. Sigrid was just one year old in 1854 when her parents found a new farm home in Wilmington, the same area where the Glasruds arrived in 1855 after first staying a year in northern Iowa.

These were people with a strong sense of tradition. While they were enthusiastic Americans, they lived with the proud values of Norwegians—solid, staunch, and strong in their pious, but not pietistic, Lutheranism.

My mother told me that both her parents spoke English as well as their native Norwegian, and added:

> They spoke English not perfectly, but adequately, I think. My father had some education. I don't know just where he went to school. But he wrote well and he was quite a reader. My grandparents didn't speak English well. My grandfather could manage all right but I don't think my grandmother ever learned to speak English.

Mathilda was born into a family that then consisted of four brothers and a sister. The following roll call indicates the ages of each at the time Mathilda arrived:

Christian. [1873-1960] He was the oldest (age 10) and was known always as Christ (pronounced "Krisst"). He lived to be 83 and became a legendary farm implement and automobile dealer who owned the first car in Spring Grove, reported to be a "White Steamer." He and his wife, Malinda ("Lindy") had two sons and six daughters: Sigrid, Julia, Maria, Peter, Borghild, Olga, Helen and George.

Julia. [1875-1902] She was then old enough (age 8) to help take care of her infant sister. She became a musician who, at age 22, married a neighbor, Cornelius Ike. They had a son, Clarence, and twin daughters, Sigrid and Maren. Maren lived only six weeks, but survived by a month her mother, Julia, who died two weeks after childbirth. By contrast, Sigrid, who was raised by her grandmother Sigrid, lived a long life, well into her ninth decade.

Peter. [1876-1926] Next in line (age 7), he was a schoolboy at that time along with his older brother. He became a merchant in Northwood, North Dakota and served ten years there as mayor. He and his younger brother, Duffy, married the Steenstrup sisters. Peter and his wife Mathilda became parents of a daughter, Lyla.

Theodore. [1879-1948] Ted (age 4) was a curly-haired, blond youngster and maintained a fair, sandy-haired look all his life. His son and grandson, both carrying on the name Ted Glasrud, inherited the appearance and the warmth of his personality. Mathilda thought that, of all her brothers, Ted most resembled his father. Ted married Abby Rosendahl in 1913 and spent most of his life in White Bear, Minnesota. In addition to their son, they had two daughters, Phyllis and JoAnn.

Adolph. [1881-1961] Always known as Duffy (age 2), he became Mathilda's playmate, especially in their pre-school years; later, in their teens, he was helpful to her when they were students together at boarding school in Decorah, Iowa. Duffy enjoyed success as an implement dealer in Fargo and became a "gentleman farmer," often flying in his own plane to inspect his crops outstate in North Dakota. He and his wife Ida Steenstrup had a son, Donald.

Those siblings were the welcoming family for Mathilda at her birth in July of 1883. But the children kept coming at two and three year intervals. These were the additions:

Edwin. [1885-1979] From childhood on, he had the strong Glasrud face, easily recognized in family photos. Like several of his brothers, he did his work stint in North Dakota before returning to Spring Grove where he became a life-long farmer. He and his bride, Gunhild Gulbrandson, were married in 1915 and raised five sons: Paul, Leslie, William, Raymond and Peter. Seven sons in all were born, but one died at birth and another in early infancy.

Arthur. [1887-1978] He followed the family tradition of farming for some years in the Red River Valley (Kittson County, Minnesota) and then returned to become a merchant in Spring Grove. He and his first wife, Amanda Myhro, who died in 1947, had six daughters—one of whom, Pernella, died at age 12. The others were Sylvia, Lillian, Dorothy, Marcella and Delores. Arthur later married Elsie Landsverk.

William. [1890-1971] Best known as Willie to his family and as Bill to some others, he had his sister, Mathilda, to help care for him in that busy household. Later she even was his teacher in the one-room school near their farm. Willie and his first wife, Lillian Johnson [1891-1962], farmed the Glasrud home farm for fifty years. He married Genevieve Hysell in 1966.

Gertrude. [1892-1893] Mathilda's younger sister, born six months before her father died, lived only six months after his death.

Left: Julia Glasrud at age sixteen. Right: Mathilda Glasrud at age eight.

Life on the farm for Mathilda was bound to be energetic and often hectic as is the case in any large family. The two sisters among seven strong and healthy brothers in that household created a vitality that made for challenges, delights, problems and many memories:

> I can well remember that in summer, even after we had the windmill and a cistern, it was so dry in August; there was no wind. Then we had to drive the cattle down

to the creek. That was two miles. We thought it was fun. We really did. We let the cattle graze along the road down to the bridge. Skadsen had a log house there before you got to the creek.

Mathilda (seated) with her brothers, (L-R) Christian, Edwin, Adolph, Peter, William, Arthur and Theodore.

Like any child would, Mathilda explored the fields, woods, valleys, flora and fauna of Black Hammer. "I walked through the woods to school for years. Oh, we saw woodchucks and skunks and things like that but I never saw anything like a fox or a wolf," she told me in a recorded talk in 1965. "I can remember Indians came around. They used to go down by the creek during the summer and they looked for herbs and things."

Mathilda wrote about the native Americans in her *History of Houston County*:

> Near Riceford are the remains of what might have been fortifications . . . They have been plowed over, and other eroding processes have been at work and now some of them are almost completely obliterated.
>
> There is also in the vicinity a cave, or cavern, that may

> have been formed or modified by human hands. It has an entrance not unlike a door, four feet square, and extends a thousand feet or so, varying in height from five to six feet. In 1882 a gold coin was found in this cavern by Peter C. Carrier, son of William Carrier. It was about the size of a $5 gold piece and bore no intelligible inscription.

Religion was the foundation of living for these Norwegian Lutheran pioneers. Their parents and ancestors in the Old Country had been grounded in faith and doctrine. They prayed and they worshipped—in Norwegian.

When Peter and Sigrid came to Black Hammer in 1872, a congregation was there to welcome them. It had been formed in 1857 as a result of the missionary work of the legendary Pastor F. C. Clausen, whose parish extended from the Root River to the Iowa River. Later the church was combined with Spring Grove and Wilmington. Until the frame church was built, just four years before the arrival of the Glasruds, worship was in homes.

An article about the history of that congregation, now known as Faith Lutheran Church, in the February 5, 1991 issue of the *Spring Grove Herald*, describes worship at the time of Mathilda's childhood:

> Services were quite different over a hundred years ago. The men and boys sat on one side and the women and younger children sat on the other side. They didn't have Sunday School, so the pastor catechized the children, while standing in the aisle after the last hymn was sung. They also had the "Churching of Mothers," which was a special blessing by the pastor of the mother and child to be baptized.

The first choir was formed in 1888 and doubtless Julia and several of her brothers were among the singers.

In a sketch about her mother, Mathilda wrote, "Sigrid Glasrud was instrumental in helping to organize the Black Hammer *Kvinde Forening* or Ladies' Aid. The first meeting was held at her home."

Mathilda explained, "We didn't go to church every Sunday. Our minister had three congregations . . . so we only had services every third Sunday for a while." She added that on other Sundays at home her father would read from the sermons of Martin Luther.

> I remember sitting and listening. Of course we had a big house. It could be around the table. They were all sermons of Luther. I have that book—*Hus Postile*—a great big book but the print is large, too. I have read some of them but it seems like they are a little bit cumbersome for us to read now because what we have now is more condensed and more concise . . . We did have the Sundays of the Church Year and the text for them in the old small hymnbooks, too—the hymnbooks without notes, you know. The language was in the Norwegian instead of English. Lots of times that Norwegian comes back to me in religion better than the English.

The spiritual life of her family had always been a favorite topic our mother would be happy to expand upon. And so she continued:

> I imagine services started at 10:30 or 11 a.m., and we would, of course, clean up and then get ready. I suppose we'd probably had a bath on Saturday night. I was kind of carefree in those days. My sister made my clothes and combed my hair and fixed me up for Sunday. I don't think we ever walked to church. I can remember when I went for confirmation I didn't even walk then because the boys loved to hitch up and take me. They'd go home and probably come back and pick me up because they liked to do that, as boys today like to drive the car.
>
> In those days . . . they didn't have any organ. But we had what they called a Klokker and he would read the opening prayer and the closing prayer and he would lead the singing. He sat in the front bench. We had a man from Riceford and his name was Andrew Vick. He led the singing. He was really musical . . .
>
> The custodian, the man who rang the church bell, would be on the watch. When he saw the minister come over the hill, he would ring the bell. So then we knew the service would start because the minister was arriving. We sometimes could be there before the bell was rung. I can't ever remember that we were late to church. I liked to go to church.
>
> And another thing about the church: We had to learn our lessons for catechization. We would line up on the aisle of the church. I suppose some of them were quite

> bashful and wouldn't say it even if they knew the answers to questions the pastor would ask, but that never bothered me. If I knew it, I'd say it.

Mathilda was a life-long reader and lover of books. She told us:

> I had learned to read quite early and had finished my catechism. My mother had taught me that in Norwegian, so I asked my father if he would buy me a "Folklaring" explanation, which he did the next time he went to Spring Grove. It was such a beautiful book to me. But, alas, like all children, being careless, I was studying outside and left it lying on the grass. It rained in the night. I remember I got a little switching for that—not very severe, but needed.

The memories were not all idyllic. There was tragedy in her life, too. The poignant recall of grief seemed, ever after, to color her approach to life and death and give it a wistful seriousness. In her memoirs, which both my brother Knute and I had repeatedly urged her to write, and in her recorded interviews, she recalled a major emotional milestone of her life. She tells this story:

> My father died in September of 1892. I was then just past nine years old. I remember what he looked like and several things about him; but of course my memories of him are limited . . . I remember that he fell ill in March and I think quite soon after that he went to LaCrosse to seek medical aid at Doctors Christiansen and Gunderson. They didn't seem to know what ailed him. Sometime later Dr. Christiansen came up to see him. It wasn't that he didn't seek medical aid; they had good doctors in LaCrosse at that time. But he seemed to gradually get worse and I know he was in bed six weeks before he died. And he wasted away.

In his 1994 book, *Glæserud—Glasrud: A Family History*, Clarence "Soc" Glasrud states that Mathilda's father, his Uncle Peter (a brother of his own father, Claus), died from stomach cancer. Mathilda wasn't so sure what the malady was. "They said it wasn't cancer. It could have been leukemia or something like that, you know."

Left: Mathilda's mother, Sigrid Qualey Glasrud with baby Gertrude, who lived only one year. Right: Mathilda's father, Peter Anton Glasrud.

Soc includes a precious letter from Peter to Claus, who had gone to homestead in North Dakota. In that letter, written less than two months before he died, Peter wrote:

> I have been sick all summer since the month of March, and now I am so very thin and weak that I can hardly write three lines and these poor lines may perhaps be the last ones you will receive from me, dear brother, in this world. It doesn't seem to be God's will that I will get well again.

And the letter (in Norwegian) went on to describe his futile doctoring; in it he gave a strong testimony to his Christian faith.

Mother told me in her recorded interview:

> I can picture the death scene in my mind now. We were all there gathered together and he had, I think, said goodbye to all of us. He called me to his bedside and told me I should be good to my mother. I always tried to obey that admonition. I don't remember which others were there. I know Aunt Sigrid was there and her sister came and helped in the kitchen. I don't think my mother did any of the work at that time because she took care of him all the time. I think they had two beds in the room above the parlor. He just closed his eyes and slept away.
>
> My mother, now widowed, just had to carry on. That was it. With a big family, you just had to carry on. She

had the baby, Gertrude, who was only six months old. And I can remember her taking the little child in the wagon and walking back and forth outside. She was composed. I think I may be a little like her in character.

He left a wife, two daughters, seven boys and an infant child. The child died the following spring.

Mathilda wrote about her father's funeral:

They said there were one hundred teams—I guess Knute Ike counted them. They said they had come from Wilmington and Stillwater. I remember that everyone came to the house first and afterwards relatives and friends came back and were served a big meal. The funerals were conducted in the forenoon in those days . . .

The spring after my father died, my mother built the barn, which is still on the place . . . My father had quarried and hauled all the rock for the basement, and also had cut the timber. The beams were all hewn in those days. Besides our own family of ten, there were two stone masons and one "tender." There were also two and three carpenters for several months.

I think of the food used, the meat butchered and bread baked. It couldn't happen today. My sister Julia was my mother's mainstay at that time. I remember they were easy on me. I usually awakened by myself long after the rest had had breakfast. I think they found me useful as an errand girl. One chore, I remember, was very tedious. We had to churn all the butter needed. We did that in the cellar. I know we did have an icehouse. It was a job to dig into the sawdust for a chunk of ice and wash it off before dumping it into the milk tank. Sometimes the butter was slow in coming, and it was no fun to sit down there alone and turn the crank of the barrel churn. To vary the monotony, I used to count the revolutions up to one hundred and start over again, keeping on, it seemed, indefinitely.

On July 3, 1893, a very tragic accident occurred during the raising of the barn that my mother was having built. During barn raisings in those days many men were assembled to help raise and put into place the heavy timbers and cross beams. My two uncles, John and Gustav Glasrud, were standing together pulling up a beam when the noose slipped off the beam and John lost his balance and fell 16 feet to the plank floor below. He was carried to the house and placed on a mattress that was placed on the floor of what we called the parlor. A physician was summoned, but could do nothing. He died the following evening, July 4th, without regaining consciousness. It was very hard for his wife and his mother who both were there at the time. It was also hard for my mother who had then witnessed three deaths in her home in less than a year.

I think all this had a sobering effect on my life . . . I became very close to my mother. My mother's lot was not very easy. The boys were good workers, but high-spirited; she was given strength to carry on. She not only had to take care of housework, but also had to oversee things outdoors like bringing in calves from the woods, looking after breaks in fences, etc.

. . . my sister was a help so I could be spared, and often when my grandparents came over I would go back with them and sometimes spend as much as three or four weeks there. Somehow I did not get homesick. I think one reason for that was that there was quite a bit of reading material about the house. The people of the community—it was called the "Switch" [a landmark by the railroad tracks just east of the village of Spring Grove]—had belonged to a library club, the books of which were housed in the Switch schoolhouse. This club later disbanded and each member took his share of the books. That was how I became acquainted with stories of adventure by Hans Christian Andersen, *Aesop's Fables* and many others I have forgotten about. All stories were in the Norwegian language, of course.

I even attended school a couple of times in that district. I suppose their term lasted longer than ours did. They had a teacher who had been there for many years by the name of Halvar Lee. He undoubtedly added quite a bit of culture to the community, but I couldn't get along with his methods. I did just fine with everything else except the spelling. We would line up in a row, spell a word, and then give the meaning in Norwegian. Not having an English-Norwegian dictionary, what could I do? It seems to me there was something about passing up to the head of the class, too. Naturally, I did not, being at the foot of the class all the time. I don't think he kept school very many years after that. He did not have the necessary qualifications for English school. Then he became ill and passed away. He was the first one buried in the west-end cemetery of Spring Grove.

The next event of importance was when I was sent to Caledonia [about 15 miles east of Black Hammer] to stay with Uncle John and Aunt Sophie. I was to work for my board and room and go to school. They lived in the house just south of the courthouse in Caledonia. The house is still there. I really learned to work while there. She was a good housekeeper and I had to scrub floors on hands and knees, even the wooden sidewalk outdoors. Uncle often brought home company for dinner; and she was a good cook, so there would be piles of dishes and pots and pans. I used to run for it when I heard the last [school] bell ring. I was there for two school years. Aunt Sophie was of the Catholic faith.

I have many pleasant memories of going to school at home [in Black Hammer], especially during the spring and summer. We walked southward down one steep bluff and up another one. It was a long mile, whereas to drive around by the road it would be three miles. There were so many wildflowers to pick, so many different birds and wild animals to see. To this day when I smell wet ferns, I have to think of the walk to and from school. Once or twice a friend and I would stop and build a snowman. I remember once we tarried so long that one of my big brothers came to look for us.

I had a couple of friends I liked to visit. They were the Vinje girls, Mathilda and Oline. They were orphans. Their parents both died of TB and their grandmother took care of them. Their farm was rented. They had a room upstairs where all their mother's clothes were kept; some in trunks and some hanging on the walls. We used to go upstairs and play house and dress up in all those old clothes. Sanitary precautions as practiced today were not observed then, but we all survived to this day.

Her sister's wedding was a great family celebration and stories about it became part of the family legends. The Glasrud farm was fairly jumping with joy that summer night in 1897 when Julia married Cornelius Ike, a neighbor who lived just a short distance away, across the road and up the adjacent field.

Here is Mathilda's own account of the gala event:

> I believe that was the biggest wedding ever celebrated in Black Hammer. The preparations went on for weeks in advance. There was a lot of sewing going on—no buying of dresses in those days. I believe they butchered a cow, hog and sheep, besides having tubs full of lutefisk. There was a lady there for a week or more beforehand. I know they made about 75 pies, cookies and cakes besides lefse [a kind of potato pancake, almost mandatory at Norwegian festivals, as was the lye-soaked codfish delicacy, lutefisk]. There were two cooks hired for the day before and for the wedding day.
>
> A big tent was obtained and set up; long tables were made for the tent. I am not sure, but I believe 75 could eat at one time. I know there were more than 300 guests.
>
> My brother Christ, next to mother, was in charge. The two of them went to Spring Grove and came back with a shining new surrey. That was a rather elegant equipage in those days. Christ had a very nice black road team hitched to the surrey. It carried the bridal party to and from the church.
>
> There were three bridesmaids. Annie Dammen, aunt of the groom, was maid of honor. Ida Knutson and Josephine Glasrud were the other two. The groom's attendants were Helmer Ike, my brother Christ and my cousin, Christian Glasrud. The flower girls were Sarah Ike and Julia Glasrud.
>
> A platform was built down in the orchard for dancing. The bridal party was surprised by the fact that the Highland Prairie Concert Band arrived and added a lot to the entertainment. Pictures were also taken of the crowd. Many of them stayed for breakfast the next morning.

My mother never mentioned or referred specifically to it in her own writings or oral history interviews but Julia's daughter, Sigrid Vaaler, told me that she had heard that her aunt Mathilda, then 14, "danced all night!"

Mathilda's older sister Julia and her bridegroom, Cornelius Ike. The Glasrud farm was the scene of their gala wedding in 1887. Their marriage was short-lived; she died in 1902 and he in 1907.

In October of that same year, 1897, Mathilda was confirmed by the Reverend Eskild Jensen. She told me:

> There were thirteen of us in the class—three boys and ten girls. We were confirmed in the first frame church. The present church, which was built of brick, was erected two years later. After the old church was torn down, services were held at different homes. On several Sundays services were held in our barn, it being empty of hay at that time.
>
> In 1898 mother's first grandchild and our first nephew was born. As he was the first we all made a big fuss over him. He was Clarence Ike, the son of Julia and Cornelius.

Mathilda often referred to her hunger for learning. She was troubled, embarrassed, and regretful that she could not have the kind of formal education that young men, including some of her own brothers, might acquire at the turn of the century. Her voice breaking, she said:

> I feel that my education was so negligible that it isn't even worth talking about. I had finished, you might say, eight grades, although there was no examination. What would you do in a six months school?
>
> In this day and age when all you children got to high school and college and beyond that and I couldn't even . . . I know I wanted to go to school so badly after I was confirmed. I can remember I cried and cried because I wanted to go to school. And I suppose my mother couldn't afford to send me. Not because she didn't want to. But, of course, it wasn't very common for [women?] . . . this idea for learning. I suppose I had the curiosity probably. I was curious about things and wanted to know.

But Mathilda did manage to go on to school, at least for a year or so. And that's a story by itself as the narrative of her life continues:

> I think my mother had finally come to the conclusion that she was going to let me go. I heard afterwards that she had to borrow some money. It didn't cost very much, you know.

CHAPTER THREE

Teenage Student, Teenage Teacher

For a farm girl from a Norwegian enclave in Minnesota such as Black Hammer, Decorah was an ideal place to go to get an education.

Decorah was Norse-friendly. The northeastern Iowa community was home to many Norsemen who found their way to the United States in the 19th century. One of the most prominent Norwegian-American newspapers, *Decorah Posten*, was published there.

Decorah was also (somewhat) ethnically diverse. It was a community with German, Irish, English, and Polish residents along with the Norwegians; very few were French, Italian or Russian. It seems probable that most inhabitants of that town at the turn of the century had never even seen an African or Asian American.

Decorah was an educational center. During the Civil War, Luther College was re-planted (from its 1861 beginning in Wisconsin) first to downtown Decorah (McCloud Hotel) and later to a hilltop at the northwestern edge of the town. The college brought students to the town—no women then of course, but several hundred young men, most of whom were pre-seminarians on their way to becoming Lutheran pastors. In those days when few high schools existed, special academies were established; Decorah had two. One was the Valder School, training students for business careers and the other was the Decorah Institute, offering college and university preparatory work and teacher training.

Decorah also was a publishing center. The Lutheran Publishing House printed and distributed religious literature and hymnbooks. All this, and more, gave Decorah an almost cosmopolitan air much beyond its size as a village of several thousand souls.

Mathilda said, "I had been nagging my mother to send me some place to attend school, as I felt that I needed more education. Times were hard and money was scarce, but in the fall of 1898 I went to Decorah to attend Decorah Institute. Perhaps it was better known as Breckenridge's School."

Going away to school was a big step for the 15-year-old farm girl. It helped that she had already spent some time in Caledonia away from her family with her Uncle John and Aunt Sophie Qualy. The vast network of relatives—there were dozens of aunts and uncles and scores of cousins—helped her now in Decorah also. On hand as a student already at Breckenridge was Gedelia Qually (each Qualley family seemed to choose its own spelling), a first cousin. Although Gedelia was two years older, she and Mathilda became roommates. Mother wrote:

> I remember that my brother Duffy and a friend, Peter Holm, took me down [to Decorah]. I believe we borrowed Stenehjem's buggy, a long affair on which the back seat could be removed to make room for my trunk. The approximately 30 miles was a long trek in those days. It took more than five hours.
>
> I roomed and boarded with my cousin, Gedelia Qually, at Amelia Ruen's. Amelia was a cousin, in turn, of Gedelia's mother. She ran a dressmaking shop located across from what was then the McCloud Hotel.
>
> She had a kind of big apartment and we slept in a little alcove bedroom off of the room where she fitted her dresses for the ladies who came to her. She had a back

> bedroom and a kitchen and an outdoor toilet. And I think—did we pay $2.50 or $2.75 a week for room and board? And what we paid for tuition, I can't remember. Perhaps $10 or $15 a quarter. It was very low.

The Decorah Institute was something of a family affair. John Breckenridge and his wife Bertha had established the school a quarter-century before Mathilda Glasrud became a student there. Because there were few, if any, high schools in the area, it offered a rare chance, for teen-agers especially, to continue their education beyond the 8th grade. Four daughters were born to John and Bertha Breckenridge and undoubtedly were educated in the Institute. One of them, Mary, went on to the University of Iowa and her sister, Anna, to the University of Minnesota. Julia taught English and Physical Culture for Girls and Clarissa taught typewriting and stenography at the Decorah Institute while Mathilda was enrolled.

Breckenridge had "an efficient corps of assistants," according to W.E. Alexander in his 1882 *History of Winneshiek and Allamakee Counties*. One of them, J. W. Rich, the assistant director, wrote:

> The Decorah Institute was established by Prof. Breckenridge in September 1874. It occupies the building formerly used by the M.E. Church, and is situated on Broadway, south of the CourtHouse. The Arlington House is used as a boarding house where students obtain board at actual cost, it being amply fitted for the purpose, as well as for rooms for many of the students. The Decorah Institute draws pupils from adjoining counties and states. There were over 250 in attendance last year, and the number this year will probably be larger, as at the commencement of the school year there are over 150.

Bertha Breckenridge's role at the Institute was later commented on by the *Decorah Journal* on July 25, 1934 when it reported her death:

> Mrs. Breckenridge was not only a devoted wife and mother, but worked side by side with her husband in the development of the Decorah Institute. There her original teaching of history and literature inspired hundreds of young people to a broader vision and a finer appreciation.

Professor Breckenridge was a charismatic, legendary character, loved and feared by his students. It is clear to us, Mathilda's children, that she was indelibly impressed by this educator's precepts, which he delivered in daily talks to the student body. Here are some of them, collected by his wife and daughter Julia, and included in a 1946 history of the school, published on the occasion of the Iowa Centennial:

> When Sunday comes, students, get up in time to neatly dress for church. Start on time to be on time to begin with the minister and his congregation in the services of the Church.
>
> Be attentive to the sermon; don't let your thoughts stray to discover some mistake in pronunciation, or to detect a grammatical error.
>
> Do all you can to train your memory and don't give up training it as long as you live. Don't let a day go by, without putting some valuable fact or some fine bit of good literature in the keeping of your mental personage.
>
> Develop an appreciative taste for good reading and think about it until the good thought of your author becomes a part of your mental personage.
>
> Treat your physical personage, your body, with respect and care . . . Regular habits of eating plain, well-cooked food, moderate use of tea and coffee, regular hours of rest and sleep, of bathing and of exercise.
>
> Give your physical personage good care and it will respond with eagerness in helping you to be of the greatest good to yourself and to those around you.
>
> Be the ruler of your Kingdom of Self.

Mathilda didn't leave us completely in the dark about her days at school in Decorah. Some letters were preserved. They capture the naivete of a farm girl suddenly thrust into a new and somewhat urban environment. (Decorah, for a rural town, was considered large, but hardly a city.) The pencilled pages reveal the flighty silliness of a teen-ager who loved a good time, who had priorities that included boys—one in particular—and who assuaged any loneliness or homesickness by conducting an active correspondence. Letter writing was a joy for her all her life.

The following letter was written shortly after the 1898-99 Christmas—New Year's break. She had enrolled only the previous September and had spent the holidays in Black Hammer.

Decorah, Iowa, Jan. 8, 1899
Dear Friend:

I will now answer you your letter which I received yesterday, as I have nothing else to do and I won't have much time for writing on week days.

. . . I like school all right again. I was afraid I would be homesick after I came back but I haven't been yet and don't think I will be either. Of course I wished I could have stayed a while longer. There must be about fifty new scholars, most nearly all boys. There must be about four boys to every girl down here. But I tell you there are some funny ones, too.

Last Friday we had a regular old fashioned spelling school. Gedelia and I chose sides and we had some fun. I wish I had been home to the dance Friday or Saturday night; but, "If wishes were horses, beggars would ride" so you see it is of no use to wish. And besides, about the dance in Yucatan, I know Mamma wouldn't let me go to that anyway. I think they had a Mask Ball here too, Friday. But I am not going to go to any dances here.

Thank you ever so much for sending the song but the trouble now is that I can't sing it.

. . . I must tell you that Christ Glasrud [her cousin] is down here going to school, too. But he goes to Valder's. Duffy and Henry like school all right I guess. They were up here Friday evening.

Next Saturday we are going out to the sister of our landlady and will be back Monday morning. Expect a good time, too, you bet.

. . . Well, I think I have scribbled almost enough now. But when I get started writing a letter I never know when to quit. I believe that this is enough for this time. I think we are going to the Congregational Church this evening as we didn't get up in time for church this morning.

Yours, Mathilda Glasrud.

P. S. Hope to hear from you soon. C.M.G.
Excuse paper and writing.

Her "friend," the one to whom the above letter was written, was none other than Knute Maurice Lee, who was 19 and who lived in Spring Grove. That's the man she ultimately married almost eight years later. I am guessing that they had been at the same party over the holidays.

My mother reluctantly gave a few details to my brother when he was pressing her to tell just how she first met our dad. She told Bill that it was at a party when she was 15—the same age she was when she wrote Knute from Decorah. Her brothers had brought her to the party in a buggy—or maybe, she said, in a sleigh—and she said they were late. The place was the Ole Lee farm in Black Hammer. Ole was a cousin of Knute's father, Aad. Knute brought along his older sister, Belle. Mother said our father was noted for being kind to his sickly sister and for escorting her to various social functions. Belle had what they called in those days, "quick consumption," a kind of tuberculosis. It was often fatal. In her case it was. She died at age 22.

Tillie became infatuated with Knute when she was just 16 and he was 20.

Here is a part of the recorded dialogue between Mathilda and her son Bill about the young man Knute:

> *As a farm girl, you had probably never had a date?*
> Never had a date—that I can remember.
> *Did you know he was going to be there?*
> No.
> *So this was a surprise? What did he look like when you first saw him?*
> Well, I don't know. He looked all right. I never thought he was a handsome man. I never did. Nice hair.
> *You had never seen him before?*
> No. (Laughter) But I could tell by the way he looked

at me. My mother used to say that—I heard her say it to others—not about your dad, especially, but, you know, I suppose there were other boys interested in me. She couldn't quite see why they would be interested in me. I was such a tomboy. You know, being raised with all those boys. And I wasn't interested in how I was dressed or anything. It didn't bother me.

But I bet you had a nice dress for the party.

Well, ordinary. Lots of people had much nicer dresses than I did. Because I took what I got, you know. Julia, my sister, sewed and I wasn't asked.

Apparently Dad saw beyond the dress. Did he catch your eye pretty quick?

How would I know?

But the succession of letters that January and February in 1899 suggest that she did know that Knute had indeed caught her eye. Some of her letters to him were saved, fortunately, but his letters to her have vanished.

Knute responded and Mathilda wrote again:

Decorah, Iowa, Jan. 23, 1899.
My Dear Friend:

I will now answer your letter which I received Saturday. Very glad to hear that you are alive yet, and I am pretty well myself, only I have a pretty bad headache just now.

I can tell you that there are several on the sick list. Mr. Breckenridge is one and Duffy is another. Mr. Langland was our teacher in Physiology, Geography and Arithmetic. And I must say that I like him almost as well as Mr. Breckenridge himself. Henry and Willie Tweten were up here yesterday and they had sent Duffy to the doctor then. It is only the grip he has, I guess. Saturday evening Edwin and another college fellow were up here.

A week ago Saturday night we were to a show down to the Grand Opera House. I tell you it was fine. The name of it was Hamlet, one of Shakespeare's plays.

. . . Do you remember that time at Lee's last spring when we played cards? I tell you I hadn't touched cards either before or after that time and don't think I will either. I don't think Duffy is going around the streets with a cigar in his mouth and I am glad you don't either. I have heard that you have had so much fun up that way these last weeks but it is always so that I am never at home when all the fun is going on but I suppose there will come my time, too, as they say.

. . . Did you have a splendid time at the Yucatan dance? They are going to have a students dance next Saturday evening but I can't go because I promised Mamma I wouldn't go to any dances and I wouldn't go anyway. I tell you Mamma is pretty strict with me. I s'pose it's for my own good.

Well, I have nothing more to scratch so I will quit. Give my best regards to your sister, Belle, if she is home. Well, good bye for this time.

Yours Sincerely,

Tillie

(That is what they usually call me here.)

Letters like these give us clues to the relationships among family and friends whose history is linked through events, places and circumstances. We become aware that Tillie's brother Duffy was also a student in Decorah, whether at the Breckenridge or at a business school or at Luther College. She refers frequently, in letters to Knute, to Julia Fredrikson. Even though Julia, a cousin, was seven years older, she appears to have had a frequent exchange of letters with Tillie. We don't quite know what the connection between Julia and Knute might be. Could Tillie merely be teasing? It couldn't have been very serious or romantic because we know that Julia was married to Martin Knutson late in that same year, 1899.

Decorah, Feb. 6, 1899

My Dear Friend:

You must excuse me for not answering your letter before but the fact is I couldn't, that's all. I have been down with the measles and am yet, although I am up now. I was in bed the day I received your letter and of course then it was doubly welcome. I have had such a terrible cough and it has left me without a voice. I haven't been able to speak, only whisper, since Thursday. It does not feel so pleasant either.

Well I suppose you spoke with Duffy, perhaps when he was home. He was up here just now but I didn't speak very much with him as all the girls were around.

The boys had been speaking of going home and they said that when they went we could go along. So they went last Friday and I was sick and couldn't go along. I wish they had waited another week. But it is no use to worry about that anymore right now.

But I must tell you a week ago last Saturday we went nine miles out in the country (that cold day you took J.F. from Spring Grove, you know) out to the home of our Landlady's sister and came back Mon. morning in the cold. I was sick then, too, but we had so much fun that I didn't mind it. J. M. Kirkeberg was along and then you might know we had fun.

I tell you I got in a fix Sunday, though. We played "Dra handske" you know and it goes by a certain number. And the one that gets that number, the others ask him or her a question each. My turn came first and Mr. Kirkeberg just hurried as fast as he could and asked: "Who took you home from the dance the 4th of July?" I wouldn't tell but I just had to. I tell you I got even with him, though. But I have forgiven him—he brought me all kinds of nice things while I was sick. I thought today that I would go to school tomorrow but I see now it won't do. I'll have to learn to talk first. But now let it be enough about this sickness . . .

Feb. 8, 1899

Well, I started your letter Monday afternoon and now it is Wednesday morning 9:30 and I have just had my breakfast. I am an early riser, ain't I? Well, I tell you yesterday I was good and homesick, sitting around here. Can't do anything and can't go to school either. This is my second week out of school. Expect I shall have to work like a good feller to catch up again. Isn't it funny? I can't speak yet and it will be a week tomorrow since I got that way. Maybe I'll never get my voice back.

I am afraid you won't find this a very interesting letter but I don't know of any news. Because I'd like to know where I'd get them. If I must say so, I am a little bit homesick today, too, for that matter but you mustn't tell anyone. I just wish somebody would come and get me some Friday afternoon. I'd go if it was 40 below. They said it was over 30 below yesterday.

I got a new picture Sunday of my Landlady and I

expect about a half dozen more from . . . you know. Duffy, Henry and Willie had their pictures taken and I am promised one. I have seen the proofs and they are good.

I wonder what is the matter with Julia Fred—-she doesn't write. It is her turn to write. I answered her letter long ago. I had so many letters last week. Two from the kids at home and they said they had been sick and you and Peter had been hauling ice. Willie wrote: "They have put up about 100 chunks, 17 chunks in one load." I had to laugh at that. He kept pretty good count.

Everybody is sick down here and I have heard that it is the same up there. S'pose you have a lot of fun, just the same.

Go and see J.F. all the time and then J.S. once in a while—ha! ha! I bet you have a big time. I did too while I was in bed—ha! ha! That's about all the big times I have just now.

Well, I am a great scribbler anyway. I beat you all to pieces. But I just write for the sake of passing my time the best I can just now. But I wonder when I will get this mailed. But you'd get it some time and then you must answer right away and I'll write a more interesting letter next time. I think I shall write a letter to J.F. to ask her what is the matter with her. I must try to fill out this page. My, I guess it is pretty cold outside, but I haven't been out to find out. That is the last thing I could think of to write so I will have to quit, although I hate to.

Don't you wish with all your might that I will get well again and . . . and . . . and . . .

Your Sincere Friend,

Mathilda Glasrud

For a homesick teen-ager away at school, Valentine's Day in February was important. And her infatuation with Knute Lee, as evidenced in these letters, gave it a special dimension that year.

We can read between the lines that Tillie loved to go to dances and was envious of those who, unlike herself, were permitted to go.

Tillie seemed also to have been the victim of winter illnesses. Considering the harsh winters of the Upper Midwest, the drafty buildings and more primitive health care, it is not surprising that there were complaints and frequent epidemics.

Decorah, Iowa, Feb. 23, '99
My Dear Friend:

I received your welcome letter today and I will now answer it. There is quite a change in the weather again—it seems as if we will have winter once more. I am now perfectly well with an appetite of a _____ but I am quite hoarse, yet it doesn't seem as if I will get over it either.

I got a very pretty valentine last evening. Suppose you don't know anything about it. I tell you I think you are almost too good. I never expected one and certainly not one as pretty as that. You were mistaken as to who sent the other one. He'd never send me a valentine. I guess he's going to get married pretty soon by the way he talks himself. He was up here to bid goodbye Sunday. He is at Solberg's now, I suppose.

By the way, do you hear from Duffy? He was up here Sunday but I'd never dare to ask him.

Last Saturday night we were to a concert up at the college. Mr. Langland took both Gedelia and myself—that is, up there. And the worst part of it was that there was somebody else that wanted to take us, too, but was too late, poor thing, and you know we were sorry (I guess not.)

. . . I had a letter from Julia Fredrikson Sat. You said you didn't have a very good time in Yucatan. She said she had a very good time. But you see, tastes differ. I thought I had a pretty good time Christmas and she didn't.

You wanted to know about the ring business. Don't you remember the time Julia gave you my ring and we said Grandpa would get after you. You said I should look under the stamp. I looked but I couldn't see a thing.

I do like Decorah quite well now. I could have had a chance to go home some time this week but I didn't care to. I had a very good time, but I suppose I would have had a better one at home. You better stick to your promise, young man, and when I get home give me that ride you know, not on a bicycle ha! ha! Miss Ruen has a wheel.

We had two examinations last week and I got 100% in both of them. We had one today in Civil Government, but I don't know how much I got in that.

One day this week I was really sick and tired of school and I could have quit any day. But I am all over it now.

I tell you, you mustn't dare show Julia this letter for

> if you do and I find it out I will never write another. That is plain truth now. Because I wouldn't want to have it for anything in the world. You are the first boy I ever wrote to. But you see I am young yet, you know, and you might take that into consideration. But please don't mind any of this nonsense. "You mustn't get mad, you know, it is only for fun." Julia would know my writing anyway.
>
> I haven't heard from home for a long time. But Gedelia got the Herald yesterday and there was something from Black Hammer. Je vil nok ha candi naa—for I haven't had any for a while but valentines are just as good ha! ha! I suppose you are the one who sent Julia hers too. I heard that they were going to have a students' dance Friday, but of course we are not going. We never do.
>
> Well, I can't think of anything else to write so I will close for this time.
>
> Very Truly Yours,
>
> Clarie Rude, Decorah, Iowa
>
> P. S. Hope for an answer soon. Excuse paper and have nothing else just at present.
>
> (That name is no lie. It is the first and last parts of my name.)

Mathilda recalls that in 1899 there was a lot of talk about the end of the century and what it all meant. But mostly she associates the year with an emotional event for the students and teachers at the Decorah Institute. She explained:

> Mr. Breckenridge died. He must have died in the night because when we came back to school in the morning it was announced that he had passed away. And he was quite a character. He had good standards. He was telling the boys, "Don't go around with your hands in your pockets. Keep your hands out!"

Likely Mathilda was among "the long line of his beloved and sorrowing students, his beloved comrades of the Grand Army of the Republic, and his faithful Masonic brethren, and his many, many friends" who, according to his biography, followed the funeral cortege to Phelps Cemetery in Decorah.

A coincidence—or was it?—relates to the stanza of *Thanatopsis* by William Cullen Bryant. The biography of

Breckenridge tells us that those verses "So live that when thy summons comes . . . " etc., were a favorite of his. Mother loved them, too, and perhaps first heard them read by him. We heard them quoted in the sermon at her own funeral 77 years later.

Mathilda continued at the school until the spring of 1900 when life suddenly changed radically for her. A decision by her mother, an older brother and a North Dakota uncle was imposed on her:

A teacher was needed in a rural school in North Dakota. The Glasrud matriarch had discovered this on a trip with her son Peter at Christmas time 1899 visiting Uncle Erick Qualley. It was decided that there was an eligible teacher in the family: Mathilda. So she had her spring term at the Decorah Institute cut short and was sent to fill the vacancy. She wrote in her memoirs:

> I was elected and cannot recall that I made any objections about taking the job. I surely did not feel prepared to teach but luckily there were only five pupils. Before starting to teach I had to go to LaMoure, the county seat, to obtain a certificate to teach.

For a not yet 17-year-old farm girl, her secondary education still incomplete, to travel alone to North Dakota was a very considerable challenge. Years later in her taped conversation she admitted that "it was a little bit adventuresome for me to go to North Dakota on my own." In her memoirs she wrote:

> How well I remember my trip out to North Dakota—quite a contrast to now. I boarded the old narrow gauge at Spring Grove, went down to Reno, and then changed at Bridge's Switch for St. Paul. Getting into the long, dark train shed and into the huge Union Station at St. Paul seemed very bewildering to me . . .
>
> I think I changed at the Union Station—I don't remember much about Union Station in St. Paul. But I do remember coming to Fargo in the morning. That would be 24 hours afterwards. And when I got there the sun was coming up. And it seemed to me that it came up in the West!
>
> I waited around—I don't remember how long—because there was a mixed train going out to Lisbon, North Dakota. I think that was probably a division point. And from there out to near La Moure—Verona was the

place. But nobody was there to meet me or anything. It took practically all day for that train to get to Verona from Fargo, possibly one hundred miles. And when I got to Verona there was no depot. Just a drop off, and a little hamlet. Maybe a house or two. But I think the Lord was with me there.

As luck would have it there was a farmer in for a load of feed. And he lived a mile from my uncle Erick. And I don't know—he probably was on the school board and knew of my coming. He knew, but didn't know when. But there I was. And I got a sleigh ride on his load of feed to my uncle's. He lived about a mile east but he took me way in.

This was in March of 1900 and in North Dakota it was still rather wintery. Mathilda arrived on a weekend and had to start right in teaching. She lived with her uncle's family.

My uncle's kids were awful mean kids, in a way. They were unruly. My trunk was downstairs in my uncle's bedroom because their upstairs was unfinished and I slept up there with the kids. But they dug into my trunk and I couldn't keep them out of there and that bothered me. I suppose they knew that I didn't like it and so for that reason they persisted. Pests! It was private. I wasn't used to that at home. The boys [her own brothers] never snooped into my stuff. I didn't like it.

And then, of course, when school was out, why then I was stranded there and I had to go to summer school in La Moure. And then I had to go to town and get a place to live. La Moure was a town like Spring Grove. It was the county seat so they had summer school. I suppose I got a [temporary] permit to teach those two months but I had to get a certificate. [It was dated March 9, 1900 and was valid for one year.] I managed to get a third grade [rating]. Second grade was a better one.

Summer school was either four or six weeks. Of course I then had to pay for room and board there. Another girl was there, too, an older girl who had been to summer school before and she was a little more sophisticated. I came from a farm family. I suppose I would just follow cues.

Back at the Erick Qualley farm, Mathilda got a notice by mail that a bicycle that her brother Peter had ordered for her had arrived at the train station in La Moure. At the time Peter was working in a hardware store in Kindred.

> The farmers were busy with their haying and harvest at that time, so I decided that I would walk into La Moure and ride the bike home again. I walked and walked over the prairie trails, passing not more than a half dozen homes on the way. It was a very hot and long walk. When I arrived at the station, there was my bicycle—crated.
>
> There were two men there and they started to uncrate it and they put it together for me. So you can't say there aren't nice people. Imagine! A young girl walking around. Of course there were no tramps out there on the prairie. I pedaled the whole way back.

Meanwhile her uncle had helped Mathilda get another teaching position at a different school about 15 miles away. She recalled that they paid $40 a month. But before the new school year started Mathilda wanted to visit other relatives in the state.

All alone on her bike, she headed for Kindred, some 75 miles away. She pedaled along and (she laughs as she tells it):

> When I got close to Lisbon, I think it was—it was a warm day—I knocked at the door of a house for a drink of water. They were eating dinner and here they invited me in to have dinner.
>
> . . . I think I managed it (the whole trip) during the day. I know I didn't stay overnight anyplace . . . I've never talked to anyone about it. I don't like to talk about those things. I think I took the train back again. I think then they took the bicycle in the baggage car.
>
> . . . Aunt Johanna Fredrikson, who was my mother's sister (and Julia's mother), lived in Kindred. A great many Spring Grove people had gone west and settled in Cass County, North Dakota and Clay County, Minnesota, or, in other words, the Red River Valley. I felt more at home there.

Earlier she had described for me that migration, including Glasruds and Stenehjems, in covered wagons. "It took them about six weeks, I think. And they had cows along so they had milk. A couple of cows. And they would have to have some feed for them and they would stop overnight and let them eat grass."

Tillie had a harrowing experience when she decided to ride her bike to the place, about 15 miles in a northerly direction from her uncle Erick's farm, where she would teach during the soon-to-start new school year.

In telling this, my mother hesitated, eyeing the tape recorder. "Is that on?" she asked. My brother told her it was but it could always be erased. So she continued:

> And here I got into a country store to ask directions. And there was a young man in there and not a single other person. I think he was tending store for his father. And out of a clear blue sky he said to me, "Let's go out in the back room and have some fun!"
>
> I tell you I backed out and got my bicycle and scooted out as fast as I could. Imagine! A perfect stranger coming into a store . . . I was never in that place again!

She began scouting a place to stay near the school where she would teach. She saw one home she thought would be a nice place to stay but they weren't willing to take anybody:

> And then I came to this other place, a kind of tar paper shack. It had about four rooms and a houseful of kids. I think they had eight kids and another one coming . . . I stayed there. And I had a room off their bedroom and one of the little girls slept with me. But she was so small she didn't bother me at all.
>
> The serenity of those lovely fall days was soon shattered. One day, I think in late October [1900], the older boy who was not in school came to the schoolhouse and told me and the other children to go to a neighbor's house to sleep. I suspected that something was wrong. Towards evening the neighbor woman came home and told us that my landlady had died. She had given birth to a baby boy. It was 25 miles to the nearest doctor.
>
> I think she bled to death . . . I stayed on with the family but it was not like when the mother lived. They had two girls. One was 16 and one was 18. Ashwill was their name—they were Yankees, originally from Illinois.

> Decent people. The mother was fixing things up in fine shape. Those girls took care of the baby. The baby survived. But it's unforgettable.

Mathilda finished her first full year of teaching and returned to Black Hammer. She had lived a lot of life even before her 18th birthday. The North Dakota experience, although adventurous and educational for her, was not a happy time. She hadn't really wanted to go. She told me in 1965:

> I was not very proud of it. It was my first teaching experience. I had such a small school and I don't think I was a very good teacher . . . and not much of any education to speak of. And no teacher training. And yet they sent you out to teach school. It's a crime, I think. I didn't do that to any of my kids. Times were different.

Somewhat sadly she said to me, "I haven't ever told any of the family and don't you tell it either."

Six years later, however, she told my brother essentially the same story, but in even greater detail. And she concluded by saying to him, "What is a year when you are so young? I didn't tell any of my girl friends. I didn't tell anyone else. But you made me tell it . . . But don't put anything like that in my obituary."

I am telling it now because this is the true story of Mathilda. And it wouldn't be complete without it.

CHAPTER FOUR

Teacher, Daughter, Sister, Bride

Mathilda had taught in two different country schools in North Dakota for a year. She was still just four months short of her 18th birthday when the term in her second La Moure County school concluded on March 1, 1901. She felt rather alien, perhaps also homesick, in that community, even though relatives were nearby. Her mother must have agreed that she could come home.

Before taking the train back to Houston County, way down at the southeast corner of Minnesota, she visited the Fredriksons again in Kindred. There were other former Spring Grove and Black Hammer folks who had also moved to that area, including Glasruds, Qualleys, Dustruds and Myhres; she might have wanted to see them again as well. Mathilda's brother Peter had left his job in the Kindred hardware store some months earlier in order to marry Mathilda Steenstrup in Caledonia. Peter was to return to North Dakota with his bride and they would spend the rest of their life there.

Tillie couldn't extend her Kindred visit for more than a week, however, because she had to hurry home. She was scheduled to be in another wedding party. Her oldest brother Christian and Malinda Seglem had set their wedding date for April 7, 1901 and Mathilda had been asked to be the bridesmaid.

Mathilda (standing at right) was a bridesmaid at her brother's wedding on Easter Sunday, April 7, 1901. Seated are Christian and his bride, Malinda Seglem. Cousin Henry Glasrud was the best man.

The wedding picture, taken at the Frank Joerg studio in Spring Grove, before the actual ceremony at Trinity Lutheran in Spring Grove, shows a serious young woman. She wore a gray wool floor-length dress with an open vest revealing a fluffy white blouse with turtle neck collar. Doubtless it was made by her sister Julia, a skilled dressmaker, who had sewn all of her clothes up to that point. Along with the bridal couple and with cousin Henry Glasrud, the best man, Mathilda posed in a rather formal and dignified stance with no hint of a smile. But that didn't disguise her natural beauty.

Mathilda was truly a beautiful young woman. She had what I call a regal bearing. Her photos from the time and throughout her lifetime attest to that. Posture was always important for her. Her children all were conditioned to hearing her steady reminders to "stand up straight, shoulders back." Doubtless John Breckenridge's daily admonition in Decorah to his students to "fill your lungs" made an impression on his student, Mathilda Glasrud.

She went back to live on the farm in Black Hammer. It was a time of shuffling of rooms and beds for that large family. Christ was moving out, of course. He and Lindy had bought a farm several miles away on the road to Spring Grove. A hilltop on their farm was the site of a legendary landmark: two primitive sculptures of women crafted from stones, creations of the previous owners. One of them still stood there 30 years later when, as a child, I would ride out with my family to "the farm" and we would wave at the stone lady and sing a little Norwegian song inspired by the landmark.

Julia and her husband, Cornelius Ike, with their son, Clarence, who had been born in August of 1898, had been living on the Glasrud home farm while waiting to acquire a place of their own. They remained that winter of 1900-1901 partly, no doubt, because Cornelius had been seriously ill with pneumonia. When he recovered he and Julia also bought a farm—the Ole S. Olsen farm just east of the Black Hammer church—and moved there just about the time Mathilda returned home from North Dakota.

The matriarch, Sigrid Qualley Glasrud, was not wealthy by any means, but neither was she poor. With the help of her sons, she became a prudent farm manager. She had the policy, according to Sigrid Vaaler, of giving each of her children $100 when they left the farm to make their own way in life. The sum seems small by today's standards, but it represented much more as seed money then. We also know she advanced loans—where else would they get the money for downpayments?—when they established their own homes. Even at the time of her death, there were Depression loans outstanding from the help she had given one or more of her heirs.

So there was room for Mathilda at home again. Returning to Black Hammer was especially convenient for her then because she had been hired as the teacher for the home school. Hers was Public School No. 69 in Houston County. She knew it well, of course, because she had been a student there herself. To get there from the farm, she could walk perhaps a mile and a half southward through woods and fields and across a creek, down one steep hill and up another steep hill. Or she could walk the three miles by road by going east to the church, then south for a mile or so and then west again. She never cared to ride horseback but sometimes may have driven a horse and buggy or had one of her brothers take her.

One of the pupils—there were about 20—was her young brother, Willie. She told me that, even though her own brother and neighbor children were in her charge at the school, "they didn't take advantage of me. But they did things they shouldn't do, you know—like they went out and smoked."

She taught three terms of six months each between the fall of 1901 and the spring of 1904 in that home school. That meant that, for at least six months of the year, she could be a full-time helper for her widowed mother. Mathilda may have wanted the chance to go to summer school but, because it was a busy farm, she was not encouraged to pursue additional higher education.

In August of 1901, just prior to her first year of teaching in Minnesota, she took her qualifying exams in Caledonia, the county seat. The testing took place during three days. She passed, of course, and got a certificate which attested to her being "a skillful teacher . . . possessed of good moral character." Her rating was 68% for "Professional Requirements" and 72% for "Skill in Teaching" (she had virtually no training for teaching, per se). Her standings, as recorded on the official certificate were: Arithmetic, 92%; Composition, 80%; Geography, 86%; Grammar, 94%; History of the U.S., 62%; Penmanship, 68%; Physiology and Hygiene, 78%; Reading, 80%; and Spelling, 84%.

She never commented on the grades as such but she commented often on her lack of teaching experience. In fact, she told me, "I don't think I was a very good teacher." After she died, however, one of her former students came up to me on the street in Spring Grove to tell me how wonderful a teacher she was.

In the spring of the next year, 1902, there was occasion for celebration in the family: Julia and Cornelius, now situated on their own farm and with a four-year-old son (Clarence), became parents of twin girls on March 21st. The happiness soon turned to sorrow, however, as tragedy struck. Mathilda wrote in her memoirs:

> Complications set in and, in spite of daily visits by Doctor Stabo, three weeks later Julia died. The twins were Sigrid and Maren. My sister was a believing Christian and her faith was strong and her prayers fervent. Rev. Jensen made many visits although he himself was ill at the time. His daughter, Stella, came with him and I remember that she stayed several days there and was a great comfort to Julia, reading, quoting the scripture and offering prayers for her.
>
> My mother took Sigrid to raise, and Maren was two weeks with Aunt Sigrid Glasrud and then was taken to Ike's (Cornelius' parents). She evidently was not as strong because at six weeks of age, she too died.

Sigrid Ike Vaaler herself, the surviving twin, at age 86 shared with me the legend of her birth that she had absorbed during the years that she had been virtually adopted by her grandmother:

> My mother lived for about two weeks after we were born. My grandmother always thought she died from a blood clot but your mother thought she got an infection after childbirth. So she passed away. And then there were the twins. So Grandma Glasrud took me and Grandma Ike took Maren. We were baptized, I suppose, at home on the farm where we were born—right there in the shadow of the Lutheran Church in Black Hammer. My mother had been organist there . . .
>
> It was such big news in Black Hammer that Julia and Cornelius had twins—twins were really something in those days. And people used to come and visit. It was usually rommegrot (a Norwegian cream pudding) that women would make and bring to the home in those days. When they came to visit my mother and the new twins, why, Grandma Glasrud said they got out their big meat platter—you know they had big meat platters in those days on the farms—and they put the two of us on a meat platter, wrapped us up, to show us off.

Julia's death was a severe emotional blow to Mathilda. Although her sister had been eight and a half years older, Julia was almost a surrogate mother for the energetic and always curious little girl. In a home full of boys, Tillie would get understanding from the only other daughter in the family. Dresses and coats were doubtless handed down. Julia had been the family seamstress. Feminine matters that would never be mentioned aloud in a male-dominated house in those days were likely shared between sisters. Julia had learned to play the parlor reed organ and later was one of the first organists at their church. Mathilda also loved music. She loved to sing and we can imagine that Julia accompanied her.

"We did get an organ at home," Mother explained to my brother, Bill:

> There was a man from the Kimball Company who came around selling organs to people. Ole Stenehjem, a neighbor, was quite interested. He was quite a "go-getter" in some ways. He went around with the organ dealer. And a lot of the people in Black Hammer bought organs from him. Mrs. Knute Ike [Julia's then-future mother-in-law] had a sister in Highland Prairie named Anne Dommen. She was a music teacher. She came to live with her sister in Black Hammer and went around giving music lessons to everybody in the area.

But, sadly, not to Mathilda. She added, "My mother wouldn't let me have lessons . . . I don't know why. She let Duffy take lessons but he wouldn't practice."

Even though her mother ruled the household with what seemed to be an iron hand and could wield great authority in spite of her quite petite stature, Tillie said they never had a clash of wills. "I respected her too much. I thought she was pretty swell, you know."

She mentioned that when her mother was seriously ill during this time when she herself was living at home and teaching at the home school, "I couldn't stand to leave her. I was close to mother."

On the other hand, she complained that her brothers didn't seem to be that sensitive. "She was so terribly sick before she had her operation. It bothered me like everything, you know. I couldn't understand the boys because they would go out to a dance as she was lying there in the bed moaning. I wouldn't think of doing it."

Nevertheless, she said that generally she got along well with the boys, especially the ones who were older than she was:

The ones that were younger, that was different. I can remember that I fought with the boys, the younger ones. They probably were ornery and boys don't like to be bossed, either. I've learned a few things in my long life. Because I probably would have said and done things in those days that I wouldn't do now.

Mathilda had a searing memory of the drama that unfolded when her mother's condition became critical:

Her illness was gall bladder trouble. She had an attack fourteen years before, a very serious attack . . . There was a Dr. Browning. She had been sick an awful long time. Uncle Andrew [her mother's brother, Andrew Qualley] came over. He lived closer to Caledonia and he knew of Dr. Browning. He said she should try to see him. I think he got word to him and Dr. Browning came over and he told her to come to the Caledonia Hospital. Well, she wasn't going. She lay there and suffered and she thought she was going to die. But I suppose it got to be too much. She was suffering and there was no change for the better.

One Sunday morning at six o'clock, I came downstairs and she said, "Call Christ. I want to go to Caledonia today."

I said, "I don't see how you can go to Caledonia. You're in bed."

"Call them!" she said, "and have them come over."

Lindy and Christ were living a few miles away on their own farm on the way to Spring Grove. At this point there was no phone on the farm. Someone had to hurry over to summon her oldest son.

He came over with a surrey. I sat in the back seat and steadied her. And she stood it until we got there. The hospital was in a house on Main Street in Caledonia. And I was along so I know it happened this way: The bed was on the second floor. And I remember that Christ picked her up in his arms and carried her upstairs, so you know she was wasted. And she had to stay there to get built up a whole week. I know afterwards how we kept track of it [her condition]; there was a telephone at the store. There were only three in the area. Tweetens had one, there was

> one at the Black Hammer store, and there was one someplace else. So we could call the Caledonia Hospital to hear how she was. And I know two weeks afterwards we went over there and she said, "Don't shake the bed!" She had had a very serious operation and had been so weak before it. She had then been a widow for more than ten years.

From today's perspective it is difficult to appreciate life without modern transportation and communication. At the beginning of the 20th Century the boundaries of communities were beginning to be stretched by the first technological breakthroughs that were destined to change our world. Automobiles in rural Minnesota were a few years off. Telephones were still new—the long distance telephone link between New York and Chicago had been opened just one decade earlier. Black Hammer farms would wait almost three decades before electricity could be delivered to them.

At the turn of the century, the horse was truly the farmers' friend—dependable both as beast of burden and as "horsepower" for travel. Horses it seemed had both character and personality. At least they had "horse sense."

"I was scared stiff of horses," Mathilda admitted:

> I can remember once, we were on the fields, and my mother—I wonder if we didn't have a hired man who was lame or something—and there was an extra team and my mother got on the horse and I got on with her. My mother used to ride horseback when she was young but I didn't have the courage to do that. I was brave about many things but I wasn't brave about that. I was afraid of horses when they were out in the yard.

But, with her brothers, it was different. They had lived and worked every day with horses. She told the story about their horse, Fanny. When one of the boys rode horseback to a party or a dance and didn't want to leave Fanny outside, he would sometimes just turn her loose and she would go home. "Fanny knew the way," Mother said. (But how did that brother get home?)

Her discomfort around horses must have been increased by a runaway experience—the first of several in her lifetime—during her early teaching days at the home school when she was alone once with a team that got out of control.

Her brother Edwin took her along when he drove from the farm at Black Hammer to the farm of their uncle, between Spring Grove and Caledonia. They were sent to pick up and bring home a bull calf that had been offered to their mother. Their father's brother, Gust, and his wife, their Aunt Sigrid (a double cousin of their mother, Sigrid), had returned in 1892 from farming in Kindred to farming in Houston County. Gust and Sigrid had been pioneers in the Red River Valley. They lived in a log house in North Dakota and experienced severe winter hardships. They sold their farm to his sister, Jorgine and her husband John Myhre. The last several years before they left the 160-acre place, their crops of wheat had been bountiful. With the profit they bought what was known then as the Anthony Huyck farm and later became the Lars Sylling farm.

Mathilda tells what happened:

> Edwin drove and we went over to Glasruds and stayed over night. Then, coming home, Edwin got off at the Switch—at the top of the ridge by the school house. Then he walked down to Qualleys, a mile south across the fields. And I took the team with the same Stenehjem wagon [it had carried her and her trunk to school in Decorah some years earlier]. The calf was in back in a crate. I must have been 18 or 19 then.
>
> Here I drove a team and one of the horses was getting blind. When we got close to that road that led down to where [later] we kept our cow—down by the Muenkel place outside of Spring Grove—there was an old slaughter house there. And when we got there a pig came out and spooked the horses and they ran away. A full-fledged runaway!
>
> And you remember where the old creamery was. I held on to the tongue so tight I was down on my knees on the floor of the rig. Even the tongue, the neck yoke, fell out. It scoured along the road. They came up a hill just a bit. And I got them turned into a bank right there by the creamery. And the tongue went into the bank and the horses stopped. Christ Sylling and Mr. Gore came running out and they took care of the team. And I think they sent for Duffy because he was working down at John Ristey's store.

She wasn't injured, but was rather shaken by the experience.

Her brother apparently came right away and she believes he must have hitched up the horses again because she remembers that somehow she also got down to the store with him. The calf's leg was broken and her brother Duffy took the calf's leg and straightened the bone out and wrapped it in splints right there at the store:

> Old Dr. Jenson was sitting in the store and he told Duffy what to do and he did it . . . That calf didn't live to grow up. Probably he was injured more than was indicated. At least he survived for some weeks.

There is irony in Mathilda's being uneasy and distrustful of horses. They were actually to become a strong motif in the life ahead of her. She was becoming romantically interested again in one of the region's best young horsemen, Knute Lee, her future husband. His specialty, in fact, was horses: buying, selling, trading, training, judging, currying and caring for them. It was not only his special interest and hobby, it later became his business.

After teaching three terms at the home school in Black Hammer, Mathilda was hired in 1904 as teacher in a small rural school just south of Spring Grove in what was then called the Gilbertson school or District 88. Classes were first held in Knud Gilbertson's home when the district was created in 1878 and the school house itself was built nearby a year later.

Her move nearer to the village brought her closer to Knute. He lived in town with his parents, Aad and Hannah. Like most of his contemporaries his schooling did not continue beyond the 8th grade. The high school in Spring Grove did not have its first graduating class until 1903 when he was already 24 and Mathilda was 20. We know from her Breckenridge letters to her "dear friend" that she had more than a casual interest in him even then.

She had known him since they first met at the Black Hammer party when she was 15—she explained this to my brother while the tape was rolling:

> He was in the background and he was a friend. In between, I suppose I went out with him. But it was a long time before I went steady. I think I had it in mind that I, like so many of the others, was going to look abroad and get somebody, the right kind of man. Of course your dad didn't have much education but, of course, he really was a smart man . . . I'll tell you this

> about him: as far as expressing himself, he could do much better than I. If you had been interviewing him, he could have told you some of this in a concise way without any breaks of anything.

And another time when my tape recorder was rolling she talked about her reaction to him after first meeting him at the party:

> I knew even then that I could have dates with him whenever I wanted to. But I didn't always want to. It's funny sometimes with girls—how do they know these things? But I always did. That's the honest truth.
>
> I don't intend, Bob, to tell you a great deal about my courtship because I think that's something that belongs to me and that's something you really don't need to go into detail about. It was on again and off again lots of times. I had other dates and other chances.

One of those "other chances" may have been young Dr. Peterson from Decorah. Sigrid Vaaler remembers Grandma Glasrud confiding to her that this physician was enamored enough by Tillie—where or how they got acquainted, she didn't know—actually to come to the Glasrud farm to talk with Mathilda's mother about a possible marriage. Sigrid at the time was just a few years old and was there when he visited and remembers that she sat on his lap. Professional that he was, he noticed that Sigrid's adenoids needed attention. The grandmother acted on Dr. Peterson's diagnosis, apparently, and took her granddaughter to LaCrosse—not to Decorah!—to have them "fixed."

"Mathilda must have turned him down," Sigrid said. "Her mother, I suppose, was flattered to think that her daughter could marry a doctor. Aunt Mathilda never talked about it with me and she never told any of her own kids. I never asked about it, either, and she would not have liked it if I had."

Apparently Knute had the personality and character she found attractive and he also displayed initiative and ingenuity. He built a house in Spring Grove several years before his marriage. It was across from the new high school with a small barn or shed for his horses. How he accomplished this, and with what funds, we don't know. Mother told us that Knute's parents lived there for a few years. When Sigrid Glasrud some years later left the farm and moved to Spring Grove for the sake of her granddaughter Sigrid's education, she bought the house from Knute. Ultimately he bought it back from her. It was the house in which I grew up.

While Mathilda was teaching school near Spring Grove, Knute was already engaged in the first job of his career: rural mail carrier. It was for that reason he needed a barn for his horses and apparently it led to his building the house as well as the barn.

"He had a mail route at that time and he figured that he had to keep at least two teams of horses for that mail route," she explained. "He couldn't use the same team every day because the route was 25 miles long. He organized the first mail route out of Spring Grove and it went north to Black Hammer and down towards West Beaver Creek and around . . . It was about the time when rural free delivery was established . . . Do you know how much salary he had when he first started? Fifty dollars a month! Later on it was sixty and, at the time he quit, it was seventy-five."

It was possible for Mathilda to walk from her country school to Spring Grove and she did sometimes, but during the school term the weather often was either snowy or cold or wet and rainy. And mud was a universal problem. She had a room at the farm home of the Kolsrud family who lived near her school and she boarded with them also. She would go back to the Black Hammer farm most weekends, weather permitting, and each spring after the school term was completed. By this time some of the farms were apparently equipped with telephones—the old party-line system, to be sure—but people used them only sparingly at first. Perhaps they didn't want to "broadcast" their private conversations.

From Mathilda's letters to Knute during that period—and a few of them have been saved, fortunately—we can guess that they were engaged during this period of her teaching at the Gilbertson school. Whether they were formally engaged or not, her writing suggests she was planning to marry Knute.

> Spring Grove, Minn. January 25, 1905
> My Dear, Dear Boy,
>
> I was so pleased to get your letter yesterday. Shall try to answer now at noon. I am all alone in the school house. The children are all out coasting. It seems so nice to be rid of them for a while. Everything is quiet. It is rather hard on one's nerves at times to take care of such a family. But I get along first rate. They are pretty good.
>
> Haven't we lovely weather today? The sun is so bright that it hurts one's eyes. I expect by this time you

are down in the valleys, driving along and singing to yourself. Or maybe you stopped some place for dinner. So you are hauling wood. You must be thinking of the future. Well, that's all right too sometimes.

I felt pretty tired Monday. Had a headache too all day. But since I have felt fine. I sleep till after seven every morning.

I walked to school this morning. Have had a ride other mornings. I have not been at all lonesome this week. When I don't come before Monday morning, that helps a lot. I do not know how to get to town tomorrow evening. Have not phoned home so do not know whether they will get me or not. And about that dance. Really, I don't know. Sometimes I think I want to go and at others I don't care a bit. So I can't decide. Probably I will see you tomorrow evening. Then I can let you know. If you don't see me I 'spose you know I have gone home or something.

So Lewis is so independent. Well, we shall kindly leave him to himself. I am sure he does not care for our company and we don't care. There are others. Don't you think I am getting stingy? I have such swell stationery. [She was writing on a sheet of ruled tablet paper.] But this is all I have just at present. So it has to be this or none.

Well, my dear, I think this will have to be all for this time, so bye bye. I am
Your own,

Mathilda

What a treasure we are missing by not having the other half of this correspondence, Knute's letters to her. We know she wrote other romantic letters also that did not survive. Our sister, Barbara, told us:

> Shortly after Dad had died [1939] and we had cleared out the attic and places like that, we found some old love letters that she had written to Dad and he had kept them—or she had kept them all these years! I don't even know if she knew they were there because they were among his things. She let me read them. And when I was through reading them she said to me, "I want you to burn these." And so I did, unfortunately. They were wonderful letters!

> And that would give you such a different impression of our mother, you wouldn't have known, ever, that Tillie had written that letter or those letters.

Knute Lee was well liked by almost everybody in the community. That was the unanimous verdict of everyone we had ever talked to about him. He was warm and personable and had a ready wit. And he went out of his way to help people.

The farmers to whom he delivered mail also liked him. This is borne out by the following (unedited) article which appeared in the local weekly newspaper, *Spring Grove Herald* (exact date unknown):

> OUR RURAL CARRIERS ARE MADE HAPPY
> They Receive Liberal Donations
> From Their Patrons
>
> That the rural free delivery is greatly appreciated and found to be a necessity goes without saying, its pleasures and advantages have long been expressed by the farmers, however, the patrons on two different routes leading out of Spring Grove also showed their liking for their carriers by bestowing upon them a liberal supply of Christmas gifts.
>
> While Knute Lee, who drives the R.F.D. wagon on route No 1, north of this place, was making his usual trip last Thursday, his horses became frightened and almost ran away, having sighted an obstacle leaning against the mail box post—they however got used to the change before long. Knute became somewhat aggravated,—wondering "who in h—l used this means to frighten the horses." On closer inspection, however, his ideas were changed, having found the obstacle to be a sack of oats on which was a tag bearing his name. This occurred at his first stopping place, and with a smiling face and a feeling of gratitude toward the giver, he placed the sack in his buggy and proceeded on his way. By the time he had reached the seventh mail box he had on six sacks of grain, and seeing that there was no end to the donations, he unloaded them again. The following list of articles are those he received from his patrons: 52 sacks of oats, 10 of corn, 1 of potatoes, 1 of cabbage and carrots, 1 buggy whip, 1 pair of gloves, 1 handkerchief and $3.50 in money.
>
> Nels Kjome, mail carrier on route No.5, west of this

place, received about the same kind treatment as that afforded Mr. Lee. From several patrons he received two sacks of grain. He has been promised some from others, and some of those who have already donated, hauled the grain to his home, thereby saving Nels the trouble of doing so. He has so far received 9 sacks of corn and 18 sacks of oats.

Andrew Kjome, mail driver on route No. 3, south of this place has received two sacks of oats, and parties on his route have hinted about giving him a good start for New Year's.

Small donations of this kind if taken singly amounts to little and will not be missed by the giver, but in adding up the whole amount, it certainly makes a good, large gift for the carrier. We are pleased to see the farmers take so much interest in their carriers. They may in return look forward to receiving the very best treatment possible from he who serves them the year around.

Tillie was in love! Reading her letters from that year prior to her marriage, there is no doubt of it. Yet, she is still feeling her youth in worrying a bit about what her mother might think of her late hours. She is active in the Y.P.S—Young People's Society—the youth organization of their Black Hammer church. And this next letter seems to have been written on the Wednesday after a Saturday night date with Knute.

Spring Grove, Nov. 28, '05
My Own Dear Boy—

Think I shall have to write to you today. You know it is so long since I have seen you.

Do you know I was up town last night. I got a ride with Peter Arnston and I stayed at Glasrud's. The weather got to be so bad that I did not even get up town.

Wasn't it fierce last night. And just think of it—I walked down again this morning. Tell you what—it was nice. But I walked on the field from Simpson's to Gilbertson's so it was not so bad after all.

Monday morning is the time that I got here early. I was up [in Black Hammer] before four and got to town before you were up. It was about seven. I guess I was at the school house before half past. Then I built a fire and then walked down to Kolsrud's and had another breakfast and changed my dress.

Were you sleepy Sunday? I slept till 8:30 and then I did not sleep after that until night. I went over to the store in the afternoon and I helped the Vinge girls take down the decorations in church. So we arranged to have Y.P.S. in the basement. We are to have only cake and coffee and we girls will make coffee. You had better bring your best girl and come. Or probably you are so good you don't go to any thing.

Mamma never said a word when I got to bed. Guess she is getting used to almost any kind of hours.

What shall I do about going home tomorrow evening. Expect the roads will be awful now as they won't come for me. Maybe it would be best for me to stay down here and not go home at all. How would you like that? If I go home I can't teach Friday, that is all. 'Spose they will think it terrible to be out so many days too.

Guess you better call me up this evening about 8:30 or so. Probably I'll know by that time. 'Spose you are disgusted with me now. I never know what I want. I'll call up home first.

I have nothing more to tell you so guess I'll say bye bye. I am a future bottle washer,

Mathilda

P.S. Am just having a noon intermission.

As the letters move into 1906, the year they were married in September, there is more in her notes about his picking her up at school, or coming to see her. He, of course, was nearby in the village and could drive his horse and buggy out frequently. However, he drove out with the mail each week day and may not always have felt that he or his horses were ready for more travel. Mathilda's continuing letters sound more and more demanding.

Spring Grove, Minn. Jan. 6, 1906
Dearest Knudt—

Do not know how to get home this trip so guess I better notify you I am teaching tomorrow [Sat.] to make up for the day after Thanksgiving. Mamma phoned tonight that they could not get to town as the roads are too bad. So I thought at first I'd better stay here over Sunday as I had no way of letting you know. But the kid here goes to the minister [confirmation class] so I can mail this. Could you come down and take me up town anyway. I 'spose the old folks would allow me to stay at least one night anyway. But I expect the roads are so bad that you will be late with the mail, and therefore can not come. If you feel it is too much trouble, why of course I am welcome to stay here.

Have had a ride to school every day since the snow. So if you come you can come down to K's as I don't know of course if you are coming or not. It will be all right if you come and it will be all right if you don't. If you think it's too bad going never mind. I feel a little more cheerful than I did Sunday evening.

Lovingly yours,

Mathilda

Excuse fancy writing and paper.

We wish we knew whether he got the note in time to fulfill her wish to spend at least part of the weekend in the village of Spring Grove. We don't know who "the old folks" are at whose home she might stay overnight but there were both Qualleys and Glasruds living in town. We note that the mail service must have been excellent in that community. She often writes one day with the expectation that Knute (or Knudt as she spells his name at the time—it varied among Knut, Knudt and Knute) would come for her the next day. Working for the post office, as he did, may have allowed him to get his own mail before others got theirs.

Friday afternoon

Dearest Knute—

Am just home from church. Saw you but you must have been terribly busy because you did not have time to stop and talk to me. I was looking for you today for dinner. But you did not come. So you have to come tomorrow whether you want to or not.

Tomorrow we will have to get ready for the Y.P.S. Clara Stenehjem will help us bake.

Your own Mathilda

Bring 30c worth of roast beef and 20c sausage meat.

Monday afternoon

You may come down for me tomorrow evening Tuesday. I have to get up town for different things. If it had not been so muddy I should have walked but as it is I shall not attempt it. You could come about 5 o'clock. I will not be ready before. I am going to be very busy this week.

We went to Myhre's yesterday. We stayed till this morning. It rained so we could not get away. Did not go to sleep before about 2 so I feel rather sleepy today. I wish it was Saturday.

Your own M.

And finally, near the end of the school term—and the end of her teaching career:

Tuesday evening (April 4, 1906)

You need not come and get me Wednesday evening. I am going to Holum's. But you may come Thursday evening. Tonight I am at G. Gilbertson. Guess we will play whist.

Yours truly,

Mathilda.

The wedding was set for September 1. That meant a very busy summer for her, and for him too. Mathilda remembered the elaborate celebration the family staged for the wedding of her late sister, Julia, back nine years ago in 1897. The memory itself was poignant, of course, because of Julia's death following childbirth in 1902 and the subsequent death also of one of the newborn twins. As a result, Mathilda and her mother decided it would be a quiet wedding in the farm home and only close family would be invited.

Sigrid Vaaler told me that she remembers the wedding. She was a little four-year old girl. She particularly recalls the pleasure she received from Knute who, when he came to the farm for the wedding, brought little Sigrid a present. It was a tiny set of china—cups, saucers, plates and all—for her to play with. She prized the gift and kept it unbroken all her life.

Aad and Hannah, Knute's parents, attended, of course. He was 60 and she 53 at the time. He died the following year. His sister Ingeborg Serise (everyone called her Belle) had died from TB seven years earlier in 1899. His other sister, Maria, who married Charlie Peterson, would certainly have been at the wedding also.

It was raining on their wedding day. This made the trip into Spring Grove for picture-taking at the Joerg Studio difficult because the bridal couple and their attendants traveled by horse and buggy. The driver, Arthur, had to be outside in the rain while the other three were under the canopy. That's why, as Mother told my sister Naomi, Arthur's suit is wrinkled in the wedding picture.

This picture of Mathilda and Knute on their wedding day, September 1, 1906, required a five-mile trip in the rain by horse and buggy from Black Hammer to the photography studio in Spring Grove.

Fortunately the editor of the local weekly, *Spring Grove Herald*, was generous in covering events like this. He wrote with the broad editorial strokes and lavish prose popular in the press of that time, leaving for us this glowing account:

> Until Death Do Them Part
>
> On Saturday afternoon at the home of the bride's mother, Mrs. P. C. Glasrud of Black Hammer, was solemnized the marriage of her daughter, Miss Matilda (sic), to Knute Lee, the Rev. Kasberg spoke the magic words which made them one and inseparable, until death do them part. Only near relatives and the contracting parties constituted the audience which witnessed the making and taking of the solemn vows.
>
> The ceremony concluded and the congratulations bestowed the gathering partook of an excellent dinner. The happy twain departed on the evening train for a wedding tour to the Twin Cities.
>
> Mr. Lee as it is well known, is one of the mail carriers from this city, a young man who has won the highest respect and confidence of his every acquaintance, a recognition he eminently merits, for the very good and proper reason that he is a man of exemplary habits, fine business ability, honest, courtious (sic) and at all times reliable.
>
> The bride was born and reared in our midst and was loved and admired by all. She is a kind-hearted, sensible, and modest young lady whose height of ambition will be to make her home the happiest spot on Earth. The bride has taught school a good many years in this county and was always liked by her scholars.
>
> That their married life may be one long season of continuous bliss is the earnest hope of the HERALD together with their multitude of friends.

Mathilda was now Mrs. Knute A. Lee. She and her bridegroom were on their way to a journey together of 33 years, during which they would share adventures, joys, hardships and establish a home. It was a home for a family of seven children who arrived at regular intervals for the next 15 years

CHAPTER FIVE

Merging Lives: Mathilda and Knute

We can imagine the handsome young couple on board the train heading for home. They had been on their honeymoon in Minneapolis. Doubtless as they rode down along the Mississippi that September day in 1906 they were enjoying the still-summer scenery of the river with its boats and its bluffs and were rehearsing their memories of the past few days and nights in the Twin Cities.

The newspaper account is the only source for our knowing about a wedding trip. It was likely the first time that either of them had actually been in the Twin Cities, although Mathilda had changed trains in St. Paul on her way to and from teaching in North Dakota.

The bridal couple would have registered for a room at a downtown hotel, probably one near the Minneapolis station of the Chicago, Milwaukee, St. Paul & Pacific railroad. Knute had already demonstrated his initiative and ingenuity and it could be expected that he would know how to entertain his bride with fancy restaurant meals and entertainment. We know from letters that they loved to dance. What better time than on their honeymoon to find a dance hall—provided it was a "proper" establishment with a good reputation.

Coming home, they again changed trains at Bridge Switch, a stop north of LaCrosse on the Minnesota side of the river. There they boarded a local mixed train carrying mail, freight and passengers. (The track had been upgraded six years earlier (1900) from narrow gauge to standard gauge.) It took them to the depot in Spring Grove located across from the tall-steepled church; it was the same depot where, some years later, Knute would spend many hours in his dray business, picking up and delivering freight consigned to local merchants.

Knute already owned a house in town. It was not the one he had built earlier—his parents were temporarily living in that one. The house he had bought several years before their wedding was on the southern edge of the village. Mathilda described it for me in our 1959 recorded conversation: "There were 20 acres and a barn and a log house with two rooms, one frame room and another. And he had wanted to buy that on account of the land so he would have pasture for his horses and a little hay; he could also keep a few cows and animals there in order to help out. And you know he was always interested in horses."

Knute had his rural mail route to return to. Someone would have had to cover for him while he was away on their honeymoon. It may have been Arthur Glasrud, Mathilda's younger brother, who was then 19 and, when not farming with Willie, liked to help Knute with his horses.

Sigrid Vaaler told me she remembers that log house at the end of what they then had nicknamed "Banana" street (for Ben-Anna; Ben and Anna Onsgard lived along the roadway that today is called 1st Avenue SW). She remembers visiting her Aunt Mathilda and Uncle Knute there and doing some errands for them. One day she was given a quarter and sent to buy meat at the butcher shop on Main Street and lost the money on the way. She remembers the embarrassment of having to return and ask for another coin.

Mathilda would learn more about her new husband each day. She would discover his natural sense of humor—he was a great story teller and would easily flip out quips. Almost like an actor, he could imitate some of the characters of the village. And Knute loved to sing. He joined a male chorus even before he was married. At least two dozen singers in that glee club would concertize seriously with an instrumental accompaniment that included cornet, flute, violin, mandolin, string bass and reed organ. Knute himself had a violin at one point and his neighbors loved to hear him play the accordion. On summer nights (radios and phonographs were years away) when he took what he called his "Squeeze Box" outside to play, people in surrounding houses would come out on their porches to listen. On his mail route, as Mathilda told us earlier, he would happily sing aloud to himself—and to his horses!—as he drove along alone. He also had artistic talent. He could sketch beautifully. Drawing horses was his specialty. His handwriting was not just legible, it was neat, clear and graceful.

Knute's wife had to relate as daughter-in-law to the elder Lees, Hannah and Aad. The relationship did not seem to be particularly warm. Mathilda gave a hint of her feelings in some comments that seemed disparaging. She thought that Aad had not been ambitious enough to be a farmer. And she added, "And he drank a little."

Aad lived less than a year after his son had married Mathilda Glasrud. (The Aad in Aad Lee, pronounced awed, it was sometimes spelled Odd.) Hannah, who later remarried and moved away from Spring Grove, had reached the age of 75 by the time of her death in 1928. The Lee family, originating in the Sognefjord region of Norway, had gravitated toward an enclave of fellow Sognings in Black Hammer. My great grandfather, Knut Amundson (son of Amund), took the name of their Norway farm near the Aurland town of Li when he left with his family to come to America. But it wasn't originally Lee or Lie or Li, but rather Ytrelie, meaning the outer lea (meadow) or farthest-out Li farm. Later, for the practical reason that few non-Norwegians could spell or pronounce Ytrelie, the family name had become Lee.

Soon after they were married, Mathilda became pregnant. In nine months (and 10 days), baby Sylvia was born on June 10, 1907. Mother rather resented what she felt were almost snide questions from her in-laws asking, "Shouldn't the baby be born soon?" when the pregnancy began to show most obviously. She sensed that they were assuming the conception was pre-marital. Anyone really familiar with Mathilda's principles would understand the basis for her smoldering anger.

Any coolness with her in-laws may have also affected her feelings toward her husband's sister, Maria Peterson. Their relationship, while always correct and polite, was never warm. This also may have been due to a subtle sense of class-consciousness on Mathilda's part, of which she was likely not even aware. The Glasruds in Norway had owned land and ran a large farm (gaard) with peasant-type workers. Knute's family in Norway were more the *husmann*, the Norwegian version of share-croppers. Some of the condescension on the one hand and deference on the other may have lingered among the otherwise equal immigrants in America.

Just about the time that Sylvia was born that summer of 1907 an event took place in Spring Grove that involved virtually everyone in the village and surrounding area. It was the first Homecoming. A call had gone out to the families who earlier had emigrated to the West—to Montana, North and South Dakota and even Northern Minnesota. And hundreds came. A festival was launched that has since been repeated each 10 years on the seventh year of the decade: 1917, 27, 37 etc.

A photograph in the story of "Spring Grove, Soil, Timber & A Spring" (By Jane Briggs Palen, *Spring Grove Area, Past Present and Future*, 1991) shows a parade of people on Main Street. Among the crowd were both a horse-drawn buggy and something obviously new to the community: a gasoline buggy! A huge arch was built bridging the roadway, stores had bunting and flags and a 50-foot banner blazed with the legend: WELCOME HOME 1852—1907. Another photo revealed almost 200 people at the railroad depot including both travelers and greeters. A sizeable delegation had come from the Red River Valley region south of Fargo where so many Spring Grove, Wilmington and Black Hammer families had homesteaded. That meant that Mathilda and Knute would see again a host of returning North Dakota relatives from Kindred, Davenport, Horace and from LaMoure and Northwood farther west and from Kittson County farther north. Among them might be Glasruds, Dustruds, Haugstads, Myhres, Qualleys and Fredriksons.

Knute and Mathilda would have Sylvia Henrietta, their first-born child, to show off!

And a second child followed almost two years later. Barbara Elizabeth Marie arrived on March 15, 1909.

We have in Mathilda's own words a dramatic and, in retrospect, humorous account of an incident later that same year when both daughters were still quite young. Word had come from the farm that Tillie's mother had fallen on the back steps of her house and had hurt her back. So Knute hitched up one of his horses so they could go out to see what they could do to help.

> I had Barbara in my lap. She was just a baby. And he had Sylvia in his lap. And he had a new horse he was trying out. And he had a buggy with a canopy top with a fringe. A single seater. Canopy tops were square tops. And he had fixed up a brake on that buggy so it wouldn't be so heavy for the horse down hill. Before reaching Alfred Halvorson's farm there's a big turn in the road. Just as we were in the turn, your Dad says, 'Let's see how this brake works!' And he stepped on the brake and it went 'Brrrrr!' And the horse just gave a spurt right in the steepest part of the hill and near the curve—and we tipped over!

Knute and Mathilda in 1909 with little Sylvia and baby Barbara at the Black Hammer store. Even in those days, advertising signs traveled with them. He had two horses where one would have been sufficient, but why not give his team some exercise on a Sunday afternoon?

> Well, he had his arm around the brace of the buggy and was driving with one hand and holding Sylvia with the other. We didn't—any of us—get hurt. I think we landed inside of the top. He didn't let go of the horse. He

> hung on [to the reins]. I remember when we stopped the horse was facing us! I remember that he must have righted the buggy—I and the children got out—and he got the horse around. I can remember that he took the whip and the lines. I was standing there with the children. He laid the whip on the horse and the horse went as fast as he could way up to Lommens there and turned and came back with him—all before he loaded us again. I don't think the children even cried. Oh, that was funny! I haven't thought of it for a long, long time. We weren't any of us hurt. He was so smart about that—he was just going to test the brake!

Knute was a horseman. He knew them. He judged them. He trained them. He "broke" them. He bought, traded and sold them. He had ideas, plans and dreams involving horses. Somehow, early in 1910, he acquired a number of horses—a dozen, more or less, or at least enough to fill one of the railroad's "immigrant cars" that allowed passage for both stock and the persons tending them. Where the steeds came from and how he bought them or brokered them on consignment, we don't know. But he took the horses—and himself as the groom—out to the Dakotas. He had a cousin by the name of Winjum who had homesteaded near Lemmon, South Dakota.

Mother's letters to him give some details both of his results with his attempts to sell the horses as well as of her life at home with the children—a lonely wife missing her husband who was out seeking his fortune. Certainly pathos can be read between the lines:

> Spring Grove, Minn., Mar. 2, 1910
> My Dear Husband—
>
> I received your last letter this morning and see that you have sold the sorrels. Well, that is all right. I hope you will do as well with the rest, but I 'spose you won't do that.
>
> Today we have just beautiful weather. Just like spring. Hope it will continue. We are just back from church to see Thora get married. It was quite something to see. She had three bridesmaids and best men and little Alice as flower girl. She looked sweetest of all. I am going this evening because Ma came up to stay with the children. I chipped in with the boys for a present. We bought a rug and bedspread.

Mrs. Asle Halvorsen died this morning. I haven't heard yet when the funeral is to be. Mrs. Stenehjem's mother died yesterday morning. Funeral here tomorrow. Sylvia and Mamma were in to see Mrs. Carl Berg. Carl is quite sick.

They are quite well at Christ's now. Christ is hauling wood. Barbara walks quite good now.

So you are going to buy land, I see. Well you will have to use your own judgment in the matter.

I have $10.00 left and a couple of dollars in silver. I gave Arthur money for two sacks of feed this morning. He is all out for the colts, too. He was down to the other place this morning. He brought me back 13 eggs. I have gotten a few before, too.

Yesterday finished the trial of Jens Skrub. He was committed to the insane asylum at St. Peter and they say that is worse than the pen. Well I think this will have to be all. I suppose you don't know anything about when you are coming home. Are you going to see the boys?
With love,

Mathilda

P.S. I'll have to hurry and mail this.

* * * * *

Spring Grove, Minn., Mar. 8, 1910
My Dear Husband—

We received your cards and letters last evening [Mon.] and I received your letter [written Sunday] this morning.

The last letter I wrote you was last Wednesday. I thought I couldn't write any more as I thought you would be leaving Hettinger so I didn't know where to address them to. And I thought also that you might be coming home soon but you don't seem to be in any hurry.

We are all well, getting along first-rate. Last week the weather was very mild but both yesterday and today it has been quite a cold wind. The roads are something fierce. They use sleighs yet. Have not heard of any [mail carrier?] appointments yet. Toni had told Arthur that he thought he would have to drive till the first of April.

The children are well. Barbara is walking all the time now.

I am good and tired this afternoon. I washed yesterday and made an apron for Sylvia and myself and today I am baking bread and washed my floor and ironed. We had soup for dinner today. Don't you wish you had some?

I see you have bought land. Are you going to farm it? It won't be much to farm, will it?

I am glad you did well with your horses. But of course you had heavy expenses, too.

Yes, I went to the wedding. Ma was at home with the children. I stayed till two o'clock. I had a very good time. You see it helped some that I didn't have any husband to look after me. Barbara is crying now. She is cross sometimes. She wants to help me write. Well, this will have to be all.

With love,

Your wife, Mathilda

P.S. Christ got out today. The rest will be set free in a few days. Arthur was going to have the mules today. Last night he didn't get back before 7:30.

We can assume that the postscript refers to the snow or mud that was blocking farmers from getting to town in the spring time. Mathilda had reason to be anxious about the land deal. We detect some relief in her acknowledging his success in selling the horses he took to the Dakotas, but she is (typically, for her) cautious in her response. Of course she is very lonely, with two very young children at home. Behind her question about "Are you going to farm it?" we can read some apprehension about the land deal. It would seem that Arthur is his backup on the mail route—unless by this time Knute had already quit that job. At any rate, his exploration of the West would inevitably bring changes for him and his family.

Spring Grove, Minn., Mar. 10, 1910

My Dear Husband—

I have been looking for a letter both yesterday and today. I have been wondering how it turned out with that land deal. But maybe you got tired of writing because you don't hear from us. But we don't know where to write to you. You may have left by the time this reaches you.

We are all well. I have been busy sewing these days. Barbara is crying now of course. She is always cross when I write. She can walk.

The roads are just fierce. Hard on the mail carriers. It

is pretty hard on Fannie, too, but he [Arthur] has had Christ's mules two days this week and today he has Willie's bronco and Pickles.

We are having eggs to eat now. We get 10 and 11 a day. They taste pretty good, too, I tell you.

Christ stayed here last night. He is deeding that land today. Well, I won't write more this time.

Hope we will see you soon.

Your loving wife,

Mathilda

When Knute returned from his trip selling horses in the Dakotas, Mathilda would discover that a new adventure was about to begin. The "land deal" she had asked about in her letter turned out to be a frontier farm he would acquire near Lemmon, South Dakota. Not only that but, as she later recalled for us, he had traded their home in Spring Grove for 80 acres of dry, sun-baked land and a sod house!

Knute was a trader. He was well known for his horse trades. Later he would often barter for other property as well—cars, houses, farm implements. On his trip he had apparently visited a number of communities in both North and South Dakota selling the horses he had brought with him. He chose places where families from the Spring Grove area had transplanted themselves, many as homesteaders. These were settlers who took advantage of the right to claim and own land that the government had offered to spur development in the vast prairies and mountains of the West. For most Midwesterners, "West" was defined as the space between Minnesota, Iowa, and Missouri and the Rocky Mountains.

Mathilda's March 8th letter (see above) had referred to her husband's being in Hettinger, North Dakota. That's just up over the line from South Dakota and about 25 miles from Lemmon, which almost straddles the border between the two states. Montana is only 75 miles to the west and Spring Grove about 400 miles to the southeast. Knute knew that a Winjum cousin of his (first name not known) had homesteaded near Lemmon and it was surely while visiting him and his family that he discovered that Tollef Ellestad, another emigrant from Spring Grove, was eager to return and would trade his farm for Knute's house and 20 acres back "home." Knute couldn't telephone and consult his wife. So he gambled: he made a deal.

Mathilda must have had mixed feelings about the move. She knew what North Dakota was like and her memories were not altogether happy. She realized that where she had taught in eastern North Dakota was considerably more developed than the frontier land 140 miles farther west in South Dakota where she and her husband would now move with two small children.

They made the move by train. They took their live stock—horses and cows at least—and whatever personal belongings and furniture they needed to have with them in an immigrant car. They thought this might possibly be a permanent relocation. A hired man named Gallagher went along to tend the animals. Somewhere along the way at a rail transfer called Midway, perhaps in or near the Twin Cities, they would have to unload and reload the livestock. Mathilda's brother Arthur also made the trip with them, travelling in the immigrant car with the live stock. Knute and Mathilda with their daughters, three-year-old Sylvia and one-year-old Barbara, were in the coach part of the train and arrived a couple of days before the immigrant car.

Lemmon was a boom town of 1,500 people in 1910. Being between the Black Hills to the south and the Badlands to the north, it had a certain magnetism for adventurous souls from the Midwest. The special character of the region is described in Kathleen Norris' 1993 book, *Dakota: A Spiritual Geography*, which has Lemmon as its setting. She writes:

> Dakota is a painful reminder of human limits . . . a land of little rain and few trees, dry summer winds and harsh winters, a land rich in grass and sky and surprises . . . We hold on to hopes for next year every year in western Dakota: hoping that droughts will end; hoping that our crops won't be hailed out in the few rainstorms that come; hoping that it won't be too windy on the day we harvest, blowing away five bushels an acre; hoping (usually against hope) that if we get a fair crop, we'll be able to get a fair price for it.

My mother told me in 1959:

> It was a new town, and I guess they thought it would grow. And for a while, it did. They had built it up in some places. Later they were even prospecting for oil—I don't think they ever found any. The Winjums were there and they were very nice people and we went to their house first and then we moved out . . .

She didn't reveal her reactions on first seeing the farm but she did say that there were 80 acres of land "with all the improvements." About the sod house her only comment was, "It was a rough experience." She said that "Arthur was there and then this man Gallagher was also there and they slept on the floor. It was really primitive, you know—like regular pioneers."

Knute had two teams of horses and Arthur had one and they lost no time in planting. It was late springtime and there was hope that corn and potatoes, to begin with, would provide food. And the horses could pull plows to prepare the hard dry soil for grain. If the summer brought rain, a crop might be harvested.

They had cows for milk, butter and cheese and there were chickens. Barbara told the family story of how little Sylvia was once chased by a rooster who attacked her and almost pecked out her eyes. She also said that there was a root cellar where food stocks could be kept, entered by a trap door. One day when Mother was about to open it, a huge rat came out! Barbara added, "Mother hated it there."

The Standing Rock Indian Reservation was not far away in the adjacent county. Mother remembered riding through it and seeing Indian women squatting on the sidewalk. She also mentioned how the prairie near Mobridge had become covered with a deep blanket of snow the winter before. When the snow melted, the bodies of cattle—hundreds of them—were found. They had frozen to death and the snow had drifted over them.

Alas, Knute was not a farmer. And the weather was not kind. The heat was merciless and baked the soil. The wind was strong as it blew through, picking up dry dust and swirling it over the flat landscape, penetrating every nook and cranny. No rain came to bring relief. The crops were failing fast. She elaborated:

> Your dad decided that he wasn't going to stay there because he couldn't see any future in it because it was so dry all summer. But he did hear that, after he left, it started to rain. We had planted potatoes and they hardly came up again. I think it was August. I stayed on a while. I thought: I'm not going back home again—we'd just moved out to South Dakota. I hated to go back and to think it was a failure.

So Knute and Arthur took their teams and went on ahead toward Minnesota, leaving Mathilda in Lemmon with her two children. The men knew that with the horses they could work along the way, making money in those more fortunate places where better weather had permitted a crop to grow so it could be harvested. And they did just that. They joined threshing crews on big farms and got paid handsomely for their own labor and for the horsepower they could deliver.

Mother said:

> They had a team and a wagon each. And they rented out their teams, too. Your dad earned quite a little money during that time. He sent it home to me so I took care of it.
>
> I think I stayed on for about three weeks. But I really didn't like it. I didn't think I would mind being there with those two little children alone. But I got terribly lonesome. If I wanted to go into town I had to walk, you know. There were one or two neighbors at quite a long distance. So then I decided to go . . . and when we got ready, we went on the train.

It was typical of Knute that he found out when the train carrying his wife and daughters would pass near to where they were working. Imagine his family's surprise and delight when, at one stop along the way, he boarded the train himself and rode along with them to the next station, about 10 miles away, where he had arranged for someone from a threshing crew to pick him up.

By this time he and Arthur had found two other Spring Grove men to join them on their working trip home. One was a Myhro, Arthur's future brother-in-law, and the other Helmer Gulbrandson. They did some plowing, as well as threshing, and travelled the whole distance by horses and wagons, camping along the way.

She said that when finally the train arrived in Spring Grove, coming from the east because she had to change trains at Bridge Switch on the Mississippi:

> I can remember so plainly that when I got to the depot in Spring Grove I thought the depot was on the wrong side of the tracks . . . Oh, I was so weary, you know, having two children in such a small space . . . and I had been up all night. We started in late afternoon, I think, probably about two o'clock, and I didn't get home to Spring Grove until evening of the next day . . . and I thought the

town looked so pretty. It was so green. And I thought it was so nice in the house and I never had enjoyed it so much as I did then. Everything had been so brown out there on the prairie.

A month later Knute and his comrades arrived home.

CHAPTER SIX

A Growing Family

After their farming failure on the frontier in South Dakota, Spring Grove looked good to Mathilda and Knute. Family and friends were close by. A promising future was ahead of them and they both were determined and ambitious. But where would they live now that the log house and barns they had traded for the sod hut out west were no longer theirs? And what would be the source of their livelihood? Knute was tired of hauling the mail. He had horses but no barns and no pasture lands.

"Things were unsettled for a while," Mathilda said. "Temporarily, we rented a few rooms over the Henry Fladager store."

Mons Fladager has been called the "Father of Spring Grove"; he was the town's third resident and had started a general store in a log cabin about 1859. After he died in 1905, his sons Henry and Peter established a ready-to-wear clothing business at the "Sign of the Lion." For over a century a bronze lion lay guarding the sidewalk on the corner of Main Street and what is now Division Avenue, the crossroads of the village. Every child raised in that town remembers sitting on it. The second floor rooms had also housed a millinery parlor and the small clinic of Dr. Thrond Stabo.

"Your dad then ran a little restaurant for a while,"my mother told me, "but I didn't like that because the hours were late, you know. I was alone so I didn't like that."

The restaurant didn't succeed. So Knute scouted for another opportunity. He discovered that a hotel in Mabel, the next village eight miles to the west, was for rent. Why not try that? They did.

> We didn't stay there very long. I think only about two months. That hotel was for rent and it was also for sale and someone up and bought it.
>
> That was a busy place because we had to get a cook, you know, and some waitresses. And there were travelling men coming and going and I didn't like that job either, because your dad was up in the office and there was always somebody—salesmen and others—in and out and I didn't like that.

Knute didn't like it either, apparently. He soon discovered another opportunity to make some money in the kind of business where he felt he really belonged—the buying and selling of horses.

He and his good friend, John Kjome, developed a scheme to go out to Montana, where wild horses could be found and caught and then domesticated. They planned to bring back a carload of them to sell to farmers in Southern Minnesota. Montana was still a frontier state and in some respects deserved the label of "Wild West." Mother recalls that the men travelled by train along the Great Northern Railroad that had recently completed a stretch of track straight across the state from the North Dakota border to Glacier Park. Among other places they stopped at Scobey, in eastern Montana, and at Choteau within sight of the Rocky Mountains. Somehow they financed and bought mares and broncos and returned to Spring Grove with their cargo of restless and kicking horses, now hopefully tamed or at least soon to be "broken."

"I stayed to wind up the hotel," Mother told me with a voice that sounded tinged with unpleasant memories. It clearly wasn't a responsibility she appreciated and, in retrospect, it hardly seems fair for her to have to do that.

> I remember one incident that bothered me a great deal. We had a waitress whose husband was a barber. They came after we arrived. She wanted a job and so he got a room because she worked with us. And he was not a very good character. Then there were some travelling men there. One night—it was the last week I was there alone and I suppose they took advantage of that—they played cards in their room all night. I didn't dare go over to say anything about it. I knew it because I was trying to sleep there in the other room. I knew what was going on. But it wasn't a very easy thing for a woman to do, you know, if they are gamblers and were drinking. At that time I didn't have the courage to do anything. Now I would have!

She agreed that it wouldn't have been safe for her to interfere. She added, "We were soon out of there. The barber's wife wasn't on the best terms with her own husband because he wasn't what he should be. And there were some foxy kind of travelling men in those days, too."

During his trip with John Kjome, Knute had time to think and plan ahead how he could translate his love and knowledge of horses into a business that would help him make a living for himself and his family. The idea he would work towards would be a feed barn where farmers could stable their horses, have them fed and curried while they traded at the local stores. It would cost money to build a barn large enough to accommodate a dozen or more teams at a time.

My brother Bill, with his keen sense of town and country, explained in a 1984 recorded interview the vital role horses played in the first few decades of the 20th Century:

> On the farm, almost all horses were more or less general purpose. The idea of heavy draft horses was really not carried out in our area of the country. Farm horses were sort of dual purpose animals. They could pull the farm equipment, machinery and wagons, hay racks and so on—plows, cultivators, harrows, discs, drags—and they could also be a road team. If the farmer wanted

> horses that could prance at a pretty good clip with a light buggy, he'd take his most sleek pair of them and he'd drive them to town. If a farmer needed a heavier horse and he was willing to trade his lighter horse, my father would try to turn a few dollars in the trade to his advantage . . . This was part of the craftiness and shrewdness of the horse trader—to profit in the long run. Of course that is part of my dad's reputation; it was a little tough to get the best of him in a horse trade.

Mother recalled that the horses her husband brought back from Montana would sell in those days for fifty or maybe seventy-five dollars. "Some of the broncos, for as low as thirty-five or as high as one hundred. I suppose they were unbroken. But he used some of them for himself. I think shortly after that he bought a dray line that he had for a long time."

The dray line, a freight delivery service, would not need to wait for capital to build a big barn. A small barn would do for his teams. Perhaps his time riding the rails all the way to Montana and back impressed him with the amount of freight that trains carried. And freight came into Spring Grove, too. Merchants didn't always want to pick it up themselves. Knute with his team and wagon could perform that service for them. He would be at the depot when the train pulled in and load the crates and boxes—some of them very heavy—and deliver them to the grocery, hardware, and clothing stores along Main Street. He would follow up by collecting from the merchants not only the cost of the freight as charged by the railroad but also his delivery fee—a modest one, to be sure, as I can attest, having personally as a child collected these bills for my father. If the freight charge were $1.75 my dad would write that on the outside of the bill and add twenty or twenty-five cents.

Meanwhile, the Lee family needed a house as their home. They were able to rent temporarily a house that had been the home of Per and Gitlaug Qualley, Mathilda's grandparents. My sister Barbara remembers that it was near the railroad tracks and a grain elevator. It was a little house that had been expanded with an added-on extra room. She told me:

> What I remember about it is that Dad made us a merry-go-round, a real merry-go round! It didn't have [wooden] horses, you know, but it had seats on it. He had a big wheel and we could push it. It had handles, so that

> two people could push it. Then we'd ride on the merry-go-round! And we had a nice big swing up there too!

In 1912 there was an important new development that meant a great deal to Mathilda. Her mother left the farm to move into town. This did not mean, however, that she relinquished control. She continued her ownership of the farm and made all the major decisions about crops, animals, and the various buying and selling that a busy farm required. She had bought the original house that Knute had built and she decided it was time to let her two sons still at home, Willie and Arthur, carry on the farming while she saw to it that her ward and granddaughter, Sigrid Ike, got a proper public school education. The two of them took up residence in the house across from the school house, just a very short distance from the place Mathilda and Knute lived with their two daughters, Sylvia and Barbara.

Knute soon took action on his plan to have a feed barn where farmers could park their teams when they came into the village to trade their eggs, chickens, meat, potatoes and other produce for groceries and for cash. He acquired as the first step a house and barn down the alley south of the strip of stores that stretched from west to east. The family moved into the small house and the small barn was a starting place for the business that he knew would thrive when a big barn could be built for the purpose he envisioned.

The move came about the time that the third child and third daughter, Juliet, was born on April 19, 1912. She writes in her memoirs, *Eighty Years of Remembering*:

> 1912, the year I was born, was a bitterly cold year. I've heard that many times on comparison radio weather reports. Perhaps I was conditioned to cold weather back then, because I prefer winter to hot summer, and always have.
>
> Sigrid Vaaler, my cousin, recalls that she and Grandma Glasrud moved to our house for six weeks to care for our family because my mother was sick for some time after my birth. I've been told that my grandmother took me to church for my baptism and that my cousin, Sylvia Meitrodt, (Arthur's daughter) was baptized the same day.

Barbara remembers the house by the barn:

> It was a small house. You walked into the kitchen.

> There was a cord in the ceiling where we could pull a string and get light. I think there was a pantry there, and then there was a little living room. We did have an organ. It was a reed organ that you pumped. I remember that because at Christmas time I got a beautiful doll and they wouldn't let me play with it. They put it on the edge of the organ. I was going to school at the time. One day when I came home, it had been broken!

She named her baby sister, Juliet, as the culprit. Barbara continued:

> Off the living room was a bedroom. Then, between that bedroom and the kitchen was a steep stairway going upstairs. There were two bedrooms upstairs. The first one, I think, that you entered had a couple of beds in it, and the second one the same. Sylvia and I slept in one of the beds. I remember that while we were living there I had scarlet fever. And Sylvia had scarlet fever too. Those memories are the easiest to remember, because I had to stay in bed, you see, and I suppose I was babied a bit.

Both Barbara and Juliet remember the bare light bulbs hanging from the ceiling. Mathilda remembers when she first enjoyed having electricity come into her home. She said that the very first appliance she ever had was an electric iron. Even with that modern convenience, however, the family still kept flat irons on the stove for at least another 15 years in order both to iron clothes in the old dependable way and also to wrap the hot flat irons in newspaper to warm the beds in the coldest nights of winter.

The new barn itself was a beauty. Just how it was built and by whom, we don't know but it was an impressive structure. Knute had it painted white and his name was boldly displayed over the main entrance on the north side. My brother described it this way:

> The barn was a large livery and feed stable and it was 100 feet long and 40 feet wide. It had a loft. It was on a slope north and south—so at the north end, the upper level, it had two stories. It had the middle floor where harness, tack room and equipment was stored—surreys, buggies, rigs. It had a loft above which held probably as

> much as a hundred loads of hay. At the bottom level they could stable fifty horses.
>
> When the farmers would bring their hogs to town on Saturdays to sell them, they'd stable their horses in there, particularly on the cold wintery days. We had to fill the loft with hay for Dad to have hay to feed the farmers' horses. The fee was "Team with hay, 50c a day" . . . If he filled the barn with fifty horses, that would be twenty-five teams and there would be some profit there.

Spring Grove could never be called a "One-horse town." In that second decade of the Twentieth Century there were horses everywhere and the automobile had not yet made them obsolete. There were a few cars—Mathilda's brother, C.P. Glasrud (Christ) being one of the first proud owners with his White Steamer. The streets were, for the most part, dirt, dust and mud.

The man who had been a legendary pastor of the local Lutheran congregation for nearly 40 years, the Rev. Styrk Sjurson Reque, died while Knute and Mathilda were in South Dakota. He had been a pillar of the community, a strong cohesive force and a symbol of moral authority. Mathilda, who had been baptized by Reque in 1883, wrote this profile of him in the booklet, *History of the Trinity Congregation*:

> He was a man of commanding personality, fearless and courageous in his convictions on both problems of morals and doctrines, and at all times deeply conscious of the responsibilities of his holy office . . .
>
> During Rev. Reque's pastorate the congregation increased from 200 families to 500. It was also due to the fearless and untiring work of Rev. Reque that the saloons were voted out of the township in 1876. As early as 1892 resolutions had passed at the congregational meeting to fight the sale of liquor both in the village of Spring Grove and Riceford.

His successor was a man who was to have a great influence on many families, the Lee family especially. He was Pastor Alfred O. Johnson. Rather than adopting Reque's confrontational style, Johnson was a soft-spoken but firm diplomat. He was a musician and his influence was felt in the musical Lee household—in our worship life, to be sure, but also as we would sing and play at home. The new pastor found an ally in Mathilda Lee and they worked closely together to develop women's organizations in the church and to launch educational projects over two decades.

A family story allows us a glimpse into the human side of Pastor Johnson. The occasion was Willie Glasrud's wedding to Lillian Johnson (no relation) on December 31, 1912. My sister Barbara Gilbertson, who was then just short of four years of age, recalls it:

> I remember the wedding. It was at the Johnson farm, just a mile west of Spring Grove. It was a very cold night—New Year's Eve—and the whole relationship was there. Reverend Johnson came out to perform the ceremony and he forgot his books. So he had to walk back all the way to town to get his books. But he walked the track, because, you see, the Johnsons lived right off the track and so did he, at the other end. But it was a mile home—and a mile back!

Willie wasn't the last of Mathilda's brothers to marry. Ted would follow the next year, 1913, and Edwin would be the last to marry in 1915. Arthur's wedding had been in 1911 and Duffy's in 1908. Peter and Christ had both been married in 1901.

In 1912, Christ and Lindy with their five children left the farm and moved to Spring Grove where he operated a meat market for a year and then a harness shop also for a few years. In 1914 he began an automobile dealership and expanded it later to include farm implements.

The Glasrud clan was becoming more and more prominent and influential in the town. Mathilda's uncle Gust, who sold his farm and moved to Spring Grove in 1910, was very successful selling new-style farm implements to eager buyers in the rural community. He served as mayor for five years until 1914 and again from 1916 to 1918.

Mathilda and Knute's fourth child, and fourth daughter, was born on March 16, 1914. She was baptized by Pastor Johnson and named Margaret Katherine. Among Margaret's earliest memories are learning letters and words while sitting in her mother's lap and looking with her at the Saturday Evening Post. For many years that magazine was our mother's chief recreational resource.

After another two-year interval, our brother Bill arrived on March 19, 1916. He was baptized with the name Knute William David. His own explanation:

> I was named Knute, the first son after four daughters. A farmer, Helmer Ike, told me once that my father was very proud when I was born after wondering whether he would ever have a son. And so I was named, appropriately, I believe, after my father . . . Of course, as a practical matter of identity I suppose, Knute in our family was the father and, naturally, the child who had two other given names should be called by one of them to avoid confusion. So I was called by the name William. I was known as William until I got into the military in 1941. My birth certificate had the name Knute and when I said my name was William Lee to a big Marine sergeant he informed me otherwise: "Your name is Knute!" So my name was Knute throughout the military . . . I finally got over the notion that Knute was a clumsy, Scandinavian name and I'm no longer ashamed of it and I think the name is okay.

Right after Bill was born, Mother's good friend, Regina Kjome came to visit and brought her own newborn baby. According to Mother, four-year-old Julie saw the two babies lying together on a bed and proudly declared, "Our baby is the nicest!"

In 1916 Mathilda's mother, with her granddaughter, Sigrid, moved to the house on the east side of town vacated by her son, Arthur, and his bride, Amanda, who had left to farm in Kittson County, far north in Minnesota. This left available the house that Knute originally built across from the school, and where his own parents, Aad and Hannah had also once lived. Knute then re-acquired it for his own growing family.

This white clapboard house, heated in winter by a coal stove in the parlor, had a kitchen with a cellar below and a dining room. The second floor had four bedrooms. It was on a corner with a front porch facing the school across the street, a north entrance to the kitchen off of what was then Black Hammer Street (today First Street NW), and a south entrance and porch with a walk that led to the outhouse and the barn and alley. Later a combination garage/woodshed/chicken coop was built.

Brother Bill laughingly pointed out years later that the garage never had a car in it. By the time it was built to enclose a small Ford, our father had traded cars and bought a big touring car that wouldn't fit. Instead it became a store house for garden tools and a place to put waiting-to-be-fixed furniture and junk-filled crates and boxes.

Mathilda and Knute with five children posed for a Christmas picture in 1916, the year their first son, Knute William David, was born. He is in the center of the circle with their father also holding Margaret. At the left, top to bottom, are Sylvia, Barbara and Juliet.

Life became increasingly busy and complicated for Mathilda. She had five young children and, while that was not unusual in those days, they were lively and demanding. Fortunately Knute was earning an adequate livelihood with his dray line and feed barn so there was always food and clothing, if little else.

This is the house that Knute built. Mathilda's mother, Sigrid, was its first owner and she and her granddaughter Sigrid lived in it before it became the Lee family home, across the street from the school in Spring Grove. It was Mathilda's home until she died in 1978.

Mathilda found healthful release from the mundane pressures of small town domesticity by seeking friends and participating in church and community affairs. Some neighbor women offered the warmth of close companionship that she needed. Regina Kjome, Nellie Akre and Louise Foss—these women would take time for a morning or afternoon kaffe klatch and sit around in each other's kitchens over cookies or cake or pie and hot coffee. (It never seemed hot enough for Mathilda!) The camaraderie of these social coffees gave these homemakers a wonderful time and place to gossip, exchange ideas and share feelings.

Even beyond the homes adjacent to hers, Mathilda had friends in other parts of the town. And she and Knute would join with other couples in evenings out.

Clara Hoegh was certainly one of Mathilda's favorites. My sister Naomi explained their friendship this way: "Mrs. Hoegh was quite a private, isolated person almost, in the community, She didn't have very many friends, but she was a very well-brought-up woman, and a fine lady, well-read and so on, I think. She had a little class. And Mother immediately related to her. The two of them had a strange friendship. They were always there for each other if they were needed, in a way, but never were the two couples together . . . I don't think that either one was ever in the other's home as a couple."

Mother and Dad particularly enjoyed the John Kjomes

because he and Knute had become close during their horse-buying trip out West and Mathilda and Regina Kjome as neighbors established a solidarity over the backyard fence, so to speak.

Actually there was no backyard fence. In that small town in those days neighbors normally did not need or want to be separated from each other. However, before the Kjomes moved next door our family felt considerable unease when the Winjums were our neighbors. They were an elderly couple in their seventies. She was insane, Mother said. There were stories of her peeking in our windows.

"I know I was so scared when we first lived there and she came out, you know. Of course I had heard about her. I remember she used to call me Rondina, I suppose she used to know somebody by that name. They used to call her 'Tulla Brita'—tulla means crazy, of course."

That tortured household next door was headed for disaster, almost like a bleak and moody Swedish movie by Ingmar Bergman. Mr. Winjum hung himself in the barn or shed that spanned their property and ours. Mathilda concluded that he had come to the end of his resources, unable to deal with his wife's mental anguish and consequent violence. "You know how things were then," she said, "It isn't like now. And I suppose he had some pride and he didn't ask anyone [for help] either."

The Lutheran congregation in Spring Grove was one of the earliest in the church body of Norwegian Lutherans in America. When the formal organization of congregations, called a synod, was established in the 1850s the community was known as Norwegian Ridge. Mathilda was thoroughly involved in the activities of the congregation from the time of her marriage on to the very end of her life. She made sure, also, that her children did their part, whether it was in Sunday school, confirmation instruction, singing in the choir or performing at programs of one or other of the numerous groups.

Her Spring Grove Ladies' Aid was the group to which Mathilda gave much time. The meetings were every third Friday. And her own published history of the church organizations reveals Mrs. K. Lee as an activist woman who was a leader. She served as secretary in 1908, 1909, 1918 and 1920. She was treasurer in 1911, 1913 and 1914 and was vice president in 1925. In the chapter about her group she described what went on when they met:

> The meetings were always led by the pastor if present; if not present, he would provide a substitute, by that

> is meant either our old Kirkesanger Glasoe, or some outstanding woman. A hymn would be sung followed by prayer and scripture reading, and if time permitted, an excerpt would be read from some religious book . . . Another hymn would be sung, followed by closing prayer. The rest of the meeting would be taken over by the ladies, the dues collected, and the lunch served.

That recitation of a Ladies' Aid meeting seems very typically Norwegian Lutheran, where formalism and tradition had the highest of priority. Some of their custom and routine also appeared strange to Pastor Johnson as evidenced by this commentary in his farewell message to the women of the congregation on December 2, 1932 (He died March 7, 1933.):

> One thing that stands out in my memory is the peculiar seating arrangement at the Ladies' Aid. Instead of facing their speaker as in ordinary audiences, they were grouped on each side of a broad aisle, facing one another. I felt at the time that the one who had invented that seating arrangement must have had peculiar ideas, but I gradually got used to it, and the custom prevailed until a couple of years ago I one day humorously criticized it, and immediately the good ladies graciously and smilingly changed to a more conventional way of seating, which I think they have found better.

By all accounts, life in the Lee household in those pre-World War I days was an enchanting experience for children. Small town life was largely free of fear and social threats. Mathilda and Knute's children were nurtured in a home steeped in pious traditions where character values were stressed. But since kids could be kids, it also was an environment of fun, laughter and play.

"My companion was Margaret," Juliet told me in a recorded conversation back in 1988. "We were always together. I don't remember playing with Barbara or with Sylvia. But of course I remember that when the folks went away, like at night, Sylvia was always in charge. She was pretty tough with us sometimes. But Margaret and I used to have a lot of fun. I remember we had funerals for the kittens. We had an old playhouse—I think it was originally used for chickens. We had plums and we pretended that the green plums were olives and we'd fill bottles with those green plums. Then we'd sort of set up a store. We'd get the old empty grocery boxes and we had a kind of store in there. I do remember one time when a couple of our kittens died, we put them in shoe boxes and we took them down the school lawn, and that's where we buried them."

There never were dogs at the Lee house, but various stray cats lingered around the premises, uninvited but seemingly always tolerated. The cats were never allowed in the house. But one memorable night, when the screen door had not been closed tight, the then-in-residence family cat, who was very much in a "family way," sought sanctuary inside. In the middle of the night little William was heard fussing and thrashing around in his bed, making quite a noisy ruckus. When Dad went to investigate, he pulled the covers back and discovered the cat and her litter of kittens in Bill's bed. So the lights came on and the whole family came to see kittens—those alive and those dead. Several, alas, did not survive the sleeping child's reflexes.

Life in the village could go on for months without much excitement. But whenever a band of gypsies would come into town, an alert was sounded. Children had heard rumors that gypsies would kidnap kids they saw on the loose. The merchants were fearful that when a group of them came into a store, a raid on merchandise could be expected. My brother remembers:

> They came with gaudy colors, colored apparel and it seems to me they had some red ribbons tied to their wagons. Some horses were tied at the rear of those wagons. They were like covered wagons. They'd come with a string of maybe three or four wagons. It was a big event when they came and they would try to spend a day or two in a town. Our dad was constable at one time. I remember once he had a revolver hanging up on the wall in the kitchen for years and years (I later learned, when I was going to trade it off for some golf clubs or something, that it didn't even have a firing pin in it, so it was incapacitated.) He came in the house with a flourish when the gypsies were in town. He grabbed that revolver. went out with the cop, and they had to spook these gypsies and get them out of town.

Juliet added that our father would tell the family to stay in the house and Mother would hide the silverware in the oven!

World War I came and changed the lives of many in the village. However, beyond the infectious fever of patriotic slogans and the stories circulating about young men going off to fight "over there," the Lees were relatively uninvolved on a personal basis. Perhaps the closest relative with war stories to share was Mathilda's first cousin, Inga Qualley, who was a Red Cross nurse among the wounded in France. Knute was exempt both because of his age, 38, at the start of the war and his being the father of five children at the time.

But another kind of war came right to the village in 1918. That was the war against the dreaded and deadly influenza that was nicknamed "The Spanish Lady." Friends and neighbors were struck down in the prime of life.

Barbara remembers that she had the flu herself at that time and was worried it was the deadly strain, but obviously she recovered well. However, she saw something that lingered searingly in her memory: "I remember standing in our north window in the living room and looking up at the Kjome house and seeing them carry John Kjome out for his burial . . . It was so contagious, you see. And there was another man up our street, two of them in fact, who died at the same time, probably the same week."

Certainly the death of Knute's closest friend, John Kjome, was a deep personal blow to him. And his widow was Mathilda's close friend. Our mother must have lived in fear that her own husband would be next.

Mathilda had an additional reason to worry: she was pregnant with her sixth child. A daughter, Naomi, was born just days after the armistice ending World War I. And, in recognition of the victorious end of the awful war, she was given the name of Naomi Victoria.

World War I, even though it didn't touch the Lee family with tragedy in a direct way, did affect the way a "foreign" language such as German, Swedish or Norwegian was accepted by the society at large in the U.S. Up until Germany became the enemy and the propaganda mills of hate began working, the polyglot culture in the Midwest was openly cordial to the mother tongues of the immigrants. This changed, especially in the farm belt of the Midwest, and speaking in a language other than English began to be out of style if not suspect. German-speaking citizens had a more difficult time, surely, than their Norwegian-speaking neighbors, but the patriotic hysteria of war caused many Norwegians to hide their ethnic pride. In Spring Grove, almost totally peopled by Norwegian-Americans, the language was more tenaciously entrenched than in most other places. Most families spoke

Norwegian some of the time and with some, all of the time. Norwegian worship services were held every Sunday. Children took confirmation instruction in Norwegian. Merchants had to be bi-lingual. A tired joke, often told, was that "In Spring Grove, even the dogs barked in Norwegian."

"I even recall that in my first year in Sunday school they started me out in a Norwegian book," my brother told me. "I believe that our class simply rebelled en masse against that and they bagged the whole idea that year . . . It was just really educational instruction, a language book and it wasn't Gospel at all. There were pictures of a cat, locomotive and a ship. 'A cat. That cat. Is that a cat? It is a cat.' That was my first lesson in Norsk! . . . You can't learn about Jesus until you learn how to speak Norwegian, you see!"

Mathilda was a transitional person. She was equally fluent in both languages. In 1909 she gave her report as Ladies' Aid *sekretaer* in Norwegian. After World War I that would change. She used her skills however to translate numerous church documents for her articles about local history. Gradually in her home the Norwegian language was used only when our grandmother was present or when father and mother didn't want the younger children to understand a conversation.

Then it was my time to be born. My arrival was three years after Naomi's. The day was November 9, 1921. My sister, Margaret, remembers it well. She tells the story of her coming home from school at noon that day and being told that she had a baby brother. She hadn't even known that Mother was pregnant or that a new member of the family was expected!

While Mother was still breastfeeding me, she decided one day to go shopping in LaCrosse (30 miles away) and left our oldest sister, Sylvia, in charge. Mother likely went on the train as usual. But it was springtime and there were floods down at Reno, south of LaCrosse on the Mississippi, where she was to change trains. So she couldn't get back in time to feed me. Sylvia was equal to the challenge and introduced me to bottle feeding.

She usually returned with fascinating purchases. My sisters were impressed with Mother's taste in clothing. She loved to wear good dresses and coats and took pride in looking fashionable. Barbara remembers one particular dress she bought in the era when hobble skirts were popular. "It was a kind of blue satin. At the bottom it had maybe a foot and a half row of pleats, all the way down. And it was narrow, long—not ankle length, but long. I think she had a hat that went with that, too. It was very pretty. Stylish, we called it . . . Dad would give her money to go. And, of course, fifty or seventy-five dollars would go a long ways in those days."

In the summer of 1922, Mother and Dad decided to take a trip in a new-to-them car, a Baby Overland. It was a way for them to have a holiday from the family. But, because I was still a baby, less than a year old, I had to go along. And Sylvia went also—to help take care of me. For years afterwards I was repeatedly told that I had traveled farther afield than most of my siblings—even across the border into Canada. Only recently did I figure out why we went into Canada: Mother's cousin, Christian Glasrud and his family lived in southern Saskatchewan on a farm near the town of Mazenod and very likely we visited them. The itinerary included Lemmon in South Dakota, allowing Dad to inspect the land he still owned there. And no doubt a host of relatives extended hospitality to us also in North Dakota.

That trip may have been considered a return visit. When uncles and aunts and cousins would come to Spring Grove from the Red River Valley, they would most often stay at our house rather than at our grandmother's. And it can be surmised that, on leaving, they would say to Mathilda and Knute, "You must now come to see us!"

My siblings who were left behind all remember the trip because they were "farmed out" to relatives. William and Barbara actually were on a farm staying with our Uncle Willie and Aunt Lillie in Black Hammer. Naomi went to Grandmother Glasrud, where our cousin Sigrid Ike, then almost 20 years old, took care of her. And Margaret and Juliet went to Decorah to spend the time with Dad's sister, Aunt Maria and with Uncle Charlie Peterson.

"I was so homesick," Julie told me, "I'd sit in that swing and rock back and forth every day. I'd just cry and look down the road to see if the folks were coming. The day after we got there I'd start looking down the road, and I looked down the road for six weeks! Aunt Maria was so good to us. She tried everything. And Margaret tried to cheer me up. It didn't bother her one bit. When they finally came after six weeks, I was so happy I could hardly stand it!"

Julie admitted that she was particularly lonesome for me. Although only ten years old at the time, she had become a surrogate mother of sorts. She seemed almost to adopt me. She tended me, took me around in a baby carriage, changed my diapers, and gave me all the love and attention that my busy mother had little time to give. "I was proud of him and wanted to show him off. I wheeled him past the school so the teachers could see him," she said. We've been especially close ever since.

The next year, an event took place that, to my knowledge, was never mentioned aloud in our house. Mathilda was pregnant again. Baby number eight was expected, but not for a few months. There was trouble this time. Mother had reached her 40th birthday. Naomi, not yet five, remembers there was a lot of commotion that day. Grandma Glasrud was there. The doctor came and went. A premature baby boy was delivered and was either still-born or expired shortly after. Grandmother baptized the child—in accordance with good Lutheran theology when no pastor is at hand—with the name of Peter, a name celebrated in the Glasrud clan. Our father took the dead child in a little box out to the cemetery and buried it.

We weren't supposed to know about it. But one of Naomi's playmates knew—having heard it talked about at home—and Naomi was sure she was lying. It troubled her and she asked Mother about it. Mother took her aside that evening as she was getting ready for bed and admitted that, yes, it was true, but they shouldn't be talking about it.

Naomi added, "She never mentioned it again and I never did. I had spoken to one other person in the family who didn't even know about it, although a couple of others did."

Also in the early 1920s Naomi was the victim of an accident. The family story has been told many times: The parents were away. Bill and Naomi were playing with neighbor children on the Model T Ford that was parked in our back yard. They were pushing it back and forth. Bill narrates:

> Everybody got in the act and there were four or five kids pushing and then Naomi got her foot into the spokes of the wheel and it crunched right against one of the brake levers and she busted a couple of toes. Of course she was screaming and seemingly in almost mortal pain and in terror. It was a traumatic incident.

Naomi was rushed to the hospital. Dr. Nelson did surgical repair. She spent most of the summer recuperating. During this time, one of the neighbor boys, Norman Foss, who had been one of the group of children pushing the Ford came by faithfully each morning after breakfast with his little wagon and would give her a ride and take her wherever she wanted to go.

Occasional serious illnesses were visited upon every family in those days. They were without antibiotics and the many other amazing medical nostrums we have now. While I don't really remember it, I have been told many times about my having a bad case of measles with consequent ear infections as a small child. But my plight was shared by my sister, Margaret. And she remembers it very well; we were both in desperate pain, she said, with what they called "running ear." Margaret believes that we both have carried the after-effects of that attack all our lives.

Our family was involved in the educational process in many ways. We could look out our window at the new brick school that rose in 1922 to replace the 1899 building that was proving inadequate for the growing population. It was a handsome two-story building covering the entire block.

We had a great advantage of getting up later than most and waiting for the first bell before running across the street to be in our places by the second bell. And we always came home for lunch, unlike many of the others, especially those who lived in the country.

Julie remembers one wintertime day when the whole town was covered with a sheet of ice and our father came to the rescue of the school children with his dray team and a big flatbed sleigh. He collected children from school and delivered them to their homes at lunch time and then picked them up again to return them to their classes. She added, "All the children liked our father!"

When Mother thought things were getting a little too much for herself, Naomi remembers, "she'd probably pack one or two of us off—or probably just go by herself and leave us in the care of our older ones—and go up and see her mother. Our grandmother's house was only a ten-minute walk across town. It was a kind of haven for her. She could get away from it all."

Grandma Glasrud was a towering presence in town even though she was a small woman, prim, straight-backed, unsmiling and stern. During those 1920s she was in her seventies. She had lived through loss, burden and stress as a widow for over 30 years and had been a mother not only to her own 10 children but also to her orphaned granddaughter, Sigrid Ike.

My siblings have various feelings about our grandmother. Some liked, if not loved, her. Others found her an uncomfortable and formidable personality.

Margaret said, "I just knew she didn't care for me. She seemed to pick on me. She thought I was too sickly and that I should be outside more. She never had anything cheery to say to me."

Julie said:

> I genuinely liked her. I really did. I don't know why, but she was always good to me. I remember one time at Easter she bought me the most beautiful hat. And I don't think she ever bought anyone else a hat. This was a white, lacy hat . . . And when I was 12 years old, my eyes were so poor and I wasn't doing that well in school because I couldn't see the blackboard. So they thought I should have glasses . . . She gave me twelve dollars. And Mother said, "You get on the bus, go down to LaCrosse and get your glasses"' Well, I would never think of sending my kids any place to get glasses, certainly not out of town! . . . I didn't think of not doing it. I think I was kind of afraid to do it, but I did it. And I remember that they mailed me the glasses. I remember coming home on that bus. I sat with a lady from Mabel. And we talked all the way home. Isn't that something? At twelve years old!

On the other hand, Naomi reported:

> I didn't get along very well with her. I didn't not get along with her, but I didn't like her very well . . . I felt Grandma was very critical of me. She was a little pompous, I thought . . . and she wasn't much fun to be around. When I think of myself as a grandmother now, with grandchildren, we have such a good time, you know, and they come running, as your grandchildren do too, and jump into your arms when they come to see you. And, boy, we never had anything like that, did we?

There is no doubt that for our family the dramatic legend of the 1920s that is most often remembered and described was of the night the schoolhouse burned.

The beautiful new schoolhouse had been completed only two years before. It was the pride of Spring Grove. Then suddenly: tragedy! It came one bitterly cold December Friday night in 1924. No one lived closer to that building than the Lees. We were there, right across the street.

Christmas vacation had just started at the end of the school day that Friday, December 19, 1924. There had been the usual class parties and Christmas trees. Could some candles have been left burning? The cause of the blaze was never officially determined.

Owen Onsgard alerted the town. He turned in the alarm when, walking home after midnight, he discovered the fire.

My father, who himself was a volunteer fireman, heard the siren and immediately jumped out of bed to dress. He didn't have to wonder where the fire was this time. He looked out of his bedroom window and saw the menacing flames already breaking through the windows of the brick building across the street.

When the fire equipment came there was no water. The hydrants were frozen and had to be thawed before the flames could be attacked from the outside. The firemen broke down the doors and were able to use the hoses inside, but it was too late. Help had been summoned from Caledonia, eight miles away, but it did not come in time to make a difference.

The Lee house became a command center and battle station. Mother made gallons of coffee. Neighbors came with food. People who had been roused out of their homes tried to carry away books and supplies from the building. And most of this was deposited on our yard and in our living room and dining room. Meanwhile, because there was a strong wind, burning embers were blown across the street and fell among the papers and books piled there. It was frightening and chaotic. And the fire won the night.

Barbara recalls that in the midst of this apocalyptic scene, several firemen came directly from a midnight game of cards—one of them in a bear skin coat and another obviously drunk.

This was no time for Mother to worry about her little children. I and my older brother were hurried off to the Bakke neighbors up the street, away from the immediate scene.

Bill recalls being bundled up again and carried by Clarence Bakke down to the corner by our house to have a look at the frightening sight.

My mother told me that for a long time after the fire, I shook with fear every time the fire siren sounded in town. Because I was only three years old at the time, I don't have any clear memory of the event. But it seems my psyche remembers!

Juliet had gone to our grandmother's house for the weekend. In her memoirs she writes, "At four o'clock in the morning, Grandma's phone rang and it was my mother. She said, 'If Juliet wants to see the schoolhouse burning she'd better walk home.' I didn't want to miss that, so on that dark, cold, bleak December morning, I watched the glow of the burning school as I trudged homeward. I shall never forget that fire. A portion of blackboard was left on our lawn, so my father had it framed and it found a place in our kitchen."

The smoldering coal bin glowed for many days and wisps of smoke continued to arise from the empty, roofless ruin as a poignant reminder of how transient our structures can be—even so-called "fireproof" ones. The heart and symbol of Spring Grove's educational establishment was devastated.

CHAPTER SEVEN

Priorities as Parents, 1925-1931

The Lee family, except for the three youngest of us who had been evacuated out of the way to neighbors, didn't get much sleep the night of the schoolhouse fire. With other townsfolk they had come in and out of our house, making trip after trip across the street carrying in books from the library and documents from the school office. About half of the collection of 2,000 books were saved. Then, as the fire spread, it became impossible to retrieve any more from the doomed building.

It was bitterly cold—17 degrees below zero! When our dining room was fully packed and stacked, the salvaged material spilled over into our living room and then onto the porch and finally onto the south lawn—never mind the snow.

Everyone pitched in. Someone had to keep the coal stove stoked. Others made sandwiches. Coffee was brewing almost constantly. Women came with doughnuts and cookies for the firefighters and our house became a virtual canteen. A merchant came with a carton of mittens for those whose gloves were wet and icy. Some firemen had their clothes covered with ice.

Knute was not only a fireman doing his desperately energetic best all night as a strong-muscled 45-year old, he was a member of the school board. They would meet in emergency session the first thing the next morning.

He probably needed a bath—who didn't after fighting a fire?—but it was denied him. The town was out of water. Once the frozen hydrants had been thawed and water had been relentlessly poured into the building, the tall, towering water tank ran dry. It would take hours for the pump to fill it sufficiently to provide pressure.

Mathilda may have wanted to surrender to some sleep—even a cat nap—before dawn, but doubtless she was too taut and anxious for that. There were a thousand things waiting to be done. When she looked out her bedroom window to the west, she saw the smoldering and smoking hulk of the building that had been the town's pride just the day before. Coal had been recently delivered to the school and it burned persistently for many days.

But almost worse than the sight was the smell! She was assaulted by the stinging fumes of burned paper and charred wood. Her house was saved—thank God!—even though it had been endangered by wind-borne fire-brands falling on the roof. The smell lingered from the books and files and assorted ash-coated detritus that had been dumped in her house during the night. Knute's overalls reeked with the acrid stench of the fire's aftermath and the smell also permeated our curtains and couches and carpets.

In the morning Mathilda and her children were conjecturing about the cause of the fire. The girls recalled their Christmas party on Friday afternoon and thought that maybe someone left a candle burning near a Christmas tree or that gift-wrapping was too close to some source of heat or electrical spark. Probably they would never know.

Suddenly plans for Christmas of 1924 also seemed to go up in smoke. Next week! It would not be the holidays as usual. Our family and every family in Spring Grove had to adjust. No one was likely to shirk the responsibility. Toddlers like me were about the only ones exempt.

When Dad came home from the challenging meeting of the school board he had a lot to report. The list of tasks the board had developed was staggering. Arrangements had to be completed sufficiently for classes to start on January 6th! There were textbooks and new chairs and desks to order. Classroom space was preempted all over town. The village hall would be partitioned. The basement of Trinity Church would accommodate several classes as would the Masonic Hall. There would be room in the new A. E. Vick store building as soon as its heating system could be installed. Uncle Christ Glasrud's implement store had space for several recitation halls. And the village approved of using its curfew bell as the school bell for the duration.

Oh, yes, Knute assured the family, Spring Grove would rebuild its school as soon as humanly possible. He had been on the board during the important construction of the now-destroyed building and he and the other board members had learned a lot from that. The insurance was good—$93,300 on the structure and equipment.

The fire was a major event in the growing-up years for Mathilda and Knute's children. The stories from that cold night and the following strange year of improvised class space would feed a legend for our family and for most others in the community for generations to come. For Mathilda it served to make even more indelible her resolve that her own children and all the children in Spring Grove would have a better education than she or her husband had been permitted to have. And she worked to make that happen.

While Knute served during most of the 1920s on the school board, Mathilda was active in the Parent Teacher Association. And she was an active parent, thoroughly involved in each class where one of the Lee children was being taught.

Some of my friends thought she was much too involved. When I was given a double promotion—skipping third grade—I was taunted by some of my former classmates, those I had left behind, that it was because my mom had somehow fixed it with the school. No doubt these youngsters were passing along ideas they had heard at home. It didn't help my cause for them to know that my sisters Julie and Naomi had also each skipped a grade. But, if Mathilda was aware of what was said about her in this regard, she certainly did not reveal her feelings. And, jealous as she was for learning opportunities for her offspring, it would have been completely out of character for her to seek special favors. I just knew it wasn't so.

A small item in the *Spring Grove Herald* reported that on Naomi's seventh birthday, our mother entertained the second grade and faculty after school. Naomi remembers that her class met in what was called the Cooper Shop. It was an empty building up beyond the church and across the tracks which presumably had earlier been used as a workshop for making or repairing barrels or casks.

My sisters also remember that each year our mother would invite the teachers of her children to a luncheon. As a former teacher herself, she seemed to understand how such a gesture would be received as a way of showing appreciation for their efforts.

Naomi said that next to "keeping arrow-straight," education for our mother was the highest priority. She continued:

> She had a quality I've admired and have not emulated particularly, but I really, really admire it. She continued her education for years and years as an adult. She took course after course in the extension service from the University of Minnesota: home-making, home care of the sick, nutrition, preserving of foods, tailoring of clothing. The women of the community would go to classes regularly at the high school. Much of it was paperwork.
>
> I remember one of these classes was in swimming, and she went down to Hokah (a small town half way between Spring Grove and LaCrosse) where Jane Talbot from Winona State Teachers College was the swimming instructor. So these women enrolled in this course went down there, and they probably didn't learn to swim, but they learned an awful lot, and did exercises and things like that.
>
> And part of the thing about the nutrition courses was that she taught us as she practiced making balanced meals, so that when the fad came for health in the sixties and seventies, none of that was new to me. The brown bread and the raw vegetables and not overcooking them—she had known that and given it to us when we were kids.

Naomi agreed that Mother wished she could have gone to college and continued her education formally:

> You know, she said to me once,"It makes me feel very strange to think that all of my children have been to college and most of them have graduated from college, and that I have not"' And that took me by surprise

> because I always considered her smarter and better-educated than I have ever been, or ever will be. She was a self-educated person. It was because of her reading and she retained what she read.

She devoured the *Saturday Evening Post* as it arrived by mail each week. She would always turn first to Post Scripts, the humor page, and laugh as she showed us the cartoons and comic stories each issue featured. She also read the church publication, *Lutheran Herald*, and enjoyed the Norwegian language newspaper, *Decorah Posten*. She enjoyed mysteries by S.S. Van Dyne and loved the "Old Country" novels of Selma Lagerlof and the American ones of Ole Rolvaag.

Not only did Mathilda enroll in extension courses, she helped to teach them as well. In August of 1925, County Agent W. D. Stegner reported in the *Spring Grove Herald* that Home Management Projects were being organized in 24 Houston County communities and that in Spring Grove Mrs. Knute Lee and Mrs. Nels Kjome would be the leaders. In October of that year, the local group elected Mathilda president.

Each group had its own reporter who dutifully sent news from the meeting to the local newspaper. Some of those items revealed the variety of topics the group studied and discussed:

> Kitchen management was the subject for discussion and all of the group seemed particularly interested in ventilation.
>
> We discussed arrangements, work centers and grouping of materials of the individual kitchens.
>
> It is planned to visit a number of homes in this tour where the Home Management work has been put into practical use.
>
> Housekeeping and Home Making were discussed by the leaders. Literature and home assignments were given out.
>
> Our leaders, Mrs. Lee and Mrs. Myhre, discussed the lesson on the care and feeding of infants. Posture tests were taken which showed improvement.
>
> The leaders, Mrs. K. Lee and Mrs. N. Myhre, discussed meal planning, showing what foods are required for the maintenance, energy and resistance of the body. Food selection score cards were checked by each member, then

> the fruit and vegetable budget was explained. Posture tests were again taken.

Mother certainly practiced her health guidelines on her own children. "Robert, sit up straight! Don't slouch!" I heard that over and over. "Bill, don't always walk with your head down." He didn't always remember, however, and one time he was running home—he was late for supper on a dark winter night—and had his head down, looking at the ground, as usual. Then, wham! He ran right into a parked dump truck in the alley and broke his nose and came home hurting and bleeding.

She often asked me. "Have you had your roughage today?" She told me I must drink some water in the morning and always have the fruit juice before I ate my breakfast so that now I really can't start eating breakfast until I've had that fruit juice. And—as another carryover from her training and admonitions—I can't eat until I have said a prayer.

She never framed it—that would have been out of character for her—but I think she treasured the Certificate of Appreciation (dated December 23, 1930) she received for her Home Management leadership from the Houston County Farm Bureau Association.

Another priority for our mother was involvement in our church, with a particularly strong emphasis on religious education. She was part of a very creative and innovative project which at that time was found only in a few, if any, other communities. It was a Parochial Day School and operated on "released time" from the public school. Those students who participated actually left the school building and went for their class period of religious training to a rented room in the home of our neighbor, Oline Onstad, who also lived very near the school.

This can best be explained by our mother herself. She wrote the history of the Parochial School in her *History of Spring Grove Church Organizations* published in 1933. Here is part of her narrative:

> The religious instruction of the young is a cause which has ever been near and dear to the heart of our beloved pastor, Rev. A. O. Johnson. In all the years that he had been preparing the young people for confirmation he felt that much was lacking in the facilities of the Sunday School, and those few weeks of summer religious school, supplemented by some instruction at home which was the system of religious training followed at that time. He felt

that a period of instruction every day would give much better results than crowding in a lot of instruction during a few weeks of the summer months.

Rev. Johnson had been thinking, talking, planning, and praying for a definite form of religious instruction for many years before the plan was realized and came into operation in Spring Grove. In 1916 he explained his plan at a meeting at Roland, Iowa, and strange to say, the plan was accepted and put into use there long before it was possible to do so here.

In the summer of 1924, Rev. Johnson appointed a temporary Parochial School committee, consisting of Julius Dvergsten, Emil Quinnell, Miss Caroline Ostlie, and Mrs. Knute Lee, who together with Rev. Johnson met and transacted such business as was necessary for the organization of the school, renting a room from Mrs. Oline Onstad, and hiring Miss Emma Skjei as teacher, and that was the beginning of the present Parochial Day School in Spring Grove . . .

The consent of the Department of Education of the State of Minnesota had to be secured before classes could be excused from the Public School in order to attend the religious school. Permits were secured which had to be signed by parents, requesting that the pupils be excused at a stated period for religious instruction. The pupils of the first five grades are excused for a period of 25 minutes every day, and the pupils in the upper grades and the high school are excused two and three times a week for a period of 45 minutes a day.

On Dec. 19, 1924, the public school building was destroyed by fire which made it necessary to find rooms here and there all over the village where classes could be held. Much to the disappointment of some of the pupils at least, who had hoped that such a catastrophe would give them a prolonged vacation, school opened on time after a two weeks Christmas vacation and part of the parochial school classes were held in the back room of the tailor shop, which lot is now occupied by the Standard Oil Company, and the parochial classes of the high school were held in the kitchen of the church basement.

Mathilda went on to describe the formation of the Religious

Education Association. She was elected as one of the board of directors. She details the fund raising for a separate building and this was built and equipped, she reported, at a cost of $3,000. The Association borrowed half the money on the basis of notes signed by merchants of the village.

The *Spring Grove Herald* carried a photograph of the cement block building in its February 2, 1928 issue together with the headline, "Parochial School Building Dedicated." The article stated that Dr. J. A. Aasgaard, the head of the denomination (then known as the Norwegian Lutheran Church in America), was a guest preacher for the occasion. The article also explained that "most credit is due to the present board, E. L. Quinnell, Julius Dvergsten, Ingeman Muller, Mrs. B. N. Onsgard and Mrs. Knute Lee."

All of Mathilda and Knute's children (except Sylvia who graduated from high school in 1925) attended those released-time classes, some of us from grade school through high school. I remember well the teachers I had—Gladys Hanson, Ruby Olson, Pastor Oscars Mikkelson and Leander Brekke and seminarian Walter Korsrud. Each of them helped to make religion a lively rather than a boring subject. Miss Hanson later became a missionary to Madagascar. Years later she wrote me that, while serving there, she and her husband had heard one of my Children's Chapel broadcasts via short-wave radio. In responding to her I was able to thank her for making Bible stories interesting enough for me as a child so that as an adult I would dramatize them on the air for other kids.

Our mother's involvement with our local church, Trinity Lutheran, was not limited to the Parochial School. She was a very active participant in the women's group, the Spring Grove Ladies' Aid. She resonated well to the chatter of women in the church basement. I went to some of those meetings in order to sing or play the trumpet for their program and I can still today conjure up that scene whenever I enter a room where fresh coffee has just been brewed. These women were her friends and she felt at home.

With my father and our whole family, Mother was also active in what was called the Church Auxiliary, a semi-social family-oriented service arm of the congregation which met on Sunday evenings.

The pastors depended upon her, too. They would come to our house to get her advice and enlist her help. First it was Pastor A. O. Johnson, whom she considered a saint, and after his death it was young and recently ordained Oscar Mikkelson, the former Parochial School teacher. Pastor Johnson invited her to collaborate on the history of the Spring Grove Church Organizations.

Mathilda was a good writer. Her style was like her thoughts—clear, succinct, factual, and reasonably objective. She was biased as one who is on the side of the angels is often biased.

These excerpts from her 1933 history of her own Ladies' Aid group not only chronicles the organization but also reveals some of her own thinking and personality:

> The village of Spring Grove is unique in some respects. In the first respect about ninety-nine per cent of the people are of the Norwegian nationality, or rather of Norwegian descent. The Norwegian language has always been, and still is, used in conducting the meetings. In the second respect it has always had only one church. It is also unique in so far as it has had only three regular pastors during a period of seventy-four years.
>
> . . . In looking through the records of our society we have a feeling that the people have been living together in unity and harmony in church and aid, and seem to have had many pleasant times together, in the days that have passed.
>
> We believe that these blessings are in a large measure due to the above-named reasons: one church, one nationality. We also believe that many of the blessings which fall to our lot today are the fruits of the faithfulness, and untiring efforts and prayers and Christianity of these pioneer women, our mothers and grandmothers, and of the faithful guidance of the pastors, Rev. Clausen, Rev. Reque, and Rev. Johnson.
>
> The chief aim and purpose of the Spring Grove Ladies' Aid has always been to work for the missions. The older members would never allow any money to be taken from the treasury for local purposes, insisting that it had never been done, although the records after 1904 show that this rule had not always been strictly adhered to in every case.
>
> . . . In the early days they tell us the ladies always wore starched white aprons to Ladies' Aid. Many would bring their knitting and crocheting. Many of them would knit as they walked along, thus making use of every available moment.
>
> Lunch in the beginning was very simple, two or three kinds of refreshments, but as time passed, each lady entertaining would in turn add something to the list. It has been

> told that twelve or thirteen varieties of cake were served at once but that may perhaps be an exaggeration. Finally Rev. Reque made a stop to this extravagance by making this statement at a meeting: "After this it must be a standing rule that not more than three kinds of refreshments are to be served at any meeting. "This rule has been faithfully followed up to the present time.
>
> Ten cents was the amount of the dues collected. In 1926 it was changed to 15 cents per meeting.
>
> As an historian, may I add that writing this little history has been quite a bit of work, still it has been a pleasure, also an honor to be asked to do the work. I have been a member of this organization all the time, except for a few months, since I joined about 24 years ago. I am indebted to Mrs. Mikkel Bakken and Mrs. Olaus Myhro who kindly helped by looking through the old records, and thus secured quite a bit of the information for me.

Neither Mathilda nor Knute was especially outspoken about religious matters, except to establish for their family unequivocal goals and parameters for church and Sunday school attendance. Some of us who taught Sunday school during our high school days (or after graduation if we were still living at home) were not pressured by our parents to do it. It was just understood that we were who we were and the definition of our family included being serious and observant Lutherans.

Our Dad preferred the Norwegian language worship service which was offered every Sunday. Mother sometimes went with him but more often she was by herself at the earlier English language worship or with one or two of her children who were not in the choir or were not sitting with friends. We were never particularly aware of Dad's activity in the congregation—although the local newspaper mentions his being teamed with a neighbor friend, Eddie Foss, visiting a dozen homes early in 1925 to raise funds to reduce the church body debt. At the end of that same year he was on the Christmas Tree Committee for the Sunday School's Christmas program.

Saying a grace before each meal was a rule in our home. It was always a memorized prayer in English or Norwegian. I do not recall ever hearing or using an improvised prayer. But no other time was set aside for reading from the Bible or praying together as a family. As Norwegian-American Lutherans we were not emotional about our faith. Yet, some of my siblings remember, as I do, that our mother gently led us in memorizing the Lord's Prayer.

Mathilda seemed to keep her distance from Knute's work. In Spring Grove at the time that may have been the way wives had for separating themselves from the tasks which belonged to the men; after all, they had their hands full doing women's work—maintaining the home and family. None of us recalls our mother ever visiting the feed barn where our father had his office, his livery stable, or later his farm implement business, his grist mill and his dealership of DeLaval cream separators and milking machines.

When anyone in the village made an out-of-town trip in those days it might be reported as an item in the *Spring Grove Herald*. From those pages we learn that Dad and his brother-in-law, our Uncle Christ Glasrud, attended an implement dealer's convention in Minneapolis each winter for a few years prior to the Depression. In 1927 the two of them also made a trip to South Dakota. We don't know why but it could well have been related to the property our father owned near Lemmon. Other than those business trips he was seldom away from home. He did make a trip to visit his mother in Twin Valley in Northern Minnesota when she was 72 years old and in failing health.

I don't ever remember seeing my paternal grandmother alive. I must have, however, inasmuch as she moved to Decorah, Iowa, soon after my father made the trip to Twin Valley. My guess is that on that trip he negotiated the move and arranged for his sister, my Aunt Maria Peterson, who lived in Decorah, to help care for their mother and their step father. Hannah died in Decorah less than a year later. I do remember that Grandma Lee's corpse was "laid out" in our living room prior to her funeral in Spring Grove in May of 1928. Her name by then was Hannah Amundson as she had married Thor Amundson in 1912 after her husband's death in 1907. Aunt Maria continued as the care-giver for Thor for at least a decade more. Grandma Lee is buried in the Spring Grove cemetery next to our grandfather and near the graves of our parents.

Sylvia, our oldest sibling, graduated from high school in May of 1925, just five months after the school burned. She had always wanted to become a nurse and our parents, in spite of their large family, were financially able to encourage her. She was accepted at famed St. Mary's Hospital in Rochester, Minnesota. Because of the adjacent Mayo Clinic, Rochester was even then one of the pre-eminent health centers in the world. Mother's cousin, Inga Qualley, was a seasoned nurse there at the time—she had been a Red Cross nurse in World War I and had served in France. She was an effervescent and assertive single woman and it would be true to her character to have smoothed the way for Sylvia's matriculation. Mathilda and Knute were reassured by Inga's being in Rochester to offer Sylvia a helping hand—and a lot of advice, no doubt—if needed.

But Sylvia ran into some bad luck. In January of 1926, after only a few months at St. Mary's, she had an appendectomy. It was necessary for her to return to Spring Grove in order to recuperate at home. She didn't return to Rochester until four months later.

That summer after Sylvia had resumed her nursing studies, another event in Rochester suddenly brought that city into focus for our family and the entire Glasrud and Qualey clans: our grandmother, Sigrid Glasrud, then age 74, was hospitalized in Rochester from injuries sustained in an automobile accident on Wednesday, July 25. She was a passenger in her brother Andrew Qualey's car which was hit by a city bus. The others in the car were not injured—her son, Christ Glasrud and his wife Melinda, and Andrew and his wife Otelia. They were enroute to Stillwater, near St. Paul, to attend the Golden Wedding anniversary of Gustav and Sigrid Glasrud. Not only was Gust a brother-in-law of our grandmother but his wife, also named Sigrid Qualey Glasrud, was a cousin of Grandma Glasrud and her brother, Andrew. It was always somewhat confusing that there were two Sigrid Qualey Glasruds of the same generation in the family.

Mathilda went to Rochester as soon as she could and stayed there a few days. Her mother remained in the hospital for several weeks. Doubtless Sylvia was able to spend time with her mother during those July and August days and, at the same time, visit her grandmother's bedside. Most likely Nurse Inga Qualey had a hand in supervising her aunt's recuperation.

And Inga also kept an eye on her cousin Mathilda's daughter, Sylvia. About that time Sylvia became romantically involved with a man whom she, as a student nurse, had helped nurse back to health. He was a charming fellow from Racine, Wisconsin, John Lueker. I remember seeing a photo of Sylvia with a handsome man standing by a handsome (and expensive) car but I didn't know much more about it until my sister Naomi told me the story:

> There was a love affair. [He] was an older man, that is, for an 18 or 19 year old girl, he seemed older. He was perhaps 28 at the time, I don't know. He seemed to be pretty well-to-do. What his work was or what his family was, I don't know. They were Catholics, I do know that.
>
> That was the problem. That, and that he was older. But

> just one or the other probably wouldn't have done it, but the two together certainly did . . . I always had a feeling that Inga Qualey had something to do with promoting the attitude that this man was not a good person for Sylvia. Inga Qualey was an old maid herself.
>
> I remember one time being at home when Sylvia cooked a meal for John Leuker, who was visiting, and everybody had gone that day. And it just happened that that was the day he was going to come to visit. But I was home. Now maybe they left me home as a chaperon, I don't know . . . So I met him, and he did seem a bit older and different from what we might have expected her to choose.And she was urged not to go back to nurse's training. And I've often wondered if there was any connection there . . .
>
> He fell in love with her. He sent her some fabulous gifts . . . I always felt that her life would have been different if she either could have been allowed to marry him—which I think he wanted—or if she could have finished her nurse's training. And I have a vague recollection of Grandma's interference here, too . . . Whenever Inga Qualey came to Spring Grove she would stay with Grandma. And then we would see them together. And she was a powerful personality!

The fortunes of first-born Sylvia, their oldest daughter, seem to have been manipulated by our parents even further. She got a job in Granite Falls, Minnesota, as nurse receptionist for a Dr. Nelson who had practiced medicine in Spring Grove and had relocated. Her nurses training, even though short of gaining her R.N. status, qualified her well for that opportunity. But how and why was the job offered to her in the first place?

Again, the local news notes in the *Spring Grove Herald* hint at what seems likely to have been behind Sylvia's employment. Knute went on a week's fishing trip to Leach Lake in August of 1927 with a party of men who also included the town dentist, Dr. Harold Lovold, our neighbor Eddie Foss, hardware merchant Neuman Myhre and C.J. Sylling, who bought and sold livestock and grain. And the newspaper added, "They visited at Granite Falls en route."

The reason for the visit was that Doc Nelson was their friend and fellow townsman. He may even have delivered some of their children. In whatever way it may have been suggested, proposed or negotiated, it was not a mere coincidence that very shortly after

Dad's visit there, Sylvia left to work for the doctor in Granite Falls.

Our mother was a good family manager. A part of her secret was delegation. Each of the daughters had some housekeeping chore. I inherited the tasks earlier assigned to my brother. These things included moving a pile of wood chunks to the woodshed from the lawn where the saw rig crew had left them, then chopping wood for the kitchen stove, and hauling chunks around to the north side of the house to toss them down the chute to the basement—during the period when we had a wood burning furnace. Often one of us was dispatched to the butcher shop or a grocery store to get supplies for the next meal. I am sure each of us can remember having to go down to find our father so we could get money to buy a quarter's worth of "sausage and hamburger mixed."

Her family management was also successful because she was a strict disciplinarian. She hadn't handled unruly kids in country school for nothing! She could scold effectively and often did. Our dad, on the other hand, was known for being "a soft touch" as far as we kids were concerned. We would fear mom but not dad. I remember only a couple of times when he was angry at something I did. He was also affectionate with us and we would climb in his lap and feel the warmth of his hugs. We weren't often invited to Mother's lap. But we were assured of her love in other ways.

One of Mathilda's priorities was being a good parent. And it turned out that her style and Dad's style complemented each other.

Dad's style of parenting was less directive than Mother's. He was a friendly negotiator and would accomplish his ends with a kind of intuitive psychology—after all, he was literally a horse trader! What made him good at that, beyond his superb knowledge of horsemanship, was his way with people. Our sister Margaret recalls how elated she felt when Dad commended her for her dusting. She always remembered his treasured words, simple though they were, whenever she began her dusting task then—and even years later when dusting in her own home.

Bill recalls, "Dad gave me opportunities to ride horses and saddle them up, and early on, I drove a truck—maybe too early! And once in a while, if I was raking leaves at the command of Grandma or of Mother in autumn from the cottonwoods, I would be doing my work and he would come by and register approval. Or he'd come by and tell me he had an errand in the country somewhere—selling a horse or trading a horse or examining a horse—something like that—and he'd say, 'Go home and tell your mother you're going with me.' And this was particularly delightful for me."

Even though we may have inherited more of our family aptitude for music from Dad rather than from Mother, she was the one who sought opportunities for us to study, perform and excel. Why else would she make deals with out-of-town music teachers to use our living room and our piano as the locus for their teaching in Spring Grove—in exchange, of course, for free lessons for her children? So John Bates from Caledonia taught several of us piano while Marian Cargen from LaCrosse and Mrs. Ingebret Dorrum from Decorah taught voice. When I reached Junior High School and only Naomi and I were left at home with our parents, I had a trumpet teacher (whose name I can't recall) from LaCrosse. It was a formative experience for me because he was a true professional. We were all impressed by the fact that he had played under John Philip Sousa!

I am sure that part of Mother's insistence that we have musical training beyond that provided by the school was that she was denied it as a child. Her sister Julia had the chance but Mathilda didn't. Perhaps Julia helped her to learn the basics of reading music and the reed-organ keyboard. Whatever her own musical experience was, she did sit me down at a certain age and instructed me on how to translate notes from the page to the keys of the piano. My siblings had the same experience. I don't recall ever hearing her play the piano, however.

Juliet was the family pianist. She would play and we all would sing. Mother arranged for Juliet to be available to provide program music or entertainment at Ladies' Aid meetings and PTA assemblies and other community events. When I was almost eight years of age, I was enlisted to perform at Auxiliary, the monthly Sunday evening church social and educational gathering. I know that Juliet played for me—but I didn't sing or play the trumpet then (I did both later). My instrument was . . . a comb! Yes, I made music with a piece of paper on a comb and hummed so that it resonated as a kind of soft reed flute. Apparently it was good enough, or at least different enough, to warrant going public.

Mathilda herself "performed," in a sense, at an Auxiliary program in January of 1927. She ran a spelling contest together with another local scholar, William R. Johnsrud.

We Lees all remember fondly that our dad liked to sing. As has been mentioned, early in their marriage Knute played the accordion. He owned a violin but we don't know if he played it. But he would sing with us. "Roses of Picardy" was a favorite, according to Julie who said he always would ask her to play it. I remember his singing "Somewhere in Old Wyoming," "Springtime in the Rockies" and

"Whispering Hope." Barbara remembers "Silver Threads Among the Gold" and "Pretty Red Wing." During a Spring Grove Homecoming event in 1987 I spotted him on a turn-of-the-century group photo blowup in the Drug Store window. He was among the singers in a men's chorus.

Mother would see that we had tickets to the Chautauqua programs during the summers when that traveling company and others would arrive in Spring Grove and pitch their tent behind the schoolhouse or on a vacant lot near the church. This was our first exposure to stage plays other than the amateur productions in the high school auditorium. We also heard comedians and musicians and magicians and lecturers.

Silent movies in Spring Grove had been popular at the Opera House. Then the school board, including Knute Lee, decided that the auditorium of the new school building could serve as a good movie theater on weekends for silent films. As a seven-year old, I was "hired" to pick up the 35mm cans of movie film at the railroad depot and haul them in my Coaster wagon to the school and carry them up to the projection booth. My pay was free tickets. So I got acquainted with Tom Mix and Rin Tin Tin and other Hollywood legends at a very early age. Juliet and her friend Lillian Gilbertson were engaged to accompany the films with appropriate piano music—fast music for the chase in cowboy features and romantic or sad or joyful songs to match the emoting of the actors.

Less than two years after the school began showing weekend silent movies, "talking pictures" came to the community—first to Caledonia and then to the Opera House in Spring Grove. The silents could not compete. In a few more years the town had its own air conditioned cinema, the Ristey Theatre. With its nightly schedule and weekend matinees, the old Opera House could not compete. And the school's "silents" quickly became passé.

When all of us siblings were together in August of 1991, we talked about our memories of home. And several mentioned how thoughtful our father had been by often bringing something special home for Mother—an Easter lily at Easter and "something nice" on her birthday: a special table or a set of Community Plate silverware. Margaret remembers that, when he bought a washing machine as a surprise for Mother, "I had to tattle and give the news away."

The 1920s were, for the most part, fairly prosperous and happy years for Mathilda and Knute. They were both in their 40s, their family was established and gradually some of the children were becoming more independent. Dad's business was active and there was income enough to feed and clothe the nine of us in the household. There might have been more money if Dad had been a careful businessman; some of his customers took advantage of his patience and laxity by not paying their bills. His labor was physically demanding—assembling heavy farm machinery, lifting bales of hay, freight from the depot or sacks of grain milled from the farmers' oats and wheat. His work was his hobby. It seems that there was precious little time just for fun. Sundays in the summer sometimes included picnics and visiting relatives. Knute did take time, however, to play cards with some fellow businessmen in a downtown cafe, sometimes until late at night, coming home when everyone else was in bed.

He was a volunteer fireman and had been elected second assistant chief. We remembered his waking in the middle of the night to the sounds of the siren on the city hall, hurriedly dressing and dashing off up Black Hammer Street to join the fire brigade.

He was elected town constable and retained that responsibility for almost a decade, beginning in 1925. There was very little for a constable to do in Spring Grove. Beyond his surveillance of the gypsy bands who occasionally worked the village on their way from east to west, we were not aware of incidents that revealed just what his official duties were. I recall his having to serve subpoenas; sometimes I would ride with him out to a farm and wait in his truck or car while he delivered the envelope.

Our father and mother did not seem to us to be overtly tender to each other. Though our mother could laugh and have fun, her decorum was always "proper." Norwegians are among the more private and undemonstrative of ethnic peoples, after all. But it can be assumed, I think, that even as Dad was warm, cuddly and tender with us in public, he would be even more loving in giving intimate comfort and sensual pleasure to his wife in private.

August 30, 1931 marked a celebration of Knute and Mathilda's Silver Wedding anniversary. It was near the end of a hot and dry summer. Percival Narveson, the local weather watcher who tracked the elements annually, recorded a record-breaking heat wave, "when for a whole week the temperature recorded from 98 to 109 degrees, "He said that summer was characterized by prolonged dry spells over the Northwest. "Some parts of Montana, North and South Dakota and Western Minnesota had total crop failures, on account of lack of rain and the abnormal heat waves." On some days, even in southern Minnesota, the sun seemed filtered by a veil of dust blown our way from the wind-swept prairies to our west.

The weather was a precursor of the era, then rapidly emerging, of an arid economic season—indeed, almost a decade—of despair: the Great Depression.

But for our family on that 1931 Sunday, festive joy was the prevailing mood as fearful financial forecasts were put aside and family fun took over. That day even the weather cooperated. The Herald reported, "The day dawned beautifully and remained perfect throughout, which enabled people to spend the day out of doors on the beautiful spacious lawn of the Glasrud home."

This home was where Uncle Willie and Aunt Lillie lived, the same Black Hammer farm where Mathilda grew up and where her wedding to Knute had taken place on September 1, 1906. Her brother Arthur, the best man, and her cousin, Minnie Glasrud Vaaler, the bridesmaid, were both on hand, together with more than 50 relatives and friends. Pastor Alfred Johnson made a little speech with kind words of praise for our parents He then presented them with "a purse of silver." This was long before the days of portable recorders of any kind, but it would have been wonderful if we could now replay the words of both Knute and Mathilda in response. The best we can do is jog our memories by looking at the posed family photo. In spite of the festive occasion, we all looked rather sullen.

Maybe we were worried, after all, about the depressing forecast of the Depression.

On Mathilda and Knute's Silver Wedding Anniversary on a hot day in late August 1931, their family poses without great enthusiasm. Standing (L-R) are Barbara, Mathilda, Knute, Juliet, Grandmother Sigrid Glasrud, Naomi and Bill. Seated are Sylvia, Robert and Margaret.

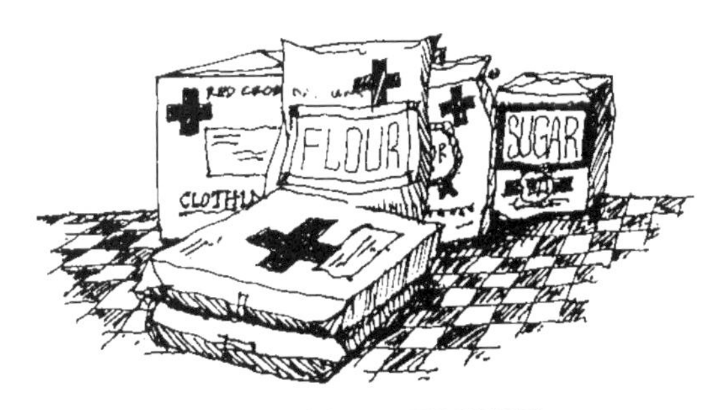

CHAPTER EIGHT

Coping With the Great Depression

The seismic shock waves from the historic 1929 stock market crash produced no panic in Spring Grove. Unlike today's world of electronic communication miracles, Wall Street and the other global financial markets were at that time remote from southern Minnesota.

Yet, the awful legacy of the crash came even to sleepy small towns in rural America, to places like Spring Grove. When the weather was good, farmers could still grow grain and raise livestock, and the food business touched everyone at the necessity level. But the economics of despair pervaded this enterprise as well. Savings, if any, were mostly eaten up or lost. Prices and sales were skimpy. The "Depression Blues" took over.

Mathilda, with her large family to manage, could no longer depend upon Knute's regular income from sales. His farmer customers couldn't pay their bills, yet they wanted and needed his services and his farm implements on credit. I.O.U.s wouldn't clothe the Lee family.

Mother told me:

> I know he had more than a thousand dollars worth of notes that were no good. And I know he had turned it over to Minnesota Twine and he had to make it good. I remember. He had to borrow the money. The notes came back, you see . . . the people didn't have any funds, so . . .

It helped that the Lees were not alone in feeling the pinch of the nation's economic constrictions. Almost everyone was in the same boat. Our sister Sylvia, while she worked as a dentist's helper after her curtailed pursuit of a nursing career, had the dramatic lead in "Depression Blues," a stage production of the local Little Theater Club. It was a comedy. People needed to laugh at their difficulties whenever they could. Sylvia played the part of a suffering mother.

Our mother, Mathilda, did not suffer nor did she let her family suffer. She was a true stalwart, having the spine of the Qualey and Glasrud pioneer immigrants from Norway. She learned from them that one had to expect hardship in life. After life in a sod hut in dusty Lemmon, South Dakota, this would not overwhelm her or her family.

She had her garden. It was not just a small plot in the corner of the back lawn. Knute helped her negotiate the use of an empty lot on the street south of his feed barn and he hitched one of his horses to plow furrows and raked them into readiness for her planting. She herself labored putting in the vegetable garden, but not alone. She had me and any of her other children who might be available. I hated it. I still remember cutting potatoes and dropping them as seeds into the holes my brother had fashioned with his spade. And there seemed to be endless assignments of weeding the rows of carrots, peas, beans and sweet corn. I had my fill of that work and ever since I have avoided planting or cultivating a garden. But, all credit to her gumption, we had food to eat from that garden each year and we could not have survived without it.

Brother Bill also remembers that garden. He had vivid memories of what the Depression was like for our family:

> It was a sad and a prolonged period and lots of privation. We weathered it better than many people. Oh, I remember in that connection the big gardens we had. We had to raise vegetables and fruit—these were canned in copious quantities.
>
> We had a household of nine people. The depression was a real trial and struggle . . . We survived and we didn't impair our health but we cut down to the bare-bone essentials and got enough food although it was just plain and ordinary kind of stuff supplemented by canning. Sometimes they would get a quarter of a hog or a beef and they'd grind up meatballs and can jars of meatballs and, of course, we could drag them out of the cellar for months into the winter. They would can peaches and can strawberries and plums and cherries for sauces, jams and jellies.
>
> We had a big heavy crock that we put carrots in. We'd have a layer of carrots laid out and then we'd have another layer of sand, and a layer of carrots, alternating way up to the top. We could draw edible carrots out of there all winter long. Potatoes the same way. So, if you could draw potatoes and carrots and canned peaches and cherries and sauce and jam and jelly and meatballs and had a sack of flour, you just about had it made. You'd buy some salt and you didn't even have to buy butter if you had a cow—you could drink milk and skim the cream and churn butter.

Our father must have traded something for a milk cow—sometimes two cows. He would often milk them himself, but his sons and at least one daughter would have that chore, too—Julie remembers going with the milk pail down to the Claus Nelson farm north of town where Myrtle and Carlton were her friends and where, at one point, we kept a cow. When I was just a kid, I would have to go to some other pasture near town (our Dad made deals when he had to) and find our cow. I'd take my pails—one with water to wash off the teats and another for the milk. This was my small assignment. It never occurred to me then, as our Mom would send me over to a neighbor widow or up to our grandmother with a small pail of milk, that it was also helping others to survive.

I remember one of our neighbors, a Mrs. Severtson, who spoke only Norwegian. When I had to make a delivery to her house, I had to memorize the Norwegian equivalent of "Would you like some milk?" Whether or not she understood me didn't matter. The milk spoke for itself.

The Depression offered Mathilda a life-changing experience—giving yeoman service to the American Red Cross. Her heavy involvement with this challenging activity was almost therapeutic for her and for our entire family. It helped mitigate any temptation to self-pity over the austerity forced on us and millions of others by the dire economic straits of that period.

In September of 1932 the *Spring Grove Herald* carried a story announcing that "Mrs. Knute A. Lee, Spring Grove, was appointed County Roll chairman for the 1932 Red Cross membership drive . . . Houston County must enroll 700 members if it is to meet the assignment made by national headquarters."

Before Mathilda could manage this new responsibility, she went to Rochester to meet with those from other counties of Minnesota who had the same assignment. The top regional official for the Red Cross, C. M. Roland, was on hand, together with the organization's Assistant National Director of Disaster Relief, Henry Baker, and Minnesota Congressman Paul Quale of Benson. Mother kept meticulous notes of what went on at that session and, reading those notes today, I can almost re-live with her the excitement and stimulation of her sudden immersion in a process aimed at helping unemployed and destitute citizens, victims of a new and sudden poverty.

Her expenses were paid: round-trip bus fare was $2.55, lunch was 75 cents and "incidentals" were 25 cents!

It was the first chapter of a very busy period for Mathilda. Her notes indicate that she was to travel around the Houston County to LaCresent, Hokah, Caledonia, Eitzen, Wilmington, and Riceford.

She prepared well, knowing that she would need to answer questions, give talks, write articles for newspapers and serve as one of two spokespersons for the agency. The other was the Houston County chapter chairman, Henry Blexrud. I remember how proud we were when she went with Blexrud to LaCrosse to speak over radio station WKBH. She called that "quite an event;" she told me she wrote the talk herself:

> It was an appeal for funds for the regular fall Red Cross drive. I know Pastor Clarence Lee of Caledonia was along. I spoke first and I think I must have spoken a minute or two overtime because Pastor Lee didn't have

so very much time—but of course he didn't have so much to do with it either.

Mathilda learned at that Rochester orientation session that the American Red Cross was first organized only two years before she herself was born. Like Mathilda, the Red Cross had grown and matured in America over the same half-century before the Depression. The agency was finally officially chartered by Congress in 1905, just a year before her own marriage.

The specialists at the meeting made a strong case for the Red Cross role as a citizen response to the Depression crisis affecting so many. Mathilda learned that, in addition to supervising the food and clothing distributions, she had to be a fund raiser. That's what the roll call was all about. She had a treasurer and a campaign captain in each community. And each week the local papers carried the listing of who gave 50 cents or a dollar (and sometimes, if rarely, $2). Somehow she was determined to enroll those 700 members in Houston County.

Support for the Red Cross has always been predicated on the power of its reputation. It earned favor in Houston County and the nation for its record during World War I, concluded only a dozen years before the Depression hit. While at the meeting in Rochester, Mathilda would, of course, visit her cousin, Inga Qualley. Inga had worn the Red Cross emblem on her nurse's uniform during service abroad in the war. Mathilda noted the "outstanding" nursing service of the Red Cross and wrote in her notebook, "If you develop nursing services well, it strengthens all other parts of the services."

The first task for Mathilda was to organize and put into motion the roll call for raising funds. It would not be easy because money was tight. Yet, when the community knew that in this case their neighbors were to be the recipients of aid—not just the flood victims in Arkansas and Mississippi nor just the hurricane victims in Florida, but the poor family down the street or on a nearby farm—it became easier.

With Mr. Blexrud, Mathilda planned a meeting in Caledonia on October 26, 1932 of the Roll Call chairmen she had appointed in every township and village within the county. In Spring Grove she had persuaded an outstanding community leader, dentist Dr. Harold Lovold, to serve. In Black Hammer township she had found her sister-in-law, Lillian (Mrs. William C. Glasrud) also willing. The annual drive would begin on Armistice Day, November 11. At the meeting she and Henry Blexrud would explain the distribution to needy families of flour and cotton cloth.

Mathilda had memorized her notes about the guidelines which had been laid down by the national Red Cross: A carload of flour would come to the railroad station. It would be stored at the C.J. Sylling elevator. The flour was only for families who could qualify for aid, for which they had to apply, and then submit the approved form. With it they could obtain one 49 pound sack (or if a large family, two sacks) at a time. The regulations said that one family could get a maximum of one barrel of flour (in equivalent sacks) to last for 90 days. Flour could not be given to an institution, only to families. "Stay away from permanent cases," the officials had told her. Transients were to be referred to the county welfare workers.

In addition to the flour, other food supplies were added from time to time. Most of the foodstuffs and clothing—oranges and grapefruit and lengths of cloth for sewing garments, and later some underwear as well—were bought by the federal government which turned it over to the Red Cross to distribute to needy families. She wrote in her notes that none of this was to be surrendered to the county welfare board to dispense to their regular clients. She added, "Congress holds us responsible."

The food and clothing depot in Spring Grove was the Lee house—our home. This was a constant reminder for all of us in the family. And many of my older siblings were deputized to help in the distribution process. People would come to the door at times when Mom was away and whichever of my sisters was home then would know what to do. The whole enterprise not only took over our dining room as a storage area, it took over much of our daily life and left a deep and lasting impression on each of us:

> Margaret: "All I remember was that our dining room had big boxes of grapefruit and maybe oranges. They were beautiful, the top of the line. And we never had any grapefruit that looked like that. And believe me, we never tasted one of those. I know we had a dining room that looked a bit like a warehouse part of the time."

> Juliet: "Our dining room was converted into a regular store . . . there was flour there, lots of fabric, lots of stockings and food like oranges. Oh, let's see, what else? Clothing, children's clothing, and then people would

come and she would dispense this stuff. And she had to keep records of everything she gave away . . . Mother was meticulous in her screening of applicants. Also she had too much pride to accept any provisions for her own family."

Naomi: "All I know was that during that time we had all kinds of things stored at our house: sugar, flour, oranges, all kinds of things. All people had to do was come and sign a paper, and she kept track of what was doled out and we could not touch it . . . I could almost tell you the size of the piece of paper they had to sign—like half a typewriter sheet—and it was a government form."

Bill: "I drove her around the county, around Houston County, delivering flour sacks and bales of overalls and clothing to some of the most critical needy families. I drove around in the old 1928 coupe and I remember coming to one farm on a cold, bitter October day when it wasn't snowing but the ground was frozen. The farmer's children were running barefooted across that frozen dirt. It was tough."

Mother: "I think I was allowed to use my own discretion. They told me their wants, you know. I know Nels Viker was the mayor then and he blamed me for giving a sack of flour to someone that he thought didn't need it. I think that was the only time I was criticized for that. What are you going to do when a woman comes in with a tale of woe? I suppose Nels Viker was a rich man and had never been in need, while I knew what it meant. I didn't have any bad conscience!"

This experience with relief supplies to families suddenly finding themselves pinched by the Depression and out of cash was profoundly moving for our entire household. Mathilda summed it up herself in her notes when she wrote, "The Red Cross is more than distribution. It is in the business of repairing bruised lives and homes." And on another page of her notes I found this quote: "The American Red Cross is the greatest mother in the world!" (And I would have to add, "It takes one to know one!")

She must have done an exemplary job as County Roll Call

chairman for she subsequently was promoted to what had been considered by almost everyone then as a "man-sized" job—succeeding Mr. Blexrud first and then Dr. Lovold as chair of the Houston County Chapter of the American Red Cross.

Mathilda was not one to remain passive in the difficult economic and social environment. She participated as fully as she could in the political process—not with passion but with persistence. She became the local chair for the Republican party in the issue-filled national election of 1932. Herbert Hoover was a revered name in our household. Franklin D. Roosevelt was scorned. Such a political bias could not help but be owned also by the youngsters in the Lee home. We had Hoover cards, brochures, posters, buttons.

Even while Mother was working on the Red Cross project, she would sometimes combine a trip to Caledonia with Republican Party business. But her notebook would carefully split the expenses.

As partisans, we bristled when we heard the campaign charges against Hoover by the Democrats. He had enjoyed only a half year into his 1929-33 term as President (having defeated Al Smith who suffered from being the first Roman Catholic candidate) before the Depression really ushered in the new austerity era. Hoover never lived down the reputation imputed to him by his opponents of being a reactionary, unwilling to help people suffering from the Depression. Mathilda found this outrageously unfair. She would tell anyone who would listen that Hoover was a great humanitarian. Not only had he managed the flood relief in 1927 for victims of the overflowing Mississippi River, he had been head of the American Relief Administration, providing post-war food and clothing to destitute peoples in Eastern Europe, and even before the war he had been a relief champion and leader for the Food Administration. Our mother saw in President Hoover a model of a person whose central ethic was helping unfortunate victims of natural disasters. Certainly that became her own ethic, too.

Naomi remembers how even we kids were enlisted in the Republican cause:

> I do remember when Hoover was trying to get reelected and failed, that particular year she was really working actively to try to get information around, and they had pledges that people signed. And she sent me with some pledges to school to ask the teachers to sign.

> And I recall asking one of my teachers to sign and she read it and said, "Oh, well, all right! I suppose so." And signed it. She really didn't want to. But I was a good kid, and she knew she was kind of on the spot. And that was a very unfair thing to have me do.

Finally the election came. Radio was at last a reality in our home and I recall listening to the returns from the presidential election on that cold day in November, 1932. I could hear the broadcast through an open window while I was outside tossing wood chunks down the coal chute to our basement for our wood burning furnace. The saw rig had been to our house to cut up a cord of firewood some farmer had given our Dad in payment for a bill. They had left a big pile of chunks along with a residue of sawdust. The news I heard was grim. So grim that when the verdict was clear, I burst into tears. It was my 11th birthday!

On a purely local level, our Dad dabbled in politics to the extent of running for office. He was easily elected to the school board, voted by his peers to become second chief of the Fire Department, and several times re-elected as village constable. But then he aspired to becoming County Sheriff. We all felt he would make a wonderful Sheriff, although we were also anxious about the danger in that job.

The *Spring Grove Herald* carried an announcement reporting that "Knute A. Lee of Spring Grove filed Saturday, March 10, as a candidate for Sheriff of Houston County. Mr. Lee is very well liked and known throughout the county."

We were proud of his paid advertisements in the paper. They carried his name in big black type but didn't include a picture. (Photos required an engraving and they cost more money.) He did have a batch of calling card size campaign cards printed and we would help distribute them around town. My brother and I would each get to ride with him in his dray truck or one of his old cars to various farms were he would stop and chat with the farmer and leave his card.

It didn't help. He lost. And in 1938—just a year before he died—he tried again and lost again. It hurt him, surely. Election losers find it hard to face the fact of voter rejection. Fortunately, his heart held very little bitterness.

Many couples with one or two children, particularly those who have not been able to accumulate savings for the future, wonder how they are going to send their children to college, given that their dream has an ever-ascending and frightening price tag. Having seen six of our own progeny through that process (albeit with considerable self-help from each) my wife and I know what the challenge is. Knute and Mathilda wanted so desperately for their family to have the benefits of the kind of education they did not get. But savings were nonexistent for them and the Depression eroded the assets and property they had—the barn and implement business, accounts payable, a second house in the village and the property in South Dakota—much of it was mortgaged and subsequently lost in the 1930s.

Mathilda tried to orchestrate her dream of getting her five daughters and two sons educated beyond high school. My brother Bill felt there was some master plan she was following. My other siblings saw her role more as an improviser and some might have thought the term juggler would be more apt.

Here, basically, is how it worked: Sylvia was first to graduate from high school, before the Depression, in 1925. She is the only one in the family to leave home "with a checkbook," as one of my sisters termed it. She didn't finish her nurse's training and this allowed her to begin earning money.

Spring Grove had a special post-graduate program of normal training—preparing young women (few if any young men) to qualify as rural school teachers. Fortunately the training was excellent. Nell Bryan, a stocky, seemingly clumsy single matron, directed the program. She became something of a legend in our small town. She was very skilled in giving her students the rudiments of teaching and arranged for the apprentice "school marms" to teach a kindergarten class each year in the spring, preparing pre-school youngsters for first grade. I was one of those Spring Primary pupils and my sister Barbara, who was in Miss Bryan's program, was one of my team of teachers.

After each had their year in that normal school, Barbara and Juliet got low-paying but nevertheless income-producing jobs in country schools in the county. Later they were able to go on to Winona State Teachers College (now part of the University of Minnesota) and qualify further for teaching in town schools. Naomi followed the same pattern.

Margaret took a slightly different path, mainly because she had a scholarship to Winona and was able, with the help of her working sisters, to begin her college after graduation. But for at least one term—the spring quarter of 1934—she remained at home and had worked at the school library under the College

Work Administration, a government program of aid. For a time during her high school years Margaret had lived with the Al Anderson family. She earned little if anything for the work she did for them but her being there meant one less mouth to feed at the Lee home.

Basic to Mathilda's plan or improvisation was (1) each of us was to work summers and during college if possible to help pay the way, and (2) those who were making money were to help those who were needing it to continue in college. As the last one in line, I received contributions regularly from Naomi and Bill, who were then unmarried and teaching, and occasionally from others in the family, but I don't remember any from my parents. But I knew the situation and didn't expect any either.

Barbara confessed to me, "I would have loved to have been a nurse." She didn't have that option. She went to "Fifth Year Normal," as it was called, and then on to two unhappy years of rural school teaching.

"I don't think anybody would be dying to get into it—probably dying to get out of it!" she said. "I taught in District 80 north of Spring Grove. I had 40 children in eight grades. Some of my eighth grade students were two years younger than I was! And then in the spring I got stuck with a little child that was to go to kindergarten. So then I had nine grades! It was horrible."

Bill remembers that when Barbara was going to go to Winona State, Mother decreed that he should forfeit his modest savings account in the bank—this was the accumulation of nickels and dimes put aside from child labor over the years so that he might have some initial educational funds later. Her thinking was, of course, that when Barbara had finished her Winona State training, she would teach and earn money and be able to help Bill when he was in college. And that is exactly what happened.

"When Barbara was teaching in Lanesboro,"Bill told me, "she sent me thirty-five dollars a month to help me keep up on my tuition at Luther College and this kind of exchange went on and on."

Barbara also underwrote Margaret so that she could take advantage of her scholarship from Winona State Teachers College. Margaret said, "What I think Mother did engineer—and I happen to know it personally—is [to figure out] whom you should help when you started earning. Instead of paying Barbara back, whom I owed and it would have been nice [for her] to get it back, Bill got it."

Not only did my sisters and brother help each other, those who had some meager income at teaching or other jobs, helped our parents, who had little income. Some of their stories are poignant:

> Margaret: "The next year [after underwriting Bill] I paid toward the taxes. And I found out years later that they had been put on the wrong thing. Instead of paying the home taxes—$30 a month out of my $70 a month check in Brownsville—it went toward the barn which was destined to be lost anyway."

> Juliet: "I remember once during the Depression—I will never forget this. I was teaching, probably my first year, and Barbara had been teaching a little while. That was really a hard time for us. We didn't have much of anything. And that Christmas I know Dad needed a coat and Barbara and I bought a coat for him. And we got gifts for all the kids. Well, nobody had a thing for Barbara and for me. And I remember it was very sad. And I went to bed and cried that night."

> Barbara: "I can remember at that time I bought a washing machine for Mother. And I have never seen her so completely in awe. She had been struggling along with this old, old, washing machine—I think it was the thing you did by hand . . . And, of course, it was a real joy for her—and for the rest of us, too."

> Juliet: "I remember one time I went down to Vick's store to get some groceries, and I didn't have any money, but I thought I could charge it because I was going to get a check the next week. And they wouldn't let me . . . and I felt pretty bad."

Barbara also remembers one time when she was teaching in Hutchinson, Minnesota, she came home for a weekend and was proud to show off a new fur coat she had bought. She thought Mother would be pleased. She was mistaken. Mother was upset. Under the circumstances of the family's financial plight, she simply could not accept what she thought of as Barbara's extravagance. And both Mother and daughter were miffed and miserable over the incident.

1933 was a pivotal year on so many levels. FDR was inaugurated president. The New Deal began. The banks were officially closed—they called it a "Bank Holiday." It was to protect the financial institutions against runs that would leave them impotent and doomed to failure because fear drove the economy. Both of the Spring Grove banks re-opened "on a restricted basis" near the end of May that year.

The local Blue Ribbon Bakery announced in the *Herald* early in March of 1933 that "Our friends have encouraged reopening the bakery, so 'If we are going to fail, let's fail trying to succeed!'"

In the same issue K. A. Lee ran this ad: "NOTICE! We have decided to discontinue feed grinding until Monday, May 1st." A feed mill was another of Dad's projects which he had hoped might change his fortunes. After all, farmers had grain and, at that time, if they were to feed oats, for example, to their livestock, they would need to have it ground. He must have had to borrow money to purchase the equipment and have it installed. And he lost it all!

1933 saw my brother graduate from high school in May and enter Luther College in the fall. My father drove to Decorah with him and his belongings. Knute had arranged with his sister, our Aunt Maria and her husband, Uncle Charlie, for Bill to room in their home. (These were very spartan quarters—no heat in his room.) That saved precious funds that otherwise would have to be scrounged from somewhere for dormitory accommodations.

A sad event in 1933 was the death after a long illness of our beloved Pastor Alfred Johnson. Our family felt close to him. He loved to tell the story of my coming up to him on the street one day when I was about six years old and asking him, "Have you seen Knute?" Everyone laughed at my naming my Dad's name rather than calling him "My father" or "My papa." I often had to go find Dad in town to get some money to buy some food item for our table and when I saw Pastor Johnson's friendly smile I knew I could ask him.

He was clearly approachable to everyone in the parish, the only church in town at that time. Mother related to him closely because of her role in the Ladies' Aid, Women's Missionary Federation and the Parochial School. When he died in March the president of the Norwegian Lutheran Church in America and other dignitaries attended his funeral.

His successor had been engaged a year earlier when Johnson's cancer was known to be fatal. A fresh graduate from the seminary, Oscar Mikkelson, was hired as the parochial school teacher. He became ordained soon after his arrival so that he could be called as associate pastor. He, too, won the hearts of the congregation; he was handsome, athletic, youthful, warm and friendly and was becoming a good preacher through on-the-job training. He was married in July of 1933 and he and his wife, Betty, had their door always open to our family. Naomi became a home helper and baby sitter at the parsonage. We all called him Mikky.

When I was 13 my sister Sylvia's life took a dramatic turn. It was big news in our family but no one had thought to tell me, the "baby of the family." (Oh, how I disliked being identified in that way.) When I was only four years old she had already been graduated from high school so consequently I grew up more-or-less detached from her day-to-day living. I remember her as a tall and commanding woman with a warm, motherly personality. (She died just short of her 58th birthday in 1965.)

One day early in January 1935, I was visiting a neighbor friend, Carlton Onstad. I loved to go to his house because it was such a child-friendly place and ours was not. Otto Onstad, my friend's father, was home and he was always a jokester and trickster. He said, "I hear your sister is married!" I didn't know what to say. Was this a joke again? Which sister? He said, "Your sister Sylvia. Didn't you know?"

I was stunned with disbelief. I hurried home and confronted Mother, who admitted that yes, it was true. In mid-February the front page of The *Spring Grove Herald* carried this article:

> DECEMBER MARRIAGE IS KEPT A SECRET
>
> Can a woman keep a secret?—we should say yes! And a man too and it's been proven to us, but imagine our surprise at learning this week when Mr. and Mrs. Knute Lee of this village announced the marriage of their daughter, Sylvia, to Fremont Deters, son of Mr. and Mrs. Franklin Deters, of Eitzen, Minnesota, December 31st.
>
> The ceremony was performed by Rev. Brekke, of Spring Grove at the Saevig home in Rushford at 4:30 o'clock.
>
> Mrs. Deters is a graduate of the Spring Grove High School and was employed by Dr. H. S. Lovold until two years ago. She has always made her home in Spring Grove, she attended the St. Mary's hospital at Rochester for a course in nurses training in 1926. Mr. Deters is a graduate of the School of Agriculture at the University of

> Minnesota. He has been engaged in farming in Eitzen until last fall, when he was elected Houston County treasurer.
>
> The Herald joins in wishing them a long successful and very happy married life.

I never did learn why Sylvia decided to get married secretly. Most likely it was related to her realization that neither she nor her parents could afford a normal wedding with all of its fuss and expense. By having it as a quiet New Year's Eve ceremony, she could have it revealed later as a fait accompli. I quickly learned to appreciate Fremont as a brother-in-law and I was proud of his being an important official of Houston County. And later when Fritzie (Robert Erwin Deters) was born in January 1936, I became an uncle and Knute and Mathilda had the joy of becoming grandparents for the first time. One has only to look back at the snapshots of both Dad and Mother with Fritzie on their lap to realize that they were relishing their new status.

Our grandmother Sigrid Glasrud died in January 1937. Even though she was a member of the Black Hammer congregation, Faith Lutheran, and buried in their church-side cemetery, her funeral was held in Spring Grove at Trinity Church to accommodate the hundreds who attended. The Glasrud and Qualley clans gathered, together with a host of others from the community who had known her as a matriarch of a large family over many of her 85 years.

For our mother it was closure on a long and trusting relationship. It wouldn't be accurate to call it close or intimate because Sigrid Glasrud was neither warm nor demonstrative and Mathilda wasn't either. But they understood one another and there was a deep respect and the kind of loyal interior affection that is found in Norwegian Lutheran families.

Another family drama opened in February of 1937, and this time fear rather than joy was the motif. The crisis came during the worst blizzard to hit the region in many years. It is best described in this account from our local newspaper:

> BLIZZARD HITS THIS SECTION
> SATURDAY NIGHT
>
> This vicinity as well as the northwest, was visited by old man "King Winter" over the weekend. Putting on all the bluster and stepping on the blower to make the snow pile up on our highways, sidewalks and everywhere.

> Travel by train, bus, automobile and foot was practically at a standstill for thirty-six hours. Very few pedestrians ventured outside their doors till the storm abated Monday morning.
>
> Then the snow shovel was the most thought of implement of the day, were it the wooden-handled one we had stored in the wood shed or the mammoth ones on our locomotives, trucks or caterpillars. They all were put to good use.
>
> . . . Mail service was resumed Wednesday morning, bringing in only first class mail since last Saturday. The highway between Spring Grove and LaCrosse has been opened, but west of us is still blocked with huge drifts so high that snow plows in this vicinity can not get through them.

There couldn't have been a worse time for getting the word that my brother Bill at Luther College had suddenly had an attack of appendicitis. Because it had ruptured, he had to be operated on immediately. His condition was grave, according to the telephone reports.

There was no way to move even outside of the house, so a trip to Decorah would be impossible. Our parents kept in touch with the hospital by telephone and may have talked with Dr. Nels Stabo, who performed the operation, whom they knew from his early practice as a Spring Grove physician. The word came that Bill might not pull through. There were complications. Finally after a couple of days Mother and Dad managed to follow a snowplow over the 20 white hilly miles to Decorah. The crisis passed and healing began. But it was slow. Bill was in his last semester of college and had to be away from his studies for about six weeks.

As if to compensate for not being a part of the first wedding in the family, Knute and Mathilda had the satisfaction and pleasure of experiencing two weddings in the summer of 1938. Margaret was married to Paul Thies, an electrician from Galesville, Wisconsin, on June 17 at "high noon" with a dinner and reception at our home for 65 guests in the afternoon. Barbara married Archie Gilbertson of Peterson in an evening wedding on August 20 with a reception following for 35 guests, again at our home. Dad escorted both daughters down the aisle for their respective ceremonies. It must have thrilled him to see Barbara wearing Mathilda's wedding dress.

That summer of 1938 was important for me, too. I had graduated from high school in May after a climactic spring season of musical accomplishments. Our high school swept the state music contest with A ratings given to our mixed choir, our male quartet (I sang 2nd tenor), the girls glee club, and my trumpet solo. I went back to Minneapolis the following week to the national contest where my performance of "Sounds from the Hudson" was then judged to be in first place in competition with other soloists from Minnesota, Iowa, North Dakota and Wisconsin. I was very proud of this but the accomplishment somehow seemed to be eclipsed by the weddings and Dad's campaign for Sheriff (he lost again, getting only 266 votes against the 1,473 for the winner and 1,325 for the runner-up.)

As if following the script of siblings-helping-siblings-get-a-college-education, my brother took the initiative for managing mine. It was fortunate because I had no plans. How could I ask my parents if I could go to college, knowing as I did that they had no money? Whether prodded by Mother or not, Bill—who now was a graduate of Luther College and had a year of teaching and band directing at Little Cedar, Iowa, under his belt—got me a summer job at the college. I don't know how he did it but it is not unlikely that he had used my trumpet solo award for all the leverage it was worth to land a campus maintenance job for me. He came to find me on Main Street one Wednesday night chatting with friends and announced that he was taking me to Decorah the next day for a summer job that would start immediately. My fate was thus sealed—and my life has never been the same since!

In spite of the New Deal's National Recovery Act (NRA), Works Progress Administration (WPA) and other political and economic nostrums aimed at seeing the nation through the Depression, our family had not fully recovered financially and austerity was still our guideline. The 1930s had been a time when Mathilda and Knute's children were maturing through teens, through high school and into college and entering the work force, such as it was. After 1933 when Bill was off to college, it was just Naomi and I who were at home with Mother and Dad. Then, after 1935 when she graduated from high school, I was the only fledgling left in the nest. Of course there was considerable weekend traffic. Students at Winona and Decorah would come home for Saturday with laundry bags and return on Sunday with clean clothes. Those who were teaching and earning money would help buy groceries. As the low man on the totem pole, I never was able to pay my share.

Mathilda's health seemed remarkably good all her long life. At least it seemed that way to us, her children. Doubtless we credited this, in part at least, to her constant emphasis on nutrition: "Drink water. Have your roughage. Eat vegetables. Easy on the sweets. Chew your food," etc. And we knew that she had experience in coming from a large healthy family and in raising a large healthy family. We also remembered those extension courses that taught health and menus and safety.

Yet, her children remembered some health problems which beset her in the years when we were living at home. In the 1920s she had a thyroid problem which resulted in a glandular enlargement at the neck—a goiter. Barbara recalls her doctoring for that:

> She was going to make sure that none of us would get it, so we had, each of us, a little box—almost like a matchbox—filled with chocolate-covered iodine pills. And every morning we'd reach on top of that little medicine cabinet that was above the washbowl in the kitchen, take our box and take a pill.

Others remember when she suffered from polyps in the nasal passages and had surgery in LaCrosse. Bill remembered that when she had them removed she kept them in a jar that stood for weeks on a window sill. He added, laughingly, "It chills me to think about it!"

Barbara also remembered her having a severe case of rheumatism. "She couldn't raise her arm all summer. And in the middle of a hot summer's day she would wear lamb's wool, a piece of lamb's wool over her shoulders, down around her arms on both sides and then she'd put a sweater on. Hot as blazes!"

Naomi added, "That's when her hair turned gray." Naomi also recalled that she was very nervous at menopause time. "I remember that very clearly. In the middle of the night sometimes, I'd wake up and she'd be really upset." She remembers how Mother cried after her teeth had been extracted and she was being fitted for dentures.

"She wasn't really happy during the time you and I were in high school, "Naomi said, "but a lot of people weren't. Those were terrible years. I have heard and read since about the Depression years, and I believe that it's felt by experts that the people who didn't live through that period have really no understanding of how psychologically abused we all were by these circumstances."

For some of those Depression era years, Mathilda would spend some lonely nights. She was an avid reader and this helped. But she would have welcomed having her husband at home, but he seldom was in the evening. He would either work late—a habit from the days when he tended teams of horses for farmers in his livery barn—or he would play cards with his men friends. I remember sometimes having to find him at night to deliver a message from Mother or to get some change with which to buy something needed at home. Several times I found him in the back room of a tavern at a card table with his buddies. The room was smoky and they smelled of beer.

While to many of us now, moderate social drinking, especially beer or wine, may be commonplace and normally acceptable, it certainly was not in Spring Grove when we were growing up. Repeal of Prohibition had only come in December of 1933. For 13 years prior to that it had been illegal to sell or buy any alcoholic beverage considered to be intoxicating. The enforcing legislation for Prohibition was the Volstead Act, named after the Norwegian-American Minnesota Congressman who introduced it. The ethos of many Norwegian Lutherans (including our mother, if not our father) was still in the mind-set of Prohibition.

Bill remembers the days when Spring Grove had a bootlegger who had a garage where private sales allegedly took place. He told me about his discovering some drunks who had passed out in the hayloft of Dad's feed barn. And a couple of times he recalls escorting a wobbly father home. We agreed, however, that Knute Lee was only an occasional drinker at most and that we would have known if there had been a serious abuse of alcohol on his part.

If there had been any serious problem, it would have been known in our small town, and Dad would never have been appointed to the job he finally got after his business failed. Dad was named as the manager of the local village dispensary—liquor store. Spring Grove was slow in licensing anything other than sales of beer, which at first could only be obtained in a tavern. It decided that the community would be best served in the new era of Repeal by controlling on-sale (by the drink on the premises) and off-sale (by the bottle, off premises) of wine and spirits other than beer through the village government. Dad needed work and while the Liquor Store paycheck was hardly a way of getting bailed out financially (the salary was all of $1,000 a year!), it was better than nothing. And it also gave him a purpose and a challenge after failure and disappointment.

It was a major embarrassment for Mathilda. And for me, too. I had been so conditioned by my religious-ethnic environment that I considered this almost shameful. One of my friends whom I admired very much taunted me about this, saying "Why don't we go down and get your dad to give us a drink . . . heh . . . heh . . . heh!"

Brother Bill was troubled by it also:

> It was terrible . . . awful. I always felt so bad about that but, you see, the way it was viewed . . . my father was asked to do this because they knew he was a man of integrity and he would do a good job, and do the things that city council people wanted. And he ran a decent place. And this was my satisfaction.

Naomi agreed and gave me an additional perspective:

> For him this was a last-ditch opportunity. It was this or nothing. And I think he took that opportunity and made it a good one. I have a picture of his shining the glasses behind the bar there—so proud, showing me how he shined them and lined them up. And knowing that they chose him for that job because they knew that they could trust him, because he would be a sober individual who would deal well with this. And I really got a feeling that he brought a little dignity to that job . . .
>
> Mother never set foot in that store. The only time she was ever in it was when he died. I had been in there several times. I saw him behind the counter, very much on the job and having a little pride in himself that he had a job that paid him a salary. He had been really desperate. He was a proud man who wanted to support his family well, and had done so well with them, and then had gotten into this terrible Depression poverty.

Nevertheless, for Mathilda it most certainly was an ignominy. Yet, it was her husband's health that worried her most. For most of his life he had been strong and healthy. It seemed to me in the short time during the 1920s and 1930s when I knew him that he was slightly overweight. He loved to eat and, like me, he would take a nap on the living room floor after the noon meal whenever he could. But he smoked cigars—a lot of cigars. They became his trademark. To this day when I catch the passing aroma of cigar smoke I get a vision of our dad. Obviously the ubiquitous White Owl cigars were injurious to his health and put an extra burden on his pulmonary system.

He began having spells and bouts of coughing. He finally quitsmoking early in 1939. That February Mathilda reported to Bill, "Dad has not smoked for over a month now and has practically quit coughing."

A few weeks later, after celebrating his 60th birthday (March 6th) with almost all his family, he himself wrote to Bill, the only one of us who couldn't be there, "I have been feeling fine all winter. But today I have been coughing more than usual. Just think—I haven't smoked a cigar since January 17th—nearly two months!"

In a separate letter to Bill on the same day, also reporting on the birthday party, Mother wrote, "I am holding my breath!" She explained that his working day regularly continued to midnight; still, he had to be up in the next morning at seven.

In June he finally went to see Dr. Rogne and had a physical exam. Some pills were prescribed. Mathilda wrote, "Dad now can't even mow the lawn." She said the diagnosis was angina pectoris. When he walked to work he had to pace himself and stop now and then to rest.

Mother told of how the two of them celebrated their wedding anniversary on September 1, 1939. They went to Evenson's restaurant for dinner and then drove over to the town of Mabel to see a movie. She added that Dad really loved seeing the horses in the film *Kentucky*.

In his last letter, Dad's comments were those of a person facing his own mortality and were poignantly prophetic: "I am feeling fairly well. I still have spells, mostly in the morning. This morning it was at 5 o'clock. I try to get up so Ma doesn't hear me. Then, when I am quiet for about 10 minutes, it is mostly over with. Still, I think some day it will get me!"

It happened on a sunny autumn Saturday, October 21, 1939, during the noon hour. Knute as usual was at his job at the Village Dispensary. An hour earlier he had been listening, as he did each morning, to me as I sang songs and hymns over the air from the Luther College radio station KWLC. At about 12:30 he was sweeping the sidewalk outside when he had a massive heart attack. His assistant, Knute Gulbrandson, said that he died instantly.

Both Barbara and Naomi were home at the time. Gulbrandson had phoned and instructed Mother, "You had better come down. Something is wrong with Knute." Someone came to get her and Naomi went along. Barbara had to stay with her baby, Kip (Christopher). Just that morning Dad had come in to her bedroom to see the baby—his second grandchild—before going to work, and Barbara said he talked baby-talk to the two-month-old infant.

Someone had phoned Sylvia and Fremont because they

arrived at the Liquor Store from Caledonia almost as soon as Mathilda and Naomi did. Naomi describes the scene:

> Dad was lying on a cot in that store and I remember Mother went over to the cot and to him and put her fingers through his hair. It was kind of touching since I had never really seen them doing any touching much, as loving as they were. It was such a simple gesture, but it said so much.

Sylvia, Barbara and Naomi wasted no time in notifying the rest of us. Bill got a telegram while he was in a band rehearsal in Madison, Minnesota where he was teaching at the time. Juliet was reached by phone in Hayward, Minnesota, where she, too, was teaching. A phone call also alerted Margaret in Galesville, Wisconsin, and she and her husband, Paul, hurried over. Fremont, Archie, and Paul—sons-in-law—were able to be of help as only they could in such a crisis: to assist in arrangements and to drive to pick up Juliet and me and, when he arrived by train, Bill also.

I was intercepted by one of my favorite Luther College profs, Francis Gamelin, as I was walking down Leif Erikssen Drive in Decorah to visit my aunt. Somehow I was able to take the shocking news with a self-control which surprised me, thanks in part to Gamelin's warm and pastoral style. My grieving came weeks later at college and I remember writing a song then as a way of giving vent to my feelings. Gamelin took me to Aunt Maria's house. When she saw me she knew something was wrong. She had a look of dread and horror on her face even before I could tell her that my dad, her brother, had died. I can still remember her uncontrollable wailing and sobbing.

When I got home I found mother in her bedroom, resting. The doctor had been there to give her a sedative. One of the first visitors had been the Superintendent of Schools, William O. Nilsen, who knew our family well and appreciated our parents and what they had meant to education in the community.

What do you say to one's own mother when her husband, your father, has just died? I have since learned that it doesn't matter because what will be remembered is the statement you make by your very presence. Nevertheless, I offered to read something from the Bible to Mom if she wanted it. She did. I grasped for something appropriate and found Romans 11:33-34: "O the depth of the riches both of the wisdom and knowledge of God! How unsearchable are his judgments, and his ways past finding out. For who hath known the mind of the Lord? Or who hath been his counsellor?"

We had an early supper that Saturday evening and Pastor Mikkelson came over. Suddenly the house was full of family again. But it was empty, too, because Dad was not there. Someone was inspired to remember one of Dad's favorite dishes and so that's what we had: oyster stew. Barbara has said she has never forgotten the Bible verse our pastor included within his prayer: "The Lord giveth, the Lord taketh away—blessed be the name of the Lord."

The next issue of the *Spring Grove Herald*, reported the death of K.A. Lee at age 60, by writing, "Although his sudden passing came as a complete shock to people of this community it was not entirely unexpected by his immediate family. Mr. Lee had been consulting medical aid for the past year and he and his family were aware that a condition of the heart was causing trouble."

It was a large funeral. While Dad's only living close relative was his sister, our Aunt Maria, there were scores of Glasruds present. Hundreds of his friends also came to show their respect. Luther College paid our family the honor of sending the celebrated band director, Dr. Carlo A. Sperati, who spoke movingly on behalf of the college family and he brought with him a student quartet, friends of mine, to sing.

Mother herself wrote the obituary. It was important for her to have it be correct and say the appropriate words to commemorate the life of her husband, lover and life's companion. I remember she asked me to type it for her. It was not just another death notice. It was written with love:

> KNUTE MAURICE LEE CALLED
> TO HIS ETERNAL REWARD
>
> Knute Maurice Lee was born March 6, 1879, in Black Hammer township. He died October 21, 1939. His parents were Aad Lee and Hannah Severson Lee. At the age of about three years the family moved to Spring Grove, where he has resided until his death, with the exception of the summer of 1900 which he spent in North Dakota and the summer of 1910 which was spent in Lemmon, South Dakota.
>
> At the age of fifteen he was confirmed by the Rev. St. S. Reque. His class being the first one confirmed in the

present church which was rebuilt after the fire which destroyed the old one.

At an early age he began to work towards his own support, at odd jobs and also, as a hired man on farms. he also took care of cream route to the local creamery for a period of two years.

In 1902 when the Rural Free Delivery became a part of the nation's postal system he circulated a petition and established Route No. 1 out of Spring Grove. Over this route he carried mail for the following eight years.

In 1906 he was married to Clara Mathilda Glasrud, daughter of Mrs. Sigrid Glasrud of Black Hammer, by the Rev. Karl Kasberg.

In 1910, he resigned as mail carrier, and the family moved to Lemmon, S. Dak., where he had purchased some land. After staying at Lemmon until August that year, it being a year of drought, he took his horses and a covered wagon and in company with three others, started for home stopping for six weeks during the threshing and plowing season, near Aberdeen, S. Dak., driving the entire distance of about 700 miles by team.

After that for a short time he operated a restaurant in Spring Grove, Minnesota, and for a few months the Hotel in Mabel. In the spring of 1912 he took over the local dray line which he conducted until 1936.

In the summer of 1914, seeing a need for a place where the farmers could keep their horses when they came to town with their load of hogs, (it not being an unusual sight to see fifty, to seventy-five loads a day) and when they came to town for shopping or otherwise, he built and maintained a large feed barn. Both of these business ventures, the draying and feed barn, were prospering for many years, but due to the trend of the times, the use of automobiles, this mode of transportation declined.

For one year he took care of the bulk oil for the Standard Oil Co., before they had a station built in Spring Grove.

He also for some years had the agency for the Minnesota Implement and Binder Twine, and up to 1936 the agency for the DeLaval Separator Co.

In January 1936 he was hired by the village council to

manage the municipal dispensary which position he held until his death.

He held the office of village constable from the year 1921 to the time of his death.

In 1921 he was appointed to fill a vacancy in the school board of Spring Grove, District 54, which position he held until his term expired in 1928. During his term of office as a school board member, the village was bonded and a schoolhouse was built in 1922—finished in 1923. In December 1924 this building burned and a new one, the present one, was built in 1925. He together with other members of the school board spent a large amount of time and effort towards the successful completion of that task.

He was a member for over thirty years of the Spring Grove Fire Department and at the time of his death an honorary member.

He was also a member of the Spring Grove Commercial Club.

His one outstanding hobby was the love and care of horses and with their passing he was somewhat lost in this modern world. He was a kind, unassuming and simple man with a sunny and cheerful disposition, a lover of children and animals, an optimist by nature.

Mathilda was now a widow. She would be living alone. Except for an occasional extended visit, none of her children would be residing in her home as a dependent. She faced a difficult personal challenge ahead. Not only would she have the loss and the grief to apprehend emotionally and spiritually, she also faced a truly dire financial crisis.

She and my father weathered the Depression through improvising: with loans and the sale of property which hadn't been lost by default, and with prayer and luck. Mostly, however, it was with diplomacy, skill and considerable help from their children who were employed. Now there would no longer be Knute's salary—less than $100 a month. Mathilda said she was dismayed and offended that the village stopped it immediately without even paying it to the end of October.

She could look forward to about $1,100 from the sale of our grandmother's farm to Uncle Willie. But first a technicality had to be worked out by the attorney for the estate.

And there was a small life insurance policy. There were loans against this policy, but Mathilda received a letter from the New York Life Insurance Company within two weeks of Knute's death informing her that, after the loans were deducted, she would receive the balance of $707.58.

Then came a cruel blow. A wealthy neighbor who owned a construction company came to see her very shortly—Barbara believes it was only a week or so—after Dad's death. He had loaned Knute money and held a mortgage that he now needed to have paid off. He came to collect it. She evidently persuaded him to grant a two-year extension and meanwhile she would continue to pay him interest each year.

Mathilda faced the new decade of the 1940s with dread, anxiety and considerable uncertainty. But she also faced it with remarkable resources—she owned her home, she had a caring and solicitous family, and she had great physical, emotional and spiritual strength. She would manage. She had met difficult challenges before during her 56 years of life. And she would again. She had faith. She had hope. And she had abundant love!

CHAPTER NINE

A Widow's Changing World

Mathilda's world would never be the same. And the universe outside of her own world was changing, too. As she faced the loss of her precious Knute and struggled to grieve with dignity and pride, the echo of Hitler's rumbling tanks in Europe could be heard even in Spring Grove at the end of 1939.

Her financial resources were meager but at least she did own her own home. She would have to figure out some way to satisfy the one loan that surfaced after her husband's death. She was determined to be independent. Her Qualey-Glasrud heritage of pride would require that. She could work—cooking, cleaning, baby-sitting or laundering. But with her keen mind and her experience of community leadership, she would wish for some way to translate her mental resources into financial resources.

The community gave her the support of its friendship and moral sustenance. Her neighbors closed in with comfort and reassurance on a regular basis. Nora Onstad, across the street, dropped in for coffee and a chat and urged Mathilda to do likewise. Belle Onstad, a mere half-block away, offered rides to church. Mrs. E. J. Foss, who had lived just across the alley, had died just six months before Knute, and Mathilda missed the almost daily contacts they had maintained for years. Perhaps she depended most upon Regina Kjome whose home was next door. When Regina came out to hang clothes, Mother would see her from the kitchen window and would go out to the back porch to exchange neighbor talk. The two neighbor widows were the closest of friends as their husbands had been.

Her three brothers in the area and their families were likewise solicitous and helped her dispose of household remnants of a lifetime which suddenly became a useless burden. And Sylvia, an earth-motherly type of woman with her own home nearby in Caledonia, found ways to mother her own mother. She phoned, she drove over to visit for a few hours, she would have her mother come back with her to babysit little Robert whom they nicknamed Fritzie. Mathilda sought business and practical advice from her son-in-law, Fremont, who was County Treasurer.

Mathilda was an inveterate letter-writer. She carried on an active correspondence, particularly with her seven children. She complained when they were lax with return letters.

Most of her letters that survive from those weeks following Dad's death were written to my brother Bill, who was teaching and directing the high school band in Glasgow, Montana. Fortunately for us, he saved almost every letter ever written to him. Less than two weeks after her Knute died, she wrote to Bill:

> It seems hard to settle down and write . . . I am feeling a little better. Have stayed home alone two nights now. The first was tough but last night I slept well . . . I will write you later from time to time and I hope I will hear from you, too, at least once a week. Sunday night I stayed with Uncle Willie and Monday, Tuesday and Wednesday I stayed with Sylvia. Time passes. [11-3-39]

Four days later:

> Today I am all alone again so I ought to have time to sit down and write a little to you. Last night I slept well all night. I have been home steady now for almost a week, and things are a little bit better. It did not seem like home at first—just like an empty house in which I had no interest. It would not have taken much for me to have disposed of my effects and to have gone and lived with someone. However, I have overcome that feeling to a certain extent. But I never knew that a mortal could feel so desolate as I did. Of course I had you children and you were all so dear and wonderful to me and so were friends and neighbors. But I guess the words "Better Half" mean exactly what they say and more. I never realized that before. I am so thankful we had this last year together when he did not feel so well. It drew us closer. [11-7-39]

A week later she wrote that Sylvia had come to get her "and I did not offer much resistance. There is not a great deal keeping me at home." And she continued:

> I had been at home since Thursday. I always like to be at home Sundays to go to church. Margaret and Robert spent the weekend with me. It seems that they change off coming home. The week before, Juliet was there. Robert is good about coming. He does not stay very long. He is quite lucky about getting rides.
>
> Things don't look quite so drab for me as they did at first. I suppose one can get used to almost anything. I am also overcoming some of my fear for the future. You must know this was quite a shock to me. And you know I had a provider and then, all at once, everything was taken away. The girls are all so good to me and seem quite anxious that I stay with them. This is what I plan to do after Christmas. Towards spring I hope to be in better spirits and hope to make some plans. I don't know what yet. [11-14-39]
>
> According to the date it is now just one month since Dad passed away. What a month! It is a good thing we

> don't know what is in store for us. Wouldn't that be terrible?
>
> . . . Sunday morning I had to get ready and go to church alone, something that had never happened before, I guess. I felt pretty blue. I was going to sit down to a solitary dinner when Barbara and Archie and the baby came over. And were they welcome! [11-21-39]
>
> I am not quite so panicky now as I was but I still get some terribly awful spells—especially when I am alone. Last night I really slept for the first time for a long while. I just miss Dad something awful. [11-23-39]

Holidays can be the roughest times for those who have lost loved ones. Memories flood in and as the family gathers, everyone is deeply aware how much a part of themselves the departed person was. Mathilda had to face Thanksgiving first. She was helped when Barbara and Archie and baby Kip came early in the week to stay through Thanksgiving Day. They brought with them a 12 pound turkey, prompting Mother to write, " . . . so we'll live high."

Naomi remembers some poignant details of that Thanksgiving dinner. Dad always had his place at the head of the table in the dining room. What to do on this occasion? While Mother was busy in the kitchen just before we all were to sit down, it was tacitly agreed by my sisters that Fremont would take that spot and he smoothly played his part. We all wanted to save Mom from having to face the empty chair when she came in to sit down.

Just then, however, she was surprised to hear a knocking on the back door. A stranger was there, cold and hungry. We used to call such people tramps or hoboes. Especially during the Depression of the 1930s they would come into Spring Grove on the rails and would hustle a meal and maybe a place to sleep before catching the next train out. Mom proved equal to the challenge. We had enough food, to be sure. And, while the rest of us, at her urging, began to eat our dinner, she remained in the kitchen to serve the visitor a bounteous thanksgiving meal. When she joined us in the dining room, she didn't seem to notice that Dad's place was now occupied by Fremont.

We all came home for Christmas of 1939. It was our first without Dad. We tried to fill the emptiness by drawing more closely together. We were a singing family and, with Julie at the piano and with the two of us brothers as trumpeters, we filled our mother's house and her life with the happy sounds of familiar carols. We enjoyed the presence of four-month old Kippy—a baby always gives an immediacy to the Christmas story—and it was fun to watch four-year old Fritzie pound the drum his bandmaster-uncle Bill gave him for Christmas.

Providentially, it seemed, January 1940 arrived with an active agenda for Mathilda. Her uncle, Gustav (always called Gust), was very ill. He and Aunt Sigrid lived in their retirement in Stillwater, Minnesota. For some time he had been afflicted with senility, the symptoms of which we associate today with Alzheimer's Disease, and his wife found it difficult to care for him alone. Aunt Sigrid urgently appealed to Mathilda to come and help her and, without hesitation and without preparations, Mathilda went soon after Christmas.

In a post card from Stillwater to me at college, Mother wrote that Aunt Sigrid "was almost starved for conversation. It must be dreary to get old under most circumstances." (Mathilda was then 56 and her aunt was 81.)So there together were two lonely women able to help and comfort each other. In a card to Bill she wrote, "The old gent is quite pert. He is sweeping around the stove right now. He makes my bed every morning and builds two fires. It is so warm here most of the time we almost smother. We listen to radio—Ford Sunday Evening Hour and Orson Welles and Helen Hayes . . ." Gust Glasrud died less than two months later.

Mathilda came home on January 19th. She might have remained longer but forwarded mail informed her that she had been summoned for federal jury duty in Winona. She wrote that she hated to leave home again because she had just rented rooms to two high school students and that required that her house be heated. However, she was able to arrange with her neighbor, Mrs. Olaf Peterson, to "have an eye on the fires," and that helped.

In Winona she stayed the first night with her daughter, Naomi, a student at Winona State. Her brother, Christian, was temporarily employed at an auto sales firm in Winona and he drove the 30 miles back to his home in LaCrosse each evening. That allowed her to spend some nights there, either at his home or with her niece, Sigrid, and her husband, Otto Vaaler, who also lived in LaCrosse. Part of the time while Mother was away, Barbara and her infant son, Kip, had come from Peterson to stay at Mother's house in Spring Grove. It seemed to be an opportunity for Barbara and it helped Mathilda too.

She returned at the end of January after the week of jury duty to resume her Spring Grove routine. In a February 4, 1940 letter to

Bill she gives an insight into the concerns that occupied her thoughts at that period:

> This letter is long overdue but it seems I have been a rather busy woman lately. Federal jury service in Winona was quite an experience and also fairly profitable. I had four dollars per day from the day I left home until I returned, including Sunday. My check amounted to $35 which was quite a lot more than I expected. Out of that we pay our own living expenses. I did not have any hotel bill, which helped some, but of course I left a little for Naomi and for Bob, and Petersons kept my fires going when I was gone so I bought yarn and made her a pair of mittens. When I came home I went down to Smerud's and bought up some yard goods. Spent $8.00 in a morning. I bought curtaining for the living room and some prints for summer use. Next week I plan to get a gas drum (for cooking) which will be another $9.00.
>
> You don't need to send me anything until I do something about my living room walls, which I expect I shall have to do this spring. However, I shall have to talk that over with the kids. I expect they will be home this next weekend. Marg and Paul, Juliet and Naomi and I suppose Barb and Sylvia will be, too.
>
> I both like and don't like to have roomers. It is company for me, of course, but then it is in and out all the time. Hard on floors and stairway. Also the two boys are like other boys—sometimes a little horseplay after they get to bed. All in all, though, they are nice kids. The Wrights bring a lot of food and Friday I cooked a chicken for them and had some myself. With the Dahl boy it is a different story. He wanted to have me get his meals and pay 15 cents a meal. We did it for two weeks but after I went away he has been bringing his eats.
>
> Later. I surely have had a time for the last half hour. Fremont brought Fritzie over this noon and he was to stay all night. Everything was fine until about 4 p.m. when he started to whimper. At bedtime he got just desperate and said, "Call my mother. I want to go home," or "Call my dad. I want to go home." I guess I heard that 50 times. I got up from my bed and went downstairs. He came after

and settled on the davenport. I surely won't keep him again if none of them are here. If the school kids had come it might have been different . . . I don't much blame the kid. It is much too quiet here, I guess.

Bob is out on his tour [with the Luther College band]. I have not heard a word from him since he started. He wrote me a letter before he left saying, "Of course I'll write you every day while I am gone." Maybe he still thinks I am at Winona. They are coming back to Decorah tomorrow night, however. I imagine you have heard from him. I plan to go to hear the band—either to Mabel on Tuesday or LaCrosse on Wednesday. If Mikkelsons go to Mabel, I can go with them.

Last night we had four or five inches of snow which was very welcome. The severe cold weather has let up for a while. It may be colder after the snow, however.

My basement is almost empty of wood now. I still have quite a bit in the first cellar. Uncle Ed and [his son] William hauled in two sled loads before I went to Winona. They used the team. I paid William a buck. He also helped some last fall so I didn't want him to do any more for me for nothing.

I spent last Saturday night and Sunday at Peterson. Had a ride with some fellows from Harmony who were on the jury. I haven't had a chance to talk privately with Barb but it seems that things are going all right . . . She was plenty anxious to get home after being here while I was away.

Guess the kid is asleep at last on the davenport. He'll be quite a load to take upstairs.

Love, Mother
P.S. I enjoyed being with Naomi. She is a hustler and knows her way around up there. She got the highest marks in psychology and physiology and an A from Talbot.

Three of Mathilda's children have their birthdays in March. Barbara on the 15th, Margaret on the 16th and Bill on the 19th. On Barbara's birthday Mother wrote to Bill for his birthday. She said that she had been listening to me on the radio from KWLC sing a birthday song for Barbara. About herself, she wrote:

> I have kept remarkably well this winter so far. Have gained a little in weight, I think. Guess it is the exercise, tending two fires, splitting most of the wood for the kitchen stove, going down for the mail every day, etc. I also have to bring in wood for the furnace. The boy [her roomer] helps sometimes but is like other kids, forgets and then he has B.B. practice till six. Last Tuesday we got down your old sled from the garage where I suppose it has been for the last 10 years, put a tub on it and filled it with chunks. Took an old harness line for rope and it works slick. I guess it won't be so bad to haul in my wood as long as the snow lasts, which it looks like it will.

On a Friday morning in late April, Mathilda was able to tune in the Luther College station KWLC and hear a half-hour program originating at the high school auditorium in Spring Grove—right across the street. It featured vocal and instrumental groups and some interviews with Superintendent William O. Nilsen and several faculty and students. It was the first live broadcast to be sent out from our home town, according to the *Spring Grove Herald*. (In my new student job as KWLC's program director I had the freedom to arrange "remotes," special programs like this to promote wider interest in the station, and I chose to begin at my home town.)

She was surprised by a Memorial Day visit from her brother Duffy. With his wife, Ida, he flew his own plane from Fargo to Spring Grove. The village had no airport but he spotted a fairly level field and set his plane down gently and, after two days visiting with the local Glasruds, took off again for the return trip. Duffy didn't need an airport runway. In Fargo he was a so-called "gentleman farmer" who lived in the city and regularly flew his light plane out over the prairie to his wheat fields to check on his crops. In North Dakota there is almost always a level field suitable as an improvised airport.

For Mother's 57th birthday on July 20th, some of the family came together in Spring Grove. Barbara and Kippy had recently returned from a visit to Bill in Montana and, with Archie, they came over from Peterson. Margaret and Paul came from Galesville, Sylvia and Fremont and Fritzie from Caledonia. Juliet had been home with Mother for part of the summer. (Bill was still out at Glasgow, Naomi was at summer school in Winona and I was working at KWLC in Decorah.)

Mathilda's family was in motion in August of 1940 also. Juliet left with four others on a three-week trip by car to California. Bill took a week from his summer band duties to return to Spring Grove to visit his mother. And Naomi had a week at home between summer school and the fall session at Winona. Her accelerated program at college would allow her to complete her course work at the end of the calendar year.

"It has been awfully nerve-wracking these last weeks but now I think everything is about shaken down," Mother wrote. "For a while I did not know where I was at or whether I would get very many roomers or not but it has turned out better than I expected."

The biggest change for Mother that September was her opening up her home to more roomers. The mothers of two high school girls from the Iowa hamlet of Dorchester were in and out, dickering with her for accommodations. And another student wanted to do her own cooking in her room, with her own equipment. Those three would bring her income of $12 per month. And then the new second-grade teacher, Lavina Larsen, rented the "east room" upstairs. Mother liked her a lot and when another teacher, a friend of Miss Larsen's, asked if Mrs. Lee could fix breakfast for her too. Mother agreed. She was pleased at the extra income, which was badly needed, especially because she had to have heat ducts installed to the upstairs and a new coil installed in the basement furnace.

She occasionally earned a few more dollars by sewing and ironing for Betty Mikkelson, the pastor's wife, and house-sitting for one of the local physicians, Dr. Rogne, and his wife while they traveled.

September 1st was her wedding anniversary, her first as a widow. A poignant note in one of her letters that autumn revealed that she was still grieving almost a year after her husband had died:

> I was so lonesome last week when I was alone. It is hard to be many, too, so I guess I am never satisfied. I seem to miss dad more and more. I would never have dreamed that it would be like this.

Nevertheless, Mathilda was undaunted in her determination to make her way financially and eke out an adequate subsistence. Her children who were working helped out when they could. Juliet, for example, paid the last installment on the taxes for 1940. With her new roomers Mother now had a full house and this meant more work as well as more money. But it also meant that she had a regular interchange with busy, active young women, and that had to be stimulating for her. The involvement with others in her home, and with friends and family, helped her on her road to emotional recovery.

Mom was able to check up on me at college by listening to my daily broadcasts over KWLC. She got worried when she didn't hear me for a couple of days and phoned the station. She was told that my voice was bad and that I had decided to "doctor up." I recall that I had sensed that I was exhausted—likely from having entire program responsibility for the radio station while taking a full load of college courses—and, with the cooperation and encouragement of Margaret Naeseth, the college nurse (and later my sister-in-law), I had checked into the infirmary for two days of much needed rest.

Another time when she was listening she also figured out something must be wrong because my daily "Hymns We Love" broadcast was recorded. She was relieved later the same day to receive my letter telling her that the president of the college, Dr. Ove Preus, had asked me to go with him to a meeting of educational broadcasters in Minneapolis.

When our family gathered for Christmas in 1940, Juliet provided the best surprise for us—her boyfriend, Marvin Skustad. During her teaching at Hayward, Minnesota, she had spent a weekend in Grand Meadow with her roommate and friend, Alta Hanson. There she met Marvin and, as she wrote in her own memoirs, she knew immediately "even before I had a date with him, that I'd marry him someday." So when he gave her a cedar chest for Christmas she figured he was close to proposing marriage and she was right. That Christmas was the first time Mother had met Marvin. She liked him right away, Juliet reports, but later commented to her that "he looks like a pugilist!" Marvin was a solid guy in more ways than one.

1941 began with the good news that Naomi, who had finished her course work at Winona State, secured a teaching position at Farmington, Minnesota, even though she remained technically a senior. She would graduate with her class in May. In Farmington Naomi would also meet the man she would marry two years later, Niles Hysell.

Barbara also returned to teaching. After substituting on and off in the fall for Alvina Larson, the teacher who roomed at Mother's house, Barbara was hired as her replacement. Miss Larsen had to resign because of health and didn't return to Spring Grove after the Christmas holidays. Mother then had the additional task of babysitting Kippy while his mother was teaching second grade in the school building just across the street.

"Kip is so lively that he pulls everything out of drawers and throws everything on the floor and climbs on tables," she wrote to Bill. "I think he will talk soon because he really tries to imitate now."

Mathilda took care of Kippy, her grandson (Christopher Gilbertson), while his mother, Barbara, returned to her career as a teacher.

It was winter and in Minnesota that inevitably brought snow and cold. During one of the cold spells Mother wrote, "I was out just now and threw down [into the coal chute] some more blocks. I am rather proficient in using the axe, too. Of course the slabs split rather easily." She had discovered that slabs trimmed from trees being used for lumber were available at a bargain and she had a load delivered. Winter is harder to weather when the economy is bad. "I always used to like winter at the time when the barn was doing good,"she said referring to Dad's business, a livery and sales barn. "Then our income was good."

There was war talk on the radio and in the *Winona Republican Herald*, the paper that came to our house. Bill and I were both facing the draft and, like millions of others, had to register. Mother told Bill she refused to get "het up" about it. "If I did I'd go nuts and I don't intend to!"

When, as a part of the nation's preparedness strategy, the Red Cross called for more clothing, Mother quickly exercised her knitting needles. "As chairman, I suppose I shall have something to do again."

She never approved of President Roosevelt and she was critical of his seeming support of U. S. intervention in the war in Europe involving England against the Germans whose Nazi army had occupied much of Europe.

> I don't know what to think of this country's situation. I guess it is best not to think. If he [F.D.R.] declares war, however, I do think he ought to be impeached. Two wars within one person's lifetime is too much. I do pray for you, William, and for all of my children and you do the same for me, will you?

Mathilda already had two grandchildren and a third one was on the way. Her daughter, Margaret, living in Galesville, Wisconsin, with her husband, Paul Thies, was expecting her first child in late February or early March. Mother decided that instead of a gift for the baby ("She has everything she needs") she and Margaret's brothers and sisters should chip in and buy some silverware for Margaret. They had given table forks to her for Christmas (Royal York Pattern) and now because of the baby and Margaret's own birthday coming up in mid-March, Mother suggested knives and recruited a dollar from each. Whether it was her own idea or Margaret's, she saw herself as being in charge of that project.

When Mary Lee Thies was born on March 1, 1941, Grandma went to visit the new mother and child in the hospital and most likely stayed to help them out at home. She reported Paul's observation about how everyone who visited would remark on what a beautiful baby this was. Paul laughed and said it was just like playing the same record all the time. She added, "She had so many visitors at the hospital . . . I got dizzy!"

Her letters in the months that followed were like a journal. Included were these items:

- Her Red Cross work continued. "I have to tag and press and pack the Red Cross sweaters today. They are not all in as yet."

- She complained that,"Bob is stingy about writing. He went to Moorhead [a gathering of students from Lutheran colleges]. He is trying out a new theme song."

- She provided each of her children with a copy of the Lutheran Hymnary with their name stamped in gold letters.

- She mused: "It seems so strange that you [her children] are all scattered all over. I so often feel lonesome for old times but there is nothing to do about it."

- Mother dickered with the man who loaned Dad money in 1930 and had secured a mortgage, for which interest had been paid each year. It was just $700 but how could she pay it off? When he came to collect she had a counter proposal. He settled for for $600.

- She attended a play at Luther College—Ibsen's *An Enemy of the People*—because her son was one of the actors. She told my brother (but didn't tell me), "Bob did well."

- Mother was proud to attend Naomi's graduation from Winona State—and noted it was with honor! "So many congratulated her on her fine record." With Mother were Barbara, Sylvia and Fremont, Paul and Margaret; and I surprised them all by showing up also.

- Her garden looked good. "I plowed it myself and got a backache out of it."

- During the summer she rented two rooms to out-of-town painters redecorating Trinity Lutheran Church.

- She acknowledged that Bill had enlisted in the Navy but didn't offer any special comment except to say, "I don't dare think about the war and you leaving and everything. We'll cross those bridges when we get to them."

- Our house never had a solid basement under the west half of the house. She had worried over what to do and finally got a bid from the lumber yard for digging it out and installing temporary supports to prop up the house while cement blocks were laid. She said she was shocked to hear the price: $300. She dickered with them and got it down to $275.

- She reported that Margaret and Paul had moved into the house they bought in Galesville. "Her place surely looks cute but Paul works at it all the time. I wish there was a Paul around here!"

- Naomi, now a wage earner again as a teacher (in Farmington. Minnesota), was able to buy Mother a new refrigerator. She got it from our Uncle Arthur's hardware store at cost. "It is a beauty!" Mother wrote.

- Naomi also sent money for linoleum, which Mom and Barbara laid with the help of Uncle Art. "You would not know the kitchen now, I guess."

- Barbara, who had begun her teaching career in a rural school, decided she needed a job again now and was hired to teach the Solum school in the country north of town.

Another challenge came to Mathilda in July of 1941 just before her birthday. It is testimony to the fact that she was known in the community as a woman of talent and ability who could write. She told about it in a letter:

> Last week a representative from the Minnesota Educational Association came here and wanted me to write the History of Houston County for a book, a sort of *Who's Who in Minnesota*. No pay, of course, only honor. I hesitated before accepting but finally said I'd try. Why they couldn't get anyone better qualified I don't know. There are to be only 3,000 words so that is going to be the hard part of that. My name goes on the article and I also get a write up or biography in the book. I guess I

> shall have to spend the next weeks on that. So that will be something to think about for a while.
>
> Last night Barb and Archie took me to Mabel to see *Caught in the Draft*. It was very funny—but not so funny after all when I think of all that gun training. I don't feel good about it all. What about saving the world for democracy now? Stalin's democracy?

She did a very good job writing the history. I have to wonder from where she could pull together all that information, including very specific items and names and dates. But it is more than that. The story she tells is a pioneer story which goes back to Indian days and the first settlement. It is descriptive of the terrain, the ethnic mix, the villages and hamlets, government, religion, economy, education—the works.

Where did she get the information? Clearly she relied on some previously published documents as she would have no way of developing all of this *de novo*—it would have taken many months. We can assume that her sources were reference books, possibly from the school library, just across the street. Her text is not annotated but at one point she writes:

> The first civilized men to gaze upon the towering bluffs of Houston County were probably Father Louis Hennepin and his two companions, Antoir DeGay Anguel and Michael Accault. A complete account of their explorations may be found in the second History of Houston County.

If there was a second, there must have been a first and probably additional county histories as well. Even so, she accomplished a prodigious task: selecting and setting forth the historical items in a flowing narrative.

I particularly like this paragraph that helps us visualize the county:

> The portion of the county along the Mississippi River has a rough appearance with many high bluffs and oval hills with rock capped summits. The bluffs vary in height from 320 feet at the spring in Beaver State Park to 595 feet above the flood plain at Brownsville. Farther into the

> interior of the county the land assumes the form of a rolling prairie with considerable timber. Still farther in the interior, it becomes a level prairie.

In describing some of the earliest aspects of the pioneer settlements, she must have been pleased to emphasize one of her own special priorities—education:

> The early pioneers never lost sight of the idea of educating their children. As fast as the children arrived, provisions were made for their education. School was often "kept" in a log dwelling with the family present in the same room.
>
> The usual method of organizing a school was for the neighbors to get together and select a lot for the building. To build a schoolhouse, a "bee" was the easiest way. Plans and estimates were improvised and each man contributed as much as he was able of whatever was needed. They brought their dinner pails, and by night, if there had not been too much hilarity during the day, the building was covered and practically completed.

The narrative concludes with a bit of prose that is about as lyrical as Mathilda would get:

> Houston County may be a small county in size and population but its productivity and general living conditions and its beautiful scenery make it second to none. It has never had a total crop failure since its organization.
>
> The present generation finds it hard to realize the trials and vicissitudes that the early pioneers endured, the undaunted courage they showed in making Houston County a "part of America."

In 1941, as in years long before and long after until almost recent times, women were identified, and identified themselves, by their husband's name. Thus her by-line in *Who's Who in Minnesota* (published by Minnesota Editorial Association 1941) was "by Mrs. Knute Lee." But in her biographical entry, where she is one of only two women among 82 men, she is LEE, MRS. CLARA MATHILDA: Homemaker.

Her listing, after reciting the obligatory statistics of birth, parentage, education, marriage and children, goes on to list some highlights of the first six decades of her life:

> 1900-01 rural schoolteacher, La Moure Co. N.D., 1901—06 Houston Co; 1906—homemaker, Spring Grove; co-author, *History of Spring Grove Trinity Norwegian Luth. Ch*, published 1934; 1924—mbr Spring Grove Parochial sch bd of religious edn; PTA, ch mbr, past pres, past secy; ARC, roll call chmn Houston Co, also Spring Grove, chmn Knitting for Refugees Com; Houston-Fillmore & Winona Co Circuit Fedn of Women's Missionary Socs, past pres; Trinity Norwegian Luth Ch, secy Ladies' Aid Soc, also past VP; hobbies: reading, gardening, handwork; res Spring Grove.

Mathilda was relieved to have that writing assignment completed. September had seemed to come too soon. It promised to be a busy fall. An immediate priority was to prepare for Juliet's wedding. She and Marvin Skustad had set the date for Saturday evening, September 27, 1941, at 8 a.m. at our Trinity Lutheran Church in Spring Grove.

Fortunately, our mother was not alone in the many tasks attendant to a wedding and reception. Margaret kindly lent Juliet the same wedding dress Mother had made for her in 1938. "It was lovely," Juliet wrote. The Herald described the gown as "white needle point fashioned in princess lines" with a long veil which "fell from a halo of sheer tulle ornamented with roses and pompons."

Our sister Sylvia Deters collaborated with Mother and our cousin Sylvia Meitrodt to organize a reception at our home for fifty guests. Julie wrote that she herself "made the chicken salad."

Others in the family had roles to play also: Naomi was the bridesmaid and I sang "O Perfect Love" and "The Lord's Prayer." And Naomi's boyfriend Niles Hysell tells about his meeting Mother for the first time that Saturday afternoon. She was in the midst of delegating last-minute tasks and her way, under pressure, of making him feel right at home and instantly part of the family was, rather abruptly, to give him his assignment: "Go up to the church basement and get folding chairs!" Years later he and Mathilda laughed about that many times.

Everyone felt the tension in our nation as the war escalated in Europe. Since March of 1941 Lend-Lease had been in operation involving U. S. Navy escorts of ships carrying munitions and armaments first to the British and later also to the Soviets. In August President Roosevelt and Britain's Prime Minister Churchill had met on warships off the coast of Newfoundland and announced a set of war aims known as the Atlantic Charter. In October a U.S. Destroyer was sunk by the German Navy and a *de facto* naval war with the Nazis was already underway. Meanwhile, the Japanese were occupying more and more territories in Asia, in China and Indochina. Our government had imposed sanctions. Relations between the U.S. and Japan were highly strained in spite of on-going diplomatic talks.

In the 1940 elections, Mathilda had voted for Willkie, who represented a more isolationist position for the United States as opposed to the Democratic posture favoring intervention. Willkie lost (45% to FDR's 55%) and this emboldened the third-term president.

Initially, small-town folks could be aloof from the debate in Washington, but when neighbors' sons were being drafted, the war fever came closer to home, even in Spring Grove. Mother knew of my pacifist sentiments (they never got to the point of being strong convictions), but she knew even more of Bill's restlessness. He wanted to be involved. He had already taken the Navy's physical and flunked the eye test. So he tried the Army Air Corps but found barriers there as well. Finally he just resigned his teaching job in Montana and drove to Seattle.

By a fluke he found a way to get reconsidered. He rented a room and was preparing to take a course in calculus at the University of Washington in Seattle. He at least wanted to be able to qualify for Navy officer's training in the "90-Day Wonder" program, a crash course to commission college students. He hoped to play in a dance band to earn his bread. But he kept thinking and dreaming of becoming a Naval aviator. One day he just went down to the main gate of the Sand Point Naval Air Station in Seattle and talked his way into the recruiting center. They had his file there and the officer in charge asked if he wanted to take the eye exam again. Of course! He told me he had practiced lining up the lights of the machine which measured depth perception. "I was able to do that pretty good by that time. I sailed through the exam like nothing," he said. So he was in the Navy and on his way to what he later termed "one of the most fulfilling four-and-a-half years of my life in terms of excitement and the things I really loved and enjoyed doing and knew that I could do well."

Mathilda remembered the horrors of World War I. And now war

was almost at our doorstep again. In those autumn days of 1941 the newspapers and radio were laden with tragedy abroad and bickering at home. Even as a woman who prized her own special awareness of current events, it would be understandable if she wanted to pretend that the conflict abroad was "their war" and not ours. She found, however, that she couldn't really escape. She prayed for peace but feared that the threat of war would never go away.

Then came Sunday, December 7th: The Japanese, in a sneak dawn attack, bombed Pearl Harbor in Hawaii. It was early afternoon in Minnesota. Her symphony broadcast was interrupted. Roosevelt called it "A Day of Infamy!" Congress declared war. The telephone rang. And rang. And rang. At last the war had come to "the land of the free and the home of the brave." It would touch every community. It would touch Spring Grove.

Mathilda's world would never be the same.

CHAPTER TEN

Weathering World War II

Spring Grove sent some of its sons and a few of its daughters off to war. It wasn't like 1917 at the start of World War I when recruits with little or no training were hustled off on troop ships to join a European war already in progress. American troops this time were, for the most part, held back in training camps for immersion in the discipline and techniques of the military. Their time for action would come, perhaps as a part of a big push later—some major deployment across the Atlantic or the Pacific Oceans.

The local weekly newspaper, *Spring Grove Herald*, did its best to promote flag-waving, figuratively and literally. Each front page beginning in 1942 carried a drawing of a fluttering Stars and

Stripes, with a quote from the Pledge of Allegiance underneath. The paper tracked the local servicemen and featured letters to the folks back home from those in uniform. The Herald generously reprinted military press releases, which often included the name of a local soldier or sailor.

Mathilda would proudly post in her kitchen any clipping reporting on Bill's progress in Navy flight training from Seattle to Corpus Christi, Texas, where he was being prepared for the important ceremony of earning his "wings" and becoming a commissioned officer.

Spring Grove people, nearly all of Norwegian extraction, tended to be stoical and outwardly unmoved by whatever fears, feelings or anxieties war talk might evoke. The newspaper dutifully printed government instructions on collections of discarded rubber and certain metals and, later, on rationing procedures for meat and sugar. These activities helped to create a sense of community participation in the war effort. It was easy to organize a patriotic pageant in the city park, preceded by a parade up Main Street.

Nevertheless, Mathilda's own family was restless. She knew we were asking about the implications for each of us in the massive mobilization of our nation's human and material resources?

Bill had taken off on his flight training adventure in Texas. He never neglected his mother's need to know what he was up to. His letters flowed then from Corpus Christi as they continued to do all through the war years and beyond. In April of 1942 he wrote to urge his mother to see a movie he had seen—the story of a Methodist minister with Frederick March:

> I see by the paper [Spring Grove Herald] that One Foot In Heaven is coming to the Ristey Theater. In your next letter to me I want you to write and promise to see it. It is positively marvelous. Don't forget this . . . You know I may still be a minister some day—if I live through this war. It depends on what the Lord wants to do with us.

Mother's frequent communications with Bill allowed her to be familiar with his plans. But she didn't have much of a clue to my intentions, mainly because I didn't either. But as my graduation from Luther College drew near, it seemed foolish for me to wait to be drafted. My brother had always been my role model. I followed him into the Boy Scouts, into playing trumpet, into Luther College. And now—should I follow him into the Navy, into aviation? But for the war and its pressure for involvement, I would never have visualized myself as a flyer. As a musician, a writer, a broadcaster, yes. But a warrior? Impossible. But my short-lived pacifism had dissolved instantly on that day of crisis, December 7, 1941.

Mathilda's sons-in-law faced the question also. Fremont, as county treasurer, was a local government official and was needed where he was. Similarly, Marvin as a farmer could see his responsibility in continuing to produce food. Archie began to see an opportunity as a worker in the defense industry. He and Bill Fossum of Spring Grove drove out to California to check out their chances in the burgeoning new ship-building industry. They got jobs. And Paul knew his skills as an electrician would be of use in some defense enterprise. He explored the possibility of employment at a submarine building facility in Manitowoc, Wisconsin, on Lake Michigan. He would move his family across the state "for the duration." And Naomi's boyfriend, Niles, like me, was exploring Naval aviation.

Meanwhile, Naomi was preoccupied with her teaching in Farmington plus a summer job at a defense plant in nearby Rosemount, Barbara was teaching near Spring Grove, both Sylvia and Margaret were mothers on duty in their homes (each with a small child), Juliet was discovering the challenges of being a farmer's wife, and I was totally involved with classes, final exams, rehearsals and broadcasts in my last months before graduation from Luther College.

Then, a week or so after graduation in May 1942, a major fire destroyed Luther's Old Main building. It proved to be more than a minor distraction. All my clothing, papers, documents, pictures and mementos of four years in college had been consumed. As day after day I looked at the stark smoldering ruin of the only "home" I then had, it somehow symbolized for me the war abroad. I decided to try the Navy, following my brother's example.

When Barbara's school term was over she decided to travel with Kippy out to California where Archie was helping to build Liberty ships in San Pedro. She recalls taking the bus to the train in Cedar Rapids and while going through Decorah she saw there the skeleton of the burned building at the college.

I remember having lunch in early June in Minneapolis with my sister, Sylvia. She was a circuit officer of the Women's Missionary Federation (WMF) and was attending their national convention as a delegate. I got a ride from Decorah with a delegate to the church body (ELC) convention, being held simultaneously with the WMF meeting, but what I really went to Minneapolis for was to try to see if I could qualify for the Navy's air cadet program. I took the exams and I passed.

That summer of 1942 brought Mom closer to our nation's war effort than she could ever have expected to be. My brother, ever the "impulsive interventionist" as I have previously dubbed him, had a scheme that he felt would serve both her interests and needs and his. He proposed that she take the train to Corpus Christi in order to attend his graduation and commissioning as an Ensign; she could share in the ritual of pinning on his "wings." Then, because he still had his car, she could ride back home to Spring Grove with him. He wanted to spend his leave with family before reporting for active duty on the West Coast.

Barbara wrote Mother from Long Beach, California urging her to go to Texas: "Don't let anyone talk you out of it. You'll enjoy the trip, I know."

In mid-July Bill wrote to her, "It was good news to hear that you are planning to come down here. I can hardly wait for the day to arrive. I sort of hate to have Uncle Bill have to give you the money but I really don't think it would hurt him to do it and it was nice of him to offer." He added that she would have to take the train and he urged her to get a berth in a sleeping car "since it's just about two nights or so and the added expense is certainly worth it . . . You sleep just as well in them as in your own bed at home."

But it wasn't as simple as buying a ticket and boarding the train. The date of the graduation kept changing. Bill had to complete certain check flights—there was even the possibility that he could still "wash out" just before graduation, although that wasn't likely. But his letters to her kept postponing the date. Then, finally, he instructed her on just what to do. It was a rough train trip for her—wartime travel was never easy. But she made it. She saw him in his new Ensign uniform. He brought her together with his good friends, Pastor and Mrs. A. B. Swan, who operated the Lutheran Service Center. Bill had arranged for her to stay at their home.

He recalled for me her arrival in Corpus Christi:

> I was able to manage the time and get down to meet her at the depot. The first thing that hit me and overwhelmed me was that she looked so old as she stepped off onto that hot, blisteringly hot, platform. My mother looked so old. And it was sort of a shock to me. Of course this is a long arduous trip and she was a widow in her sixties, I guess. I suppose we envision parents at a different time and I had been away from home for almost a half a dozen years now—not that I hadn't been back periodically. The festivities out at the base were extremely brief,

> which was maybe thirty minutes, no more. We threw my bags in the car and we went screaming off for thirty days of R&R in Spring Grove, Minnesota.

When Mathilda returned home, the summer was almost over. Irene Langlie came to live with Mathilda at the beginning of the new school term in September of 1942. Long a member of the parochial school board, Mother participated in the selection of Irene as the teacher. It was a formidable assignment: about 200 students in grades one through twelve were excused from the public school several times a week for less than an hour and walked to the little one-room cement block building on the edge of the school playground. The classes covered the gamut of Christian education from Bible stories to catechism to rather advanced theological issues.

Irene knew what she was getting into because she herself had graduated from the high school in 1936. She had been teaching rural school (20 pupils in grades one through eight) and when Pastor Oscar Mikkelson discovered she was looking for a job, he proposed she apply.

In a letter, Irene told me about the experience:

> Your mother was a member of the parochial school board. She offered me a place to live. I was grateful that she had, because she gave me a lot of moral support.
>
> My most vivid recollection is sitting in the living room after the evening meal and taking turns reading from the Book of Job and then discussing what had been read. She contributed much more than I did. She was a very intelligent woman and could have taught me much, but I could not take advantage of it. Classes and preparations kept me busy during the day and school and church events at night kept me occupied much of the time.
>
> She had a most regal bearing. I can still see her walking off to church and conducting Ladies' Aid meetings. She was a leader, but I wonder how much she was challenged, especially intellectually.

Irene had depended upon Pastor Mikkelson to give her guidance in her daunting assignment, but that help did not materialize. The reason was that he was joining the Army as a chaplain. His family would remain in Spring Grove during this leave of absence.

Like many in the congregation, Mathilda was both disappointed and pleased. It would be difficult to forego Mikky's warm sensitivity as a pastor, a true shepherd, well-loved by his flock. At the same time no one would openly complain, knowing that he was representing them in ministry to soldiers fighting a war. "They need him more than we do," was an often-heard declaration that all would agree to.

An ambitious send-off party, in true Spring Grove style, honored Mikkelson and his wife, Betty, on September 13th at the church. There was band music, choir music, singing by the Sunday school primary department, a vocal duet and an organ solo . . . and 19 "brief greetings" from church and community organizations, including one by Mrs. Knute Lee representing the Board of Religious Education. Mother had worked closely with Mikky on a number of projects and he was a valued counselor for her. And, indeed, she had also been a counselor for him. She would miss him.

Irene and Mother, together with Nettie Larson and Mrs. Emil Quinnell, were a committee that organized a candle-lighting service at Trinity Lutheran Church on Sunday evening, December 10, 1942. The committee sent out a notice that read, in part:

> It is desirable that the mother, father, or wife be present to light the candle for each family member in the service. Another relative or friend may substitute in the absence of the mother, father or wife. As more than eighty families are represented, it is necessary that the committee be informed as to who will assume this responsibility.

It must have been a moving ceremony for our Mother as she lit a candle for Bill and for me.

Christmas of 1942 would be different again for Mother and for her children, too. Bill reported that he was flying a patrol off the coast of Oregon on Christmas Day and had a real scare when he thought he was running out of fuel while still out over the ocean. (Finally, he was able to switch to the reserve tank and land safely.)

I was finally in uniform—officially. I completed the secondary flight program of Civilian Pilot Training (CPT) at Coe College in Cedar Rapids and at last the Navy had room for me at Pre-flight school at the University of Iowa in Iowa City. Before reporting there I had managed a few days leave in November in Spring Grove with Mother. But on Christmas Day I was playing "I'm Dreaming of a White Christmas" on the piano in the cadets' lounge and missing the family at home.

Perhaps Mother's best Christmas present that year was a visit from Barbara who came all the way from California with Kip for the holidays.

On New Year's Eve a Navy seaplane, a Catalina (PBY), crashed off the coast of Oregon. When Mother read about it she was worried because that's where she understood Bill was stationed. So she queried him and he replied that he knew all about it. "I was sent to investigate the accident and interview the lone survivor," he wrote. "I got a commendation from the Thirteenth Naval District and my squadron commander for my investigation and report. But that's not pleasant news to write home about. Six were killed."

Mathilda was getting training in tracking a far-flung family. It was a good preparation for the years ahead both during the war and afterwards when her children and grandchildren would scatter almost like a giant geographical game of musical chairs. At the end of January 1943, for example, Bill was being transferred from Oregon to Hawaii and would leave from San Francisco.

About that time I was transferred from Iowa City to the Naval Air Station in Minneapolis for Primary Flight Training. In Minneapolis we had to learn the Navy way of flying and put the "civilian" version of CPT behind us. (I later learned that one of the other cadets with me there at the time was future President George Bush.)

Mother knew I had been dating Elaine Naeseth. It began at Luther College. When she came from Janesville, Wisconsin, where she was teaching, to see me in Minneapolis the weekend of May 8, 1943, we became engaged. I went home to Spring Grove on a weekend pass to tell Mother the news and her only response was, "Aren't you a little young to think of marriage?" Of course she overlooked the fact that she was my age when she was engaged. I realize now that she was thinking of the war—was it prudent to make such significant decisions in the face of a perilous future?

In Spring Grove in those first months of 1943, Mathilda focused on the demands of home, church and community where she remained active as well as on her children who had flown the nest—a couple of us rather literally! During a snow-filled winter in Spring Grove, Mathilda heard from Bill, who wrote of getting sunburned on Waikiki beach in Hawaii and enjoying summer on New Caledonia with side trips to Australia and New Zealand.

Mother complained that spring about having a bout of rheumatism. In May she wrote to Margaret that it was better but still had not left. "It bothers me to get down on the floor and also to stretch.

I still limp a little." She was writing to thank Margaret for the gift of small towels for Mother's Day. And she continued:

> I got so many nice things for Mothers Day. Bill sent me flowers. Snapdragons—eight sprays with ferns. Also some glassware. A low flat vase on a standard with a high vase to put in the center of that. It is Tiffany Glass, whatever that is. Anyway it is lovely. Robert sent me more records, the New World Symphony and Grieg's Norwegian Dances. Naomi brought me a pair of blue gloves and took me to dinner at Evenson's besides coming home. Juliet sent me a pretty hanky and a box of chocolates. The Deters were over and they brought me a pair of stockings and Barb sent me $2.00 so I was pretty well taken care of . . .
>
> The weather is so cold all the time. I have not missed a single morning building the fire down at the Parochial School so far. Maybe half a dozen days in all I haven't had a furnace fire (at home) but then I have had a kitchen fire.

She knew Margaret's second child was due that month—she thought the expected date was May 19th—and she added, "I was thinking if I come up to see you [in Manitowoc] after the 19th and stay a couple of weeks, then you could come home with me and stay for a while if everything goes O.K. You had better insist that your breasts get emptied this time. I think that is important." She remembered Margaret's difficulty following the birth of Mary two years before.

She wrote that letter on May 13th without knowing that it was the very day that a son, Jack, was born to Margaret and Paul. The new father sent a telegram which had to be phoned to her from Winona. Mathilda immediately wrote again and said:

> "I hope you both are getting along fine. Poor Mary, I suppose she is lonesome now. It is too bad you are so far away. . .. Paul did not say how you were but I suppose when you feel able you will write. I was going to send a bouquet of tulips but I don't have any decent ones this year. They are all so scrawny and then I don't know your hospital address so it would take pretty long to get them there . . . I am anxious to hear from you."

When I was transferred from Minneapolis to Corpus Christi, Mother at least had an accurate mental picture of my situation, having been there a year earlier to attend Bill's graduation and commissioning. Mail was important and it kept coming from me, from Barbara in Compton, near Los Angeles, from Margaret in Manitowoc and, now a little less frequently, from Bill "down under" in the far South Pacific.

Later she discovered some of the reasons for not hearing from Bill. That was the time—it was August 1943—when he rather remarkably had "engaged the enemy!" When his exploits were finally revealed, she realized that he had had the primary responsibility for sinking a Japanese submarine, the I-17. It brought him both an exhilarating sense of accomplishment and, at the same time, a haunting sadness and traumatic realization of the lives lost as a result of his doing what he was sent there to do. He could be proud of receiving the Navy Cross but, as his later book, *Survivor,* would eloquently explain, he had to live with a troubled conscience.

Mathilda was also given the news that summer in July that Naomi and Niles were married out in California. Naomi had traveled out to spend some time with Barbara and Archie. She said she had wanted a change and had told Niles not to come out, adding, "But if you do, we're going to get married!" Mother, of course, had known of their engagement. Niles had discovered that his war service would not be as a pilot and he was already exploring options other than the Navy. He opted first to go to California.

By the time I had my "wings" in mid-September and came home for a leave prior to my going to California, Mother told me that she was ready to go out there also. Because I would be traveling by train, she wanted to travel with me. She could stay with the Gilbertsons—they were expecting another baby—and be with Naomi as well. After their July 17th wedding in Long Beach, and a trip back to Farmington and Spring Grove, Naomi had returned to California where she had already landed a teaching position. Niles meanwhile had joined the Army Air Force.

What a memorable trip Mother and I had! First we went by bus to Cedar Rapids and there we boarded the "City of Los Angeles" Zephyr—we called that type of train a "streamliner" then—bound for the West Coast. She hadn't been there before and neither had I. She loved traveling and during her life managed to do quite a bit of it. I discovered that one of the joys of her life was having one of her sons escort her to new and fascinating places.

My duty was in San Diego and Mother was with Barbara and

her family in Compton, south of Los Angeles, near Long Beach. On some days off I was able to make the two-and-a-half hour trip up to see them.

Mother's second granddaughter, given the name Naomi, was born on December 7, 1943 to Barbara and Archie. Mother and I were asked to be sponsors at her baptism at Our Savior's Lutheran Church in Long Beach. We enjoyed the baptismal party at the Gilbertson home in Compton on a December Sunday afternoon.

Christmas in California that year of 1943 was special. The flavor of it might best be conveyed first-hand in this portion of my letter of December 27th reporting back to Bill:

> Dear Bill:
>
> Back in San Diego again after being "home for Christmas." I am exceedingly thankful that my situation was such this year that I could join the family for a few days. I had a ride up with Lt. (jg) Hensley (who knows you from Corpus Christi) right to the door, arriving at 20:00 Christmas Eve!
>
> Mother was so thrilled to receive your letter—so beautifully and appropriately timed—on Christmas Eve. It was written the 19th, apparently and I think it nothing short of a miracle that it reached her (in spite of the Christmas mail congestion) in five days. It was great that you got a leave in Australia—we all enjoyed hearing the many details of it.
>
> I brought Mother an orchid (her first) from both of us and that helped to brighten her Christmas. She wore it on her coat to church Christmas Day in Long Beach. I gave her a beautiful dress (Naomi selected it) and she got many nice gifts. I do believe your letter topped them all, however.
>
> Yes, it was a Christmas Eve that brought back many pleasant memories. We all got a big bang out of watching the kids open their gifts.
>
> Sunday we visited with Uncle Duffy, Aunt Ida, Donald, Harriet and Donald Jr. [Mother's brother and his wife had come from Fargo to be with their only son and his family.] It was good to see them, and Duffy and I did considerable hangar flying.

I don't know how Barbara and Archie managed to accommodate

so many of our family. At that point they had two children and two extra adults, Mother and our sister Naomi. Then, just to strain the facilities even further, my closest friend Chuck Nelson and I had a few days leave prior to boarding a ship at San Pedro harbor for Hawaii and our assignment to a patrol bombing squadron at Kaneohe Bay Naval Air Station. We both came to stay with the Gilbertsons also. (Where did we all sleep?)

Most meaningful to me, and I think to Mother, were the moments of farewell at our leave-taking for overseas. She told me she wanted to walk Chuck and me a few blocks over to the bus which would take us to the San Pedro dock. So she did. Chuck was discreetly understanding and allowed Mom to have some last minutes alone with me. We felt the emotion of the departure. This was not just some "goodbye" on anothe trip. This was her second son going off to war . . . off to the Pacific where there would be action. Now she would have both of her boys placed "in harm's way." We waved as the bus left but we both saved our tears for later.

A few weeks later she wrote to me:

> I hope you will always be able to send me word about your where-abouts (if not directly) and the condition of your health and so forth. Knowing me, you would know I would always like to know even if news isn't good news. You know I can take it. We can't expect that you may be as fortunate as Bill seems to have been in that direction. Knowing both of my boys, and having faith in them, I hope I shall have fortitude to accept whatever may befall.

Meanwhile, Mother remained in California with Barbara for a couple of months. In mid-February she took the bus to San Diego. She had been invited to spend a week with her cousin, Julia Rowell, daughter of her Aunt Sigrid. "I thought I'd better try and go, knowing we would have a good time going over old times, being such close relatives. When I was a girl our families were together all the time."

She wrote to me in March that upon her arrival back in Minnesota she was greeted by the "worst blizzard of the winter!"

She had heard from Bill both about his promotion from Ensign to Lieutenant (Junior Grade or j.g.). But more importantly, she had the news that he was due to come home on leave. She expected him some time in April. He would be receiving new orders. (These would involve training on the East Coast for more duty in the Pacific—this time as a fighter pilot.)

While Naomi continued teaching in California and living with Barbara and Archie, Niles was transferred in the Army Air Force to Texas and Florida on the way to a longer-term duty station at Tonopah, Nevada. This was bleak desert country. Its only advantages were that Niles and Naomi could finally establish their first home and it was relatively close to family in California.

Then it became clear that after six months of patrol flights over the Pacific from the Mariana Islands, my squadron VPB-13 would also return to the States to regroup and prepare for its next duty even farther west in the Pacific. We would then fly west to get to the Far East! Suddenly Elaine and I could plan our wedding during that summer of 1944. I wanted Bill to be my best man and this would be possible only if we could schedule our date to coincide with his availability. We settled on July 29th which was later than Elaine had wanted it, but it did give us more time to make all the arrangements and invite friends and family to attend.

Mathilda had most of her family together in 1944 at Spring Prairie, Wisconsin, when Bob and Elaine were married. (L-R) Bob, aunt Maria Peterson, Mathilda, Sylvia, Barbara, Juliet, Margaret and Bill. (Naomi, then living in Nevada with her Air Force husband, Niles, was unable to attend.)

Mother was there, of course. It was her first trip to Spring Prairie, twenty some miles north of Madison, Wisconsin. She would discover, as I had earlier, that it is not a village or even a post office address but rather a community radiating from a parish where Elaine's father was the pastor. It was one of the very first immigrant congregations established (in 1847) by Norwegian Lutherans and as such was historically significant for our branch of the Lutheran church. For Mathilda's there was another connection between Spring Grove and Spring Prairie: our own beloved pastor, the late Alfred O. Johnson, had served there before coming to our village.

Mother was accompanied to the wedding by four of my five sisters—Naomi could not come—and their husbands. Bill had arrived from Florida to be my best man. These were precious days for Mathilda, surrounded again by almost her entire family that had been scattered by the war. But, all too soon her family had scrambled again and scattered. Elaine flew with me to California; San Diego was our new home and we could now readily go up to see Barbara and Archie and, on some weekends, also Niles and Naomi who would come over from Tonopah.

It is difficult for young persons to really appreciate how dependent their parents may be on communication with them. (I am now in that same position.) Mother scolded me for not writing often enough that fall of 1944 when Elaine and I were newly-weds. And then, she felt guilty, as we Norwegian-American Lutherans are so prone to do:

> I realize, Bob, that the tone of my last letter was slightly acid and I hope you will forgive me. I promise it will not happen again whatever the provocation. I hope I can rise above feelings of self-pity or whatever one may call it. Had I waited a few days before writing I would have cooled down. I guess I am not above temptation no matter how old I get. I didn't think it was in me to get riled up about anything any more. Guess I still have maybe a little of the (Old Adam) original sin in me.
>
> This is what I have to say in justification: You, admit it, have been a little more than lax in your correspondence with me since you got out west. I am sure you don't realize it, but two short notes, maybe both prompted by Elaine, is all I have heard from you directly until last week. Then getting that big fat letter and not seeing any sign of your handwriting except the signature, I must say I was rather bothered. I wondered why? Don't you like to write me? You know I gave you rather definite ideas on the subject while you were home and you

> remarked, quote, "The difference between Bill and me is that I like to write and he doesn't."
>
> I am sure Elaine in her loving kindness is willing to do everything to make you happy and as you could by nature become, let us say, a little indolent, you are willing to let her do things you ought to take care of yourself. I am not saying this altogether for selfish reasons but partly for your own sake. Rather mostly for your own sake. I have always been proud of you and I want you to grow into a fine mature person that both Elaine and I can be proud of.
>
> Please don't misunderstand me and think that I don't care to hear from Elaine because I certainly do. I love her and as time goes on we will be more closely knit together, I am sure.
>
> You two boys have always been something special to me and especially now during war time, I want to feel close. That is all I have of either one of you. I am very happy that you are enjoying your time together out there. I realize too that it means so much more, that as inevitably you will have to be parted for a time. God bless and keep you both.
>
> Lovingly,
> Mother

On October 21, 1944, the fifth anniversary of our father's death in 1939, his sister, our Aunt Maria from Decorah, came to be with Mother for a few days in Spring Grove. Again the tension between the two sisters-in-law could be felt. Maria brought flowers to decorate the altar in church and wanted also to bring them to her brother's grave. So she sat through two services in order to retrieve them. She couldn't take them to the cemetery until the next morning because on Sunday noon Naomi and Niles dropped by for a brief visit and Sylvia and Fremont came to invite Aunt Maria and Mother to their home in Caledonia for dinner. Mother expressed frankly her feelings to me:

> The next morning she wanted to bring the flowers to the cemetery. I told her I didn't think it did any good for anyone to bring flowers over there now and let them freeze. When she came back she said, "Now I am satisfied" and intimated that I had neglected the graves, etc.
>
> I was over there for decoration day and I keep things

> planted but, you know, I am not quite as sentimental in some ways. So I asked her if she thought I had forgotten Dad. I said I had been through that awful nightmare and now was adjusted and didn't care to have things raked up again. I think I went through my share of loneliness and grief but now am back to normal. I told her I had things to do for the living.
>
> It is sort of hard, when a person can't act natural with someone but has to be so careful what one says and does. . . . Of course I see her point of view too. Of course she has no one but Charlie and I suppose it is lonely for her. I know she has lots of friends, though. They have a card party I think almost every week. I guess it is here that she is reminded of those that are gone.

Her daily routine of living changed considerably. Her Aunt Sigrid came from Stillwater to spend the winter. Mathilda was very fond of this 86-year-old double cousin of her mother and sister-in-law of her father. She was eager for the companionship Sigrid's being there offered:

> I know it will be more work, but it is just for the winter. I know it is better for me to have to do more cooking. If you want to know what she is like, she is just an older edition of Julia Rowell—same memory for details. I think if I find time, I am going to prompt her to tell some things about long ago and put down a few things on paper. You know I can't remember things that are just told to me now. I hope she remembers some things about my grandparents on both sides.

She got more of Sigrid's memories than she expected, apparently. Later she wrote:

> I am kept rather busy. It is no small task to keep Aunt Sigrid either. She seems to be contented and as happy as possible. She seems to dwell in the past such a lot. I hear about her father and mother, sisters and brothers and my grandparents and parents and all old acquaintances all the time. She just loves to talk and tell things . . . It is pathetic, though, to get as old as that and no one of her children feel that they can care for her. I won't do it any longer than till spring. I know she won't be able to stay alone any

> more. She is so stiff that when she has been sitting it is hard for her to rise. She has a lot of pain, too. I feel very sorry for her. She is sleeping a lot—is sleeping now.

Mathilda was happy to be teaching Sunday school. She had eight 12-year-old boys. "I teach them New Testament Bible History, which is familiar ground, and I hope I may do them some good," she said. Just before Christmas she invited her entire class to her home where she served them a meal at the dining room table. She named the group: Neil Rauk, Roger Ellingson, Robert Tweito, Norris Storlie, Winton Blexrud, Verdon Erickson, Donald Nesheim and Milo Bjergum. Mathilda said, "They were all well-behaved and seemed to have a good time. They were pretty busy with scrapbooks and all the other souvenirs of you boys which I had. They also heard the records." Elaine and I had made records of some songs which we sent to Mother for Christmas. She played them for anyone who would listen and for her class. "'Is that him singing now?' one of the boys asked. I said yes it is."

She was very busy in December with the third annual candle-lighting service in church. "I was on the committee and it was a lot of work to check all the names and names of parents. The church was packed and the services were very impressive. The stand was in the form of a V [she drew a picture of it]. I lit my candles on the table inside the V. There were several gold candles which were not lit." The unlit candles represented those local soldiers or sailors who were killed, missing in action, wounded or in prisoner of war camps. "We were rather fortunate here for a long time but things seem to change."

When I went overseas again early in December, Elaine went to spend Christmas in Miles City with her sister Margaret and her husband, Pastor Norval Hegland. She returned to be with her parents in Spring Prairie, visited Margaret and Paul, and went to Spring Grove for a visit with Mother. She then returned to Long Beach where she had a job as hostess in a Lutheran Service Center.

For a time near the end of January 1945, prior to Elaine's visit, things were in a turmoil for Mother with several unexpected complications. Her words describe it best:

> I told you in my last letter of my furnace causing trouble—smoke and soot coming up. Monday was the big day. I got up before daylight and built the kitchen fire. Five below that morning. Went down and got the mail and a few groceries. Brought breakfast up to Aunt

> Sigrid. She had orders to stay in bed. My kitchen was 60 degrees and the living room 55. By nine o'clock my chimney sweep was here. Cold for him on top of the roof, too. Then Uncle Art came and took the pipes apart. I needed new ones. When the pipe came away from the furnace the iron collar that joins furnace and pipes was broken. I think that was what clogged. Then they were in a quandary, but decided to get a new ring welded. They did. The pipes were full of soot—so was the chimney. Also the floor was covered. Uncle Art took the old pipes along for measurements and called up saying he would not be back before afternoon. I worked down below sweeping and cleaning. I also cleaned out the inside of the furnace. Blegen carried out the soot and ashes.
>
> Then I had to try and wash the floor. I used six or seven pails of water. I had hot water which helped. I had to have the window open so it was cold but I had several layers of clothing, so was O.K. Then to get lunch for us. Aunt S. dressed well and came down. I pulled the table close to the kitchen stove which was roaring. Then I sent her upstairs again. At one o'clock, Mr. Bergsgaard, who has worked on furnaces, brought the pipes and set to work. I had to help hold things. By three o'clock the fire was going again and, oh, what a draught! After that I washed clothes. Washed everything I wore, too. I don't think you would have liked my looks. I am thankful everything is okay again.

She was particularly relieved to have that behind her. It was bad enough to have all that dreadful soot permeating her house. But Aunt Sigrid was there. And in a couple of days Elaine would be visiting. Even more critical, however, Juliet needed a place to rest from her trauma of a miscarriage. A week earlier she had arrived from Grand Meadow to be with her mother. She and Marvin had been happily expecting their first child, due in April. However, while at Mother's, problems arose with Juliet's pregnancy and she had to be rushed to the Spring Grove Hospital. Once Julie was back at Mother's home, Marvin planned to come to get her on the weekend. Then the weather intervened. A huge snowfall blocked the rural roads and delayed him several days.

I had been impressed with Mother's narrative ability in her letters and wrote encouraging her to write some sketches about her life now and how it had been years ago—as Aunt Sigrid supplied some of the details. She responded:

> "I am very much afraid that you greatly overrate my powers, so far as my ability to put my thoughts on paper. I have not a very vivid imagination, besides I have no memory for details. I ought to have Aunt Sigrid's—as, for instance, this morning's conversation (a small part of it):
> She: I suppose you have Ladies' Aid this week.
> *I: Yes, we have.*
> She: Who entertains?
> *I: I don't remember . . . Mrs. Ellingson is one.*
> She: I suppose none of the ones who were members when I was are left.
> *I: Oh yes, Mrs. Schansberg and Mrs. Carrie Newhouse.*
> She: I remember Mrs. Schansberg and Mrs. Wein entertained and they had rusks and cookies.
> *I: How in the world can you remember what they had to eat at that time?*
> She: I can remember that just like it was written in a book. I can remember it because my sister, Caroline, was there and she expected to get butter and didn't get it.
> *I: I can't remember what they had to eat at Aid last time. Now you tell me.*
> She: I remember you said they had peas and carrots.
> *I: Well, they did. I guess I never did care too much about food. That is, I mean it isn't too important.*

I had sent her the manuscript of an article I had written, later published in our church magazine, *Lutheran Herald.* It was a spiritual profile, from his letters home to his parents, of my squadron roommate, Roland Johnson, who had perished when his plane crashed into a volcanic island off the U.S. West Coast. We had flown together in the Pacific during our first tour of duty. My memorial was mostly in his own words. She gave me constructive feedback:

> I read with great interest your article. I hope you get it published. Towards the last there were a couple of places where I think you could improve the wording or the phrasing. You use a dictionary, no doubt. Be very careful of the exact meaning of words, as for instance, I think you would "move your chairs farther in to avoid the rain"

> instead of evade it. You avoid something concrete or tangible while you evade something unpleasant. These are constructive criticisms. One thing my reading has done for me has been to teach me the shades of meaning in words.

By the end of February, 1945, Mathilda was beginning to become weary of her role as caregiver for her aunt. She was counting the weeks until spring. But she quickly added:

> I am not complaining. It would be a shame to do that when I think of the millions of people in service who are under military discipline and privations. But it is sort of a worry to care for such an old person. It was my own doing and I am glad I have been able to do it for her. She thinks she has had a good home, which is something.

It was more important than ever, then, that she could have a little fun. She was called in as a substitute actress for a skit, *Family Album* at a school carnival:

> I don't often say no, so I went. With Mr. Quinnell I was supposed to look over an album of family pictures and they were to be shown in the form of tableaux . . .They were dressed in costume and we were to hold a conversation about the pictures. I thought we would have a script but all we had was the inscription on the page over the picture. So we had to ad lib and it worked pretty well. We had three showings and by that time we were going good. I guess it is like being a good liar. One doesn't remember what was told the first time and added to it each time. Any way, lots of people came to me afterwards and said it was good. I thought it was fun, too.

Bill, meanwhile, was training in the Atlantic off the East Coast as a carrier pilot and soon would be aboard a carrier heading for action in the Pacific. I had moved on to Saipan and later would edge closer to Japan from our seaplane base at Okinawa. As the eventful year of 1944 receded into history and the world moved into the even more dramatic year of 1945, Mathilda again resumed her vigil of watching, waiting, praying and tracking her sons who had gone off to the wars.

The momentum of action was accelerating both in Europe and in the Pacific. The spectacular D-Day Normandy invasion of the previous summer and the massive military follow-up assaults gave Americans the sense that, in Europe at least, we would win (not that it was every really doubted.) Mathilda, like so many others, was buoyed by the expectation of success but, practical woman that she was, she never for a moment forgot the cost in terms of human lives—on both sides.

When, suddenly, in April of 1945 our American President, Franklin Delano Roosevelt, died, Mathilda had to come to terms with her own conscience. Here was a man she disliked and distrusted for his political views. At the same time she respected the office he held and accepted his leadership as the Commander-in-Chief of our armed forces. She didn't talk or write about her feelings during those days of national mourning. As a Lutheran Christian, however, she would surely be mindful of and have her attitudes conditioned by the Pauline words in the New Testament, Romans 13:1: "Let every soul be subject unto the higher powers. For there is no power but of God; the powers that be are ordained of God."

Soon after the President's death, the climax in Europe came in May of 1945 with victory. She would quietly celebrate VE Day while knowing that the war was not yet over.

Meanwhile the Japanese forces in the Pacific were gradually being forced to retreat back to their islands. It was no secret that an invasion was planned. The Japanese knew it and were taking desperate measures to fend it off. With both of her sons involved in the air campaign against Japan, Mathilda found herself becoming more nervous, more anxious, more fearful for them. She prayed harder.

As Aunt Sigrid's season with Mathilda drew toward a close, Mother was involved with a rather packed schedule of social engagements as visitors came to pay their respects to Sigrid her before she left and invitations out to meals multiplied. Mother herself presided over a big farewell party:

> We had a party honoring Aunt Sigrid and the relatives turned out en masse, almost. Anyway it seemed as if most of the arrangements fell to me, or I thought they did. I felt sure no one had thought of any program so I also took care of that. Juliet came home in the morning so she played the hymns. We sang *My Faith Looks Up to Thee* and *What a Friend We Have in Jesus*. I read the 46th Psalm and then gave a few highlights of her life as she

told them to me at different times. I called on Emil Quinnell. He told of Uncle Gust's work in clearing the old buildings away from the lower end of the park [Sigrid's husband Gust was mayor at the time] and getting the whole park in shape. Ove Fossum and Styrk Stenehjem responded as did Uncle Willie. Henry Glasrud presented the gift. She got $43 in all so it shows the esteem that people have for her. Nearly everyone gave $1. It seemed very sad and touching especially as no one of her close family were there. It was hard to talk because I could see tears in so many eyes. Before the program was over, however, [her daughter] Minnie and Paul and his family arrived. Aunt Sigrid was as though transformed. She was so happy. Minnie has been ill.

Earlier her letters had been largely a report of what she was doing, and where she had been visiting. They gave her far-flung family reassurance that she was managing her life all right. That summer of 1945, however, she wrote letters furiously, dispatching a flurry of messages every few days, hoping that most of them would catch up with her sons, wherever their squadrons were situated in a large ocean that was anything but pacific. Those letters are almost like a journal as they record not only her domestic pressures but also her feelings about the war. That correspondence conveys in her own words how she saw herself and the world and tell us how she was weathering the war:

May 27, 1945
Dear Bill,

I have a piece of perhaps startling news. I have rented my house furnished for next year. It is not quite as bad as it sounds. I have reserved the room above the kitchen for myself. And reserved the right to stay here if I feel like it. It is to three of the teachers for the school year. Irene L. and two girls with her. One is the Home Ec. teacher and the other the second grade teacher. They have both been here with Irene so I know them. The two have boy friends in the Pacific so they won't be gadders . . .

I also stipulated that if you or Bob or Naomi came home I would have to take care of you, which was O.K. If Bob comes this early fall they could have my bed and you know there is a bed davenport here too.

Margaret wants very much for me to stay there some and if everything goes fine for Sylvia, she will need some help, too. [Sylvia was pregnant, their baby due in October.] Then, if I can check back again here off and on then I will feel better about leaving the house . . .

The food situation is getting sort of acute. Yesterday they didn't have meat in town. The restaurant served eggs. We have to get along on five pounds of sugar till August. I barely have time to mail this. I would like to hear from you.

Love,

Mother

* * * * *

May 30, 1945

Dear Bob,

This morning, today being Memorial Day, we went to the park for the program . . . and to the cemetery afterwards. It looks very nice out there. Supt. Hjelle gave the talk today. He did quite well, I thought . . . The papers every night are full of the doings out your way. Seems that the going is not so easy. I am wondering more and more now—I will not say worrying—about your comings and goings but I know you will be all right.

* * * * *

Grand Meadow, Minn.

June 6, 1945

Dear Bill,

You see by the heading where I am. I came up on the bus on Sunday night. It seems that Juliet and Marvin never can spare time to come down any more. They surely are busy out here on the farm. They work from morning till late at night . . .

Juliet and I have been pretty busy too. On Monday we washed and ironed 17 feed sacks. No small job to get the color out of them. Now I am making up two sheets and some towels and dish towels out of some of them. We are sending the sheets to Barbara. Sheets are not available most of the time. Neither are other cotton materials. They all go into the service, it seems. There are lots of shortages in other supplies, too.

The San Francisco conference [establishing the United Nations] is not going so hot. They are at a standstill on the veto question. Then there has been the French Syrian uprising, with England having her say. Guess it is easier to make war than peace.

The radio and papers are full of the doings at Okinawa and vicinity. I keep wondering if you're out in that direction now. God bless and keep you.

Mother

Mathilda was elated when her sons got together on board a ship in an anchorage at Okinawa. We had sent separate notes to Mom in the same envelope. Her response to each of us reflected her excitement:

June 12, 1945
Dear Bob,

It surely was thrilling to come home from Grand Meadow and find mail from both you and Bill. In his first letter he told of plans to see you so I could hardly wait to open your letter of June 1. And, sure enough, there were notes from both of you.

* * * * *

Wednesday, June 12
Dear Son Bill,

It surely was thrilling news to hear that you and Bob got together. That should boost both of your morales. I got the news when I got home from Juliet's on Friday, June 8. Of course I tell everyone I see and they all think it was swell . . .

{She wouldn't know until later how amazing that accomplishment was. Bill actually hitch-hiked on a PBM seaplane flying from Saipan, where his squadron was located temporarily on shore, to Okinawa where I lived on a seaplane tender, the U.S.S. Kenneth Whiting, and flew flying boats on long 10 hour patrols up to Korea and around Japan. He had told his skipper he wanted to visit his brother but he neglected to add that I was at Okinawa, over 1,000 miles away. We had two wonderful days together.}

> . . . Talked to Mrs. Langland yesterday. It seems that Joseph has been through the concentration camp and was pretty riled up and bitter about it. He was so incensed about what this Hutchins of Chicago U. wrote in *TIME.*
>
> Ben Hibbs of the Post had an article last week about the atrocities that is the worst I have read. Well, we can't dwell on it too much. There is so little we can do.

{While some of the points Robert Maynard Hutchins made on V-E Day as reported in *TIME* (5-21-45) are unimpeachable, one can readily understand why Joe was outraged at the University of Chicago President's remarks under the headline, "All Men Are Human."

"I venture to predict," said Hutchins, "that the present excitement about war criminals will seem ridiculous a few years hence." Ben Hibbs, editor of the *Saturday Evening Post*, on the other hand, had graphically pictured the horrors of concentration camps in the article, "Journey to a Shattered World" (6-9-45), which Mathilda had read and commented upon. Like Langland, Hibbs was actually in the camps just days after their liberation by American troops.

After being at both Dachau and Buchenwald, Hibbs wrote, "When you come out, you feel that you will never be clean again. You want to take a bath in chlorine. You know that as long as you live you'll never quite be able to get the stink of the place out of your nostrils, nor forget the scenes of abject misery you have seen."}

> . . . Well, I think if the world is to stand a while yet, we can't lump the whole German people under one, give a blanket verdict and say they are all evil. No more than we can say we are all good. If we are Christians, we build not tear down. Christ forgave. So should we.
>
> I guess there is much indifference to religion and good living right here at home. Parents send their children to Sunday school. Then they stay home themselves. It is almost impossible to get those youngsters to stay for services. You were never asked. You went. I suppose it is easy to get self-righteous when one gets older, but so many of the parents are so slack.
>
> I wish you could see the yard now. The bridal wreath is finishing. I have all sorts of iris. A yellow rose bush and peonies full of buds. I cut the grass last night. The potatoes are big but the rest is pretty small yet.

Mrs. Kjome and I enjoy each other. Sometimes she eats with me and then I with her. She is so good.

Monday, June 18, 1945

Dear Son William,

Another weekend passed and another Monday. I did a big washing this a.m. Nothing to that now. There is hot and cold water and a drain in the basement. Struck a fine day. The sun is out but the air is still cool. The nights are very cool. Not at all good for the corn. Gardens are slow too. I have cut the back lawn. It seems easier now. Shall do the front tonight.

I have to go down and get me some provisions and mail this. Do you know we can only get five pounds of potatoes at a time? Saturday they didn't have any at all. The shelves are so empty. I have managed with my points so far, but I don't eat much meat.

I have been gratified by all the letters I have received from you lately. I suppose now that you have moved I won't hear for a while. You said not to send clippings from *TIME* but I can't resist sending this speech by Judd. I have heard him over the radio. I think it is more timely to read now than to save, seeing that you are out that way . . .

I walked over to the cemetery yesterday, Fathers Day. There were several things blooming and there will be more later. I picked up a four-leaf clover on the grave. I shall enclose it.

Had a letter from Naomi today. She sounds busy. She thinks Niles will have a furlough in August . . . I have had just one letter from Bob since you were there.

The flowers in my yard are just gorgeous now. I didn't see any prettier ones in California. I have a late narrow-leafed iris, dark purple. I am sure the top is as big as a wash tub, just loaded. Also a yellow rose bush, just covered with buds and flowers. Too bad there aren't any films around.

Our congregation has to raise 1,800 dollars for Lutheran World Action [LWA]. It seems the orphaned missions haven't fared well and the Catholics are ready to take over all our buildings and holdings. Besides they [LWA] help the service centers so I suppose I shall have to do something about that.

Love,

Mother

July 5, 1945
Dear Bill,

Got your missives yesterday. Was relieved. Hadn't heard since you moved. You and Bob both are so intensely cautious about giving any news of your operations. I sometimes read a little between the lines. I notice by the papers that some of the boys tell quite a bit about where they are and what they are doing. Well, Bob will be home soon I hope. Wouldn't it be swell if you could come home for Christmas? I shall be here then.

There are a hundred things to get ready before September. I papered upstairs last week. This week I am making a fancy wool quilt for Naomi. She doesn't know about it yet. I had the wool so thought I better make it up now. Should make one for Elaine, too, but that will have to wait. I have the wool for that too.

Juliet was home on Sunday. I sent a lot of junk home with her to store and some things she could use for herself. Sylvia and Fremont were here too. They have moved out of their house and are living in their bedroom and have cooking privileges upstairs in the house they are going to live in. It seems that the people who have been there won't take their furniture until August 1.

Juliet had a flat tire on the way home but managed to get home on the spare. She sent me a card . . .

Well, I have to go downtown now so must quit. I keep thinking about you boys most of the time. Things are more uncertain out there. We hear of so many who are gone. Langlands lost a boy in Okinawa.

God bless you and keep you.

* * * * *

July 10, 1945
Dear Son Bill,

I am starting my third letter this afternoon. Somehow I have not been in the mood for writing this week.

The weather is so cold. I am wearing a sweater all day. My feet are cold right now. There is a cool wind and clouds obscure the sun much of the time. There was an eclipse of the sun yesterday morning but I wasn't up in time to see it. People are haying but the weather is not too favorable. It rains too often. I am not working quite so hard this week as last. I have been finishing the quilts I made and some other sewing I had neglected. I was glad to hear from you and to find out the name of your ship. I thought this clipping perhaps meant your outfit but saw a paper down town and the carriers were listed and yours wasn't mentioned. Which one are you connected with 1st, 2nd or 3rd? Wish I had some clue . . .

There are some roses on the table beside me, giving out some wonderful perfume. I shall put in a few petals. All my love, and God's peace be with you.

Mother

* * * * *

July 17, 1945
Dear Son William,

I am anxiously waiting to hear from you now. I know there are momentous things going on out there where you are. I heard from Bob yesterday. He said he was relieved to think that they were resting for a few days. He presumably wrote to you too. He is looking forward to coming home. Sylvia and family are living with me for a little. They can't get into their house until August 1st. They were at the house in a room for a while but the farmer tenants came back to see about their things so that didn't work out so well. There is lots of room here and they bring lots of groceries and meat so everything is fine . . . Guess the baby is coming in November. So far, so good . . .

* * * * *

July 23, 1945
Son Bill,

I received your birthday letter July 21 when I got back from Juliet's. Sylvia and Fremont were here so we went up to Juliet's on my birthday, returning Saturday. I shall be glad to get the tea set at a later date.

I am thinking about you a lot. I know you have been busy lately. Bob has been back at Saipan for a rest. I don't know if that means that this will be the start of the return. I had a nice letter from Elaine, too. She is counting time till he can get back.

The war news sounds very good now. Maybe it will be over before we think.

This is the 5th letter I have written so far this afternoon. To Aunt M., Elaine, Mrs. Mork, Niles—I had a nice letter from him this a.m.—and now to you. I have Barb, Bob and Marg left. Hope my letters get to you. You try and write often, too.

Mother

* * * * *

August 1, 1945
Dear Son William,

I hope by now there is not so much cause for worry. The papers of course are so optimistic but of course we know there are more casualties than they admit until later.

There are many things I would like to say but can't. If you are right on spiritual matters that is the main thing.

We are having a heat spell which is good. We have enough moisture too. The corn should catch up now. The garden is growing fast too. The potatoes are almost ready. Do you know that for a month potatoes were so scarce we could only buy 5 lbs. Then lots of times they didn't have any.

My house cleaning and painting will be slackening up now. I still have a few things to do. I have to clip the hedge, if I can scare up a clipper. My lawn cuts easy now. Guess the grass was too tough in the spring. Mrs. Kjome and I have visitors. A mole or moles are very busy. This a.m. we carried water and poured into the openings hoping to drown them. They surely have long tunnels. It seems in life one always has to be fighting something. Nothing is ever perfect.

Saw Melvin Trehus at the P.O. yesterday. Asked where you were. I told him. He said, Oh Bill will take care of himself. Maybe it isn't always so easy to take care of yourself. But I think Somebody does take care of you. I am so glad to hear you accept this: "Thy will be done."
Lovingly,

Mother

August 13, 1945
Dear Son William,

War news has been so exciting lately. As yet we have had no word of peace. I heard today that the carrier planes are out again and I thought that likely you were too. Had a letter from Bob today and he says as he has said before that weather is such a hindrance.

Do you know what your status will be when war is declared (over)? Will you be released or will you have to wait around as so many of the fellows in Europe have to do. I suppose only time will tell. I do know the country is entirely unprepared for peace-time conversion. I guess the task is too great. There are both of the theaters to think about. I am wondering about Barb and Archie. I suppose it will mean his job will up fold up too. I feel sort of bad about having rented my house now but it is too late to do anything about it. There is no job for anyone in Spring Grove anyhow.

I wonder what Bob will be planning. Did he say anything to you about any future plans? Guess it is not very easy to think of any thing else to do than what he is doing out there. In one way I think you are fortunate having decided what you will be doing and having a little laid by to make it possible . . .

While Mathilda was anxious for word from Bill, she could not know that he had been under water in the U.S.S. Whale, a Navy submarine in the waters off Japan. She could not know—nor could I at the time—that while I was flying a patrol along the Japanese coast, I had made routine radio contact with that very same rescue submarine. Its crew had picked him out of the water after he had been forced to ditch his fighter plane. He could not get back to his carrier because he had been circling over a small Japanese island in the harbor near the Kure Naval Base, their target for the day, that day near the end of July. He was desperately trying to fend off any Japanese attempts to capture or kill his downed wingman, Johnny Hantschel (of Appleton, WI) floating in a rubber life raft while Bill gave him cover for almost two hours. Bill then had only enough gas left to get to the sub off shore. Hantschel did not survive and Bill never did find out exactly what had happened to him.

Mathilda's prayers for her own sons' safety were not in vain. (He best describes his exploit in *Survivor*.) While he was in seclusion in the protective bowels of the sub, the atomic bombs were dropped on Hiroshima and Nagasaki and World War II was over. Bill discovered this only as he finally stepped ashore at Guam.

Everyone was stunned by this cataclysmic event, prepared for in absolute secrecy to all but a tiny elite. The dropping of the atomic bombs was too shocking and initially incomprehensible for any of us to come to terms with it and make any judgment other than the bald realization that, whatever its ultimate implications for the world, the war was finally won. We had to deal with the particulars and pressures of that. Little were any of us able to apprehend the profound truth that, although fighting had stopped, a new era on our planet had begun.

It was late in August before Mathilda learned what had happened to Bill. She wrote:

> Aug. 25, 1945
> Dear Son William,
> After a month of silence I was very glad to hear from you. I had a feeling that everything wasn't exactly right. I am glad the boys [in his squadron] didn't write then. I would really have worried. All is well that ends well. I also had your letter of Aug. 14 and the one you wrote after the war was over. I hope by now you are back to your ship again. It must have been a close call, but it seems you are to live, I hope, for better things . . . It surely was a relief to hear from you again and that everything was O.K. I said the war ended for me that night!

Mother probably would not learn until later that Bill and I were able, amazingly, to rendezvous early in September in Hawaii on our way home. I had arrived there and was waiting for transportation to San Diego by ship when I learned that his carrier had come into Pearl Harbor. I was able to telephone from my base (Kaneohe) directly to him on the U.S.S. Randolph, and we spent a couple of wonderful reunion days together.

In San Diego, where Elaine welcomed me—one of the happiest moments of our lives, certainly—I suddenly discovered I was being discharged from the Navy.

Naomi at this point was in Compton with Barbara, who was eager to get back to Minnesota again. So four of us eager adults, Naomi, Barbara, Elaine and me, two children, Kip and Naomi, and a dog took to the highways and headed for home.

Certainly it was ironic, as Mother had noted herself, that she had worked all summer to rent out her home and its furnishings only to find suddenly that her family was coming back to Spring Grove now that the war was over.

Things happened quickly, one event upon the other, that autumn. We gathered at Margaret and Paul's home in Galesville and loved being there with the children. From there I went in my uniform to Minneapolis to see if I could get a radio announcing job. I had three auditions at three stations and got a position (the uniform helped!) at WMIN, starting immediately.

Finally, we did celebrate the end of the war as a family together. We were invited to Caledonia, to the new home of Fremont and Sylvia. It was early that November, 1945. Bill had returned from some minor surgery at the Naval Hospital at Great Lakes, Illinois, and Niles was at last able to get back from his Army Air Force duty. And Barbara and her children and Naomi were still in the area. Elaine and I came down from St. Paul, Margaret and Paul and children drove from Galesville, and Juliet and Marvin from Grand Meadow.

When World War II was won in 1945, the family gathered at the Deters home in Caledonia. (L-R) back row, Margaret, Paul, Juliet, Mathilda, Bill, Sylvia, Fremont, Niles, Elaine and Bob. In front are Naomi and Mary Lee Thies.

The occasion for it was special and important on its own merits: We had been invited to be present to witness and participate in the Holy Sacrament of Christian Baptism for little Joseph Deters, who had been born on October 18, 1945. Sylvia had been trying to schedule the christening event at a time when all of us could be there.

For Mathilda it was a sacred ceremony on several levels. Being together again at last with her seven children (and most spouses) and her six grandchildren was the culmination of her hopes and dreams and prayers. On that November day in Caledonia, she was able to celebrate her new grandson's reception through baptism into God's family and at the same time welcome him into to her own reunited family. The official holiday date for Thanksgiving would come a few weeks later, but for Mathilda—and for her family—that Sunday became our own very special day for giving thanks!

CHAPTER ELEVEN

New Beginnings in the Post-War Era

"It was sort of a letdown after everyone left. I was very tired and needed rest. I did not feel so well, either, but am fine now," Mathilda wrote to Bill early in January of 1946.

Her weariness was doubtless linked to worry over the question, "What's next?" Suddenly the whole country was energized for the new period opening in the Twentieth Century. The war was won. The scattered military and civilian defense workers had returned and then scattered again. Everyone, it seemed, was making decisions. Some could resume their lives where they left off before the war disrupted their lives. Others pursued new opportunities for employment or education.

Her own family had begun to make their decisions—teaching, farming, selling, serving, broadcasting and studying. Now she would have to make hers.

Bill was temporarily at Columbia University in New York City. She wrote to him there:

> I was glad to hear from you again. I had not heard from anybody since they left [until] I had a letter from Margaret yesterday. Have been wondering about Naomi, how she is faring. She has had sort of a rugged time lately. Sylvia came over for Rev. Solum's funeral yesterday and I went back with her for a little. My plans are rather indefinite but I suppose I shall go up to Margaret's after a while.

She had rented her house to three teachers with the understanding that she could have her own room there. Over the Christmas and New Year's school holiday, our Mother was again able to be hostess for her own family in her own home. She even arranged a party and invited our Aunt Maria and Uncle Charlie (our Dad's sister and brother-in-law) from Decorah. But for the rest of the winter and spring of 1946 until June, she would feel more comfortable visiting in her children's homes and giving her renters the privacy they deserved.

Irene Langlie, who had earlier rented just a room from Mother and was now renting the entire house with two teacher friends, wrote me years later just what that privacy meant in 1946:

> It might have been questionable, yet, I think your mother would have understood.
>
> My two housemates [Vivian and Marcine] were engaged to be married that summer to recently discharged servicemen. A couple times, as I recall, they came in late spring to visit. There was no hotel in Spring Grove. It would have meant their going to Caledonia to sleep a few hours. Time and gas were at a premium. I suggested that they stay with us in the Lee house. I would chaperon and take full responsibility. All went well. There were no repercussions, as far as I know. The three of us left in June, very grateful to your mother for letting us share her home for an enjoyable year . . .

Even when she regained the full use of her house in the summer of 1946, Mathilda's life was still unsettled. Like some of us of her children, she was almost floundering, still seeking some security and wondering just where she belonged. She would spend time in Caledonia with Sylvia and Fremont, in Galesville with Margaret and Paul, in Grand Meadow with Juliet and Marvin, and in Peterson on the Gilbertson family farm with Barbara and Archie—these were the nearest of her children.

She happily accepted her role as grandmother-in-residence as her extended family grew. She was available in August of 1946 when Juliet's baby Mark arrived after a difficult thirty-two hour labor and delivery. At the beginning of that September just as Barbara was about to resume her teaching career—this time in the Rushford, Minnesota, public schools—her son Kip became seriously ill with nephritis and had to be rushed to the hospital. Mother was again available to come over and save the day so Barbara could teach. Sylvia and Margaret each had two young children and at their homes a visit from Grandma was similarly welcome. Giving the young mothers a reprieve from the constancy of child care helped her feel useful and fulfilled.

Meanwhile our brother Bill had made decisions, too. He had returned from a brief educational foray in New York City, where he had audited some courses at Columbia and Union Seminary to prepare for the Christian ministry in the Lutheran Church. He had enrolled at Luther Theological Seminary in St. Paul. He had a dormitory room on campus. He would earn extra money by flying some weekends with the U. S. Navy Reserve from the air base at Wold Chamberlin airport in Minneapolis. And he fell in love. Impulsive as ever, being a man of action, he was engaged after a two-week whirlwind courtship to Shirley Foster, a student of nursing at Fairview Hospital. They were to be married in New Rockford, North Dakota on September 8, 1946.

Mother would go to the wedding, of course. But of Bill's siblings, only Sylvia and I were available to accompany her. I had been asked to sing. My wife, Elaine, had given birth on the first of September to Peggy, our first-born. We had just moved to a different apartment in St. Paul where I was an announcer and program director at radio station WMIN. Juliet's Mark was just a month old. Barbara was teaching and had two young children. Naomi was awaiting her first-born within about three months—she and Niles lived in the Prospect Park section of Minneapolis.

The plan was for Mother, Sylvia and me to drive to Fargo where we would connect with our Uncle Duffy and ride with him and Aunt Ida from there to New Rockford (about 160 miles away) and back to Fargo that same night.

I don't remember much about the wedding itself, but I certainly remember the trip back to Fargo. It was night and Duffy was driving fast. Everyone in North Dakota seemed to drive fast! The roads are often in a straight line without a curve for miles and miles and invite pressure on a car's accelerator. I was in the front passenger seat and Mother, Aunt Ida and Sylvia were in the back seat. I had turned my head to talk with the women in back when—Wham! A sudden crunching scraping sound—we had been sideswiped by an oncoming car—or, rather, I believe, Duffy was a bit over the center line and probably the other car couldn't avoid slicing us on the driver's side or getting sliced by us. At any rate, Sylvia was thrown forward against the front windshield but her trajectory was cushioned by hitting me first. We ended up in the ditch along highway 281 just north of Carrington. It was eerie—I remember most the sound of the engine whining and the horn blowing and my Christian Science Aunt refusing to get out of the car and holding both hands high in the air and chanting "I feel the presence of God . . . I feel the presence of God." Sylvia was bleeding and Duffy seemed to have some bruises on his leg but Mother and I and Ida were virtually unscathed, except perhaps emotionally. We were able to get into Carrington for some first aid. But Ida refused, on the basis of her religious convictions, to accept medical attention for herself or for her husband.

Somehow we made it back to St. Paul after an overnight stop in Fargo. Sylvia, with a bandage covering the cut on her forehead, had to return to Caledonia and I had to report for work the next day at the radio station. And it had been planned as a part of this excursion that Mother would finally get to meet her latest granddaughter, little more than a week old, at our apartment on Stryker Avenue in St. Paul.

Elaine has never forgotten that meeting. Peg was having a nap when her grandmother arrived. Then, when she woke up and cried, Grandma went in to look her over. Elaine cringed in embarrassment as her mother-in-law loudly declared, "Why, this baby is sopping wet!" A perfectly normal comment while inspecting a wee infant just awake from a nap, of course, but this was our first baby and Elaine somehow took it personally as a criticism of her.

The Twin Cities came to have a family magnetism for Mathilda. Elaine and I with a new baby were on the heights in St. Paul looking down on the Mississippi River bottoms; Naomi and Niles were in

Prospect Park, almost at the intersection of Minneapolis and St. Paul; and nearby on Franklin Street, Bill was resuming his seminary courses while Shirley continued her own nursing studies at the University of Minnesota rather than at Fairview Hospital. In November of that same year, 1946, Mother spent a month with the Hysells before Nick was born on December 10th. She remained for a couple weeks to help Naomi adjust to motherhood and then returned to Spring Grove.

Naomi recalls that she couldn't seem to handle the situation alone and, when the baby got sick with a cold, Niles summoned Mathilda to return and she did. When she walked in the door, even before she had removed her hat and coat, she took a look at both mother and child and said to Naomi, "You look a lot worse than the baby does!"

Mathilda stayed long enough to be present at Nick's baptism. Our Spring Grove pastor Mikky came up to officiate in the Hysell's apartment. Elaine and I and Bill and Shirley were there and it possibly was the very first time the two Lee brothers and their wives were together with Mother.

Often in the past Mathilda had reason to be anxious about her children but seldom had we had occasion to be anxious about her. But, on one of her visits the following spring, she had us worried. Mother had decided to spend some days with us in St. Paul and some with the Hysells in Minneapolis. Fortunately the two locations were conveniently connected by a trolley line that went from our street, Stryker Avenue, down through the St. Paul center city and up by the State Capitol, continuing toward Minneapolis on University Avenue. When she was ready to return to the Hysells she had no qualms about traveling alone, even though it was almost 9 p.m. I escorted her to the streetcar and saw her safely aboard, making sure she would get off at the University Avenue stop by the KSTP studios at the city line where St.Paul becomes Minneapolis. There, either Naomi or Niles would be waiting to bring her the two short blocks to their apartment on Seymour Avenue.

We phoned the Hysells and said, "She's on her way. Give her about twenty minutes." They went up early to University Avenue to wait. And they waited. And waited. Our phone rang and Naomi's anxious voice said, "She hasn't arrived. What should we do?" There was nothing to do but wait. So they returned to the rendezvous point and waited longer. And they called again wondering if we had heard anything. Should we call the police? Naomi was almost frantic and we were plenty worried also.

Just when Naomi was ready to dial the police, they spotted a taxi slowly cruising by searching for the right address. They went outside and—what a relief!—out of the taxi stepped our Mother. Naomi was almost crying. But Mathilda was laughing. Her first words were a joke: "I got drunk!"

But those were not her last words. After the Hysells paid off the driver, she began unfolding the real story. The trolley was on its last trip for the night and, instead of continuing on University Avenue to Minneapolis, it turned north on Snelling and headed for the trolley yards off Como Avenue for the night. When it came to its final resting place, Mathilda was the only passenger still on board. This dark part of the city certainly didn't seem right—it didn't look like the busy junction on University Avenue between the Twin Cities. She explained her dilemma to the tram driver. He couldn't solve her problem. But he didn't just leave her out on the cold dark street that time of night. He kindly took her over to a nearby factory building where he saw the only light. They found a night watchman on duty in a small side office. His English was limited so she had difficulty explaining her predicament—she didn't even know where she was. He finally got the idea and helped her phone for a taxi. It seemed to take an inordinately long time for its driver to find the watchman's office and meanwhile she struggled to converse with the stranger. Finally the cab came and brought her home. Mother didn't panic. But we almost did!

Back in Spring Grove as Mathilda looked ahead, she recognized that her very meager income wouldn't be adequate for sustaining her livelihood as an independent woman. She needed to take some action.

The first part of her plan towards a solution was to decide to move upstairs. She would convert the upstairs to an apartment for herself and rent out the downstairs. It also meant converting the downstairs and adding a bathroom down there. Julie and Barbara came to the rescue and re-decorated—painted and papered—and thoroughly cleaned both the downstairs and upstairs apartments. An outside stairway was built on the east side of the house and a door cut to enter what had been our largest bedroom that now was transformed into Mathilda's kitchen.

Her children had serious misgivings about that rather steep stairs and the danger it represented, particularly in winter ice and snow. Juliet said she protested to her, saying "Mother, I don't think you should be living upstairs. What would happen if you would just fall down the steps?" Juliet said she simply replied, "What difference would that make?"

Naomi added, "The same thing happened to me. I was so concerned that she was up there, and I fussed about it and finally she brought up the subject herself once. She said, 'I just want you to quit fussing about that. I'm up there, and I walk up and down long stairs. I haven't fallen so far, and I probably won't, but if I do, it's not your fault.'"

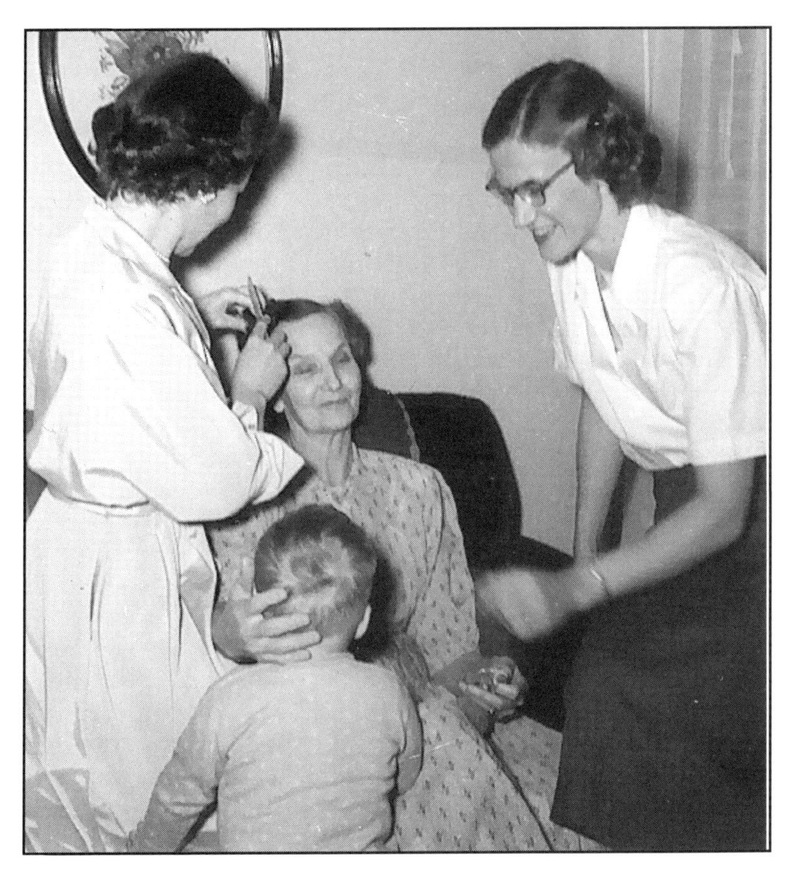

In Minneapolis in 1952, Mathilda gets a beauty treatment from daughter Naomi, while grandson Jon and daughter-in-law Elaine observe.

Julie has written, "It was necessary to have an auction. Things had to be sold to make room for the apartment. Money was needed, too, so some valuable things had to be sold. I dreaded to see some of the lovely old dishes go on the auction block."

Barbara remembers that Mother had happy experiences over the years with those who rented her downstairs apartment. One couple thankful to be there was Ernest and Elizabeth Ellingson. She was the daughter of Mathilda's long-time neighbor and dear friend, Regina Kjome. Another renter who became a life-long friend was Rose Storlie. Mother's downstairs apartment was Rose's last home and it grieved Mathilda when Rose died from cancer some years later.

Rent money helped. It was not enough, however. The second part of Mathilda's strategy was not quite so simple to accomplish. She decided she needed a job. She had earned a little now and then doing some odd jobs like ironing or knitting dresses or babysitting but her sense of security called for something more structured. Likely Pastor Mikkelson was instrumental in finding her an opportunity at the local hospital. He was chairman of the board at the time; his wife, Betty, was a nurse on the staff. Mother's work there included doing all the hospital laundry. It was menial labor, heavy and difficult.

To begin with, she enjoyed it. She told Margaret, "I like it because I have a long walk, and I like to walk and get some exercise. And I get a good breakfast." Later on, however, the circumstances of her job changed or at least the attitudinal climate shifted. The hospital stopped the free breakfasts and expected her to pay for them. She became uncomfortable because people who were her friends from the community and church were now in a more elite class and she felt, apparently, that they were condescending toward her as just a laundry worker. As in other institutions, there developed a professional class system.

Naomi thought that Mother may have contributed to whatever tension developed. When our siblings were together and discussing this, she commented, "She wasn't a very sociable person, you know. In a group of women of mixed ages like that, she wasn't necessarily very personable. If they wanted to be jolly and she wasn't exactly in a mood to be jolly, there was no question that she would be a little aloof."And our sister Barbara added, "I think the others were probably a little afraid of her—intimidated, intellectually intimidated!"And someone else quipped, "Weren't we all?"

She participated, however, in the annual Christmas party at the hospital and, in 1947 when the entire staff drew names for gift giving, she got the name of one of the nurses and knit a beautiful pair of mittens for her.

Barbara observed that Mother's hospital job served as an introduction to her wearing slacks. She was of the old school where women would seldom don trousers. The long walk in bad weather from her apartment to the hospital would have made long pants welcome, however, and Mathilda was, if anything, a practical person.

After Elaine and I moved from St. Paul to Great Falls, Montana, where I began a new project for our church called Sunday School at Home by Mail and Radio, Mother followed our Children's Chapel radio broadcasts. She gave me feedback by mail when she had heard one of the programs from WCAL at St. Olaf College, Northfield, Minnesota, or WNAX in Yankton, South Dakota.

Mathilda always had a fascination with history. She seldom discussed family history with us. This was mainly our fault, not hers. We were no different from children or young adults today who often are much too absorbed with the present and the future to worry about preserving, documenting or exploring the past. A second cousin of hers, Carlton C. Qualey, a professor at Carleton College, Northfield, Minnesota, had distinguished himself as an expert on Norwegian-American history. At one point he had written about his roots in sketches concerning the Norse-American enclave of Spring Grove, his own home town. As a history buff herself she must have been proud of him. When in 1947 he was speaking in Caledonia, Mathilda was in the audience listening. He came to assist in organizing and to promote the establishment of a Houston County Historical Society. She wrote to me, "He knows his history!"

Having a son in training to become a pastor was a source of considerable pride for our Mother. She had invested much of her life in church work and, like most early Scandinavian Lutherans, had put her *Prest* (pastor) on a pedestal.

She was also pleased, I think, when I left commercial radio to work in broadcasting for our national church body. She never heard me preach as far as I know, though in those days even as a layman I was sometimes invited to preach and conduct Sunday school workshops as an extension of my activities under the churchwide Board of Parish Education.

She did hear Bill preach, however. In April of 1948, his senior year at Luther Seminary, Barbara had arranged for him to be invited to preach at their church in Peterson, Minnesota. She remembers that his sermon title was "Spare-tire Christians." Bill himself reported that "Spring Grove turned out en masse." By that he meant that 23 of those in the congregation that day were his relatives.

Mother wrote, "I thought Bill did quite well. He has improved a lot since last year. He seems to feel much more sure of himself."

Mother wrote to me on May 18, 1948:

> The time seems to slip away so fast. When I come home from work, I am pretty tired and hit the sack for a while. Then there are a few things to tend to around here, too. I have not started house cleaning yet. Guess there won't be too much of that done. I have put in a little garden which is peeping through. I just came in from digging now and found it is already five o'clock . . .
>
> Last Sunday after church Art took me out for dinner at Canton. That seems to be a popular place to eat on Sundays. I asked him to come home with me for dinner because we were both alone. [His wife, Aunt Manda, had died a year and a half earlier.] But he said, "No, you come with me and we will go out to eat." Everything looks nice around here now. Today is perfect. The weather has been cool and rainy.

The big event of the summer of '48 was Bill's ordination in Spring Grove. He had negotiated the date with Mikky, taking into consideration the fact that, although he had a call to Bremerton, Washington, he had not finished all of his course work at the seminary and was still taking classes or producing papers up to August 7, 1948. The date was set about a week later, August 15th.

By then Elaine and I had moved back from Great Falls to continue our work from the Twin Cities and this allowed us to be present also. When I recall the ordination service—or when I listen to my tape recording of it—I hear the haunting plainsong strains of *Veni Creator Spiritus* sung that day with stanzas between the Scripture readings by pastors from the southeast Minnesota area. These same pastors all gathered around Bill for the "laying on of hands" as he knelt during the rite of ordination. It was an impressive ritual, marred in my mind only by an ugly loud feedback squeal from my tape recorder—one of the first instruments of its kind, having been introduced to the public only after World War II.

For Bill himself one of the most impressive aspects of that day was his initiation into pastoral acts by officiating at the private confirmation of our brother-in-law, Niles, who had taken instruction from Bill and had chosen to become a Lutheran.

The new pastor and his wife and baby son—David was then almost a year old—left for the West Coast to a challenging congregation in Bremerton, Washington, on the Olympic Peninsula, a ferry ride from Seattle Mathilda followed about six months later for a visit so she could help the family during the time that their second child, Robert Foster, was born on March 20, 1949. In a letter she told about taking baby David out in his stroller for a walk while Shirley was in the hospital for the delivery. On this first trip to the Pacific Northwest, she traveled by train, though on later trips to that area she would fly.

About her job at the hospital, she wrote to me that "the work is as usual." What had started out as a fulfilling activity that produced some additional income became more and more unpleasant. She was looking ahead both in terms of how she wanted to spend her remaining years and how she might manage financially. At least the hospital job had brought her within the social security program. She needed to work longer, however, to qualify for the minimum for retirement. But what else could she do?

Something Margaret had mentioned once stuck in her mind. Although Margaret hardly remembered saying it, Mother got the idea that Margaret, who had been trained as teacher, would like to get back to it. She had left teaching when she was married and began raising her two children, Mary and Jack. Margaret remembers that at a family gathering in Peterson at the Gilbertson farm, Barbara had announced, "I'm not going to teach this year." After the war Barbara had resumed teaching and had been commuting daily to nearby Rushford. Mother heard, or thought she heard, Margaret wondering if somehow she herself should resume her career as a teacher. In 1988 Margaret gave me the story:

> I know it was 1949 that I began work. Mother called up one day and said, "Well, Margaret, if you want to do what you said you would, I would come up and stay with you." I was completely taken aback. I just honestly did not know what she was talking about. I didn't want to say I didn't know so I just answered, "What exactly did I say?" And she said, "Well, you said that . . . "I don't remember exactly what she said but, in effect, she made the offer that "if you want to go back to teaching, then I would be glad to come up and stay with you." I told her I'd have to talk to Paul and I would let her know.

Mathilda posed proudly with daughter Margaret who had received her M.A. degree in 1955. Margaret was able to complete her education and teach, with her mother helping to manage household, in Galesville, Wisconsin in the 1950s.

She and Paul did talk about it and felt it would be worth a try. They worked out an arrangement for paying her and she moved to Galesville where she remained for the school year and each summer planned to return home. Margaret got a job teaching in Centerville, half way between Galesville and Winona. Margaret said, "We helped her to earn a few quarters of social security by filling out the necessary papers and paying the necessary part, which didn't amount to that much. I remember that it was a big nuisance later, because long afterwards we were still getting these letters from the government. It didn't bother us—we had to ship them back, that's all. But I do know that she had that chance to get a little start on social security."

Thus began a special mother-daughter relationship that extended longer with perhaps greater depth than with any of her other daughters or sons. It continued for about 12 years—except for a rather dramatic interruption for four months in 1951.

Bill sent her an urgent S.O.S. Suddenly he had been given an offer he found he couldn't refuse. He felt it was more of a mandate inasmuch as it came from the head bishop of the ELC, Dr. J. A. Aasgaard. He wanted Bill to serve as a civilian chaplain in, of all places, Northern Greenland! Up near the Arctic Circle at Thule, the United States Air Force was building a huge air base as a strategic defense against the Soviet Union during the early days of the Cold War. Many of the construction workers were from the Upper Midwest and, principally because so many of those being recruited were Lutherans, our denomination was asked to provide a chaplain. The workers, only men, would be gone from home and family for months at a time, isolated among Greenland's icy mountains in the darkness of winter and the round-the-clock light of summer. That gigantic undertaking had the code name Project Blue Jay. The construction company offered the job but the church body made it a call in the spiritual sense.

The call did not come to Bill at a convenient time. It was spring of 1951—the same spring during which Shirley and Bill's third child, their son John, was born on April 22nd. And John came into the world with some digestive problems that worried them. What were the implications of husband and father absenting himself to the top of the world for months or maybe years? And what of the church he would leave behind? He had overcome some major problems already and now there was a chance really to grow. But, certainly after considerable prayer, Bill felt that, because it came from the Bishop, it was as if the call came directly from the Lord. Dr. Aasgaard had even summoned him to a personal meeting in Seattle. Bill met with him for an hour and a half in his hotel room and afterwards he realized "I was on my way to Greenland." His only solution to the family problem seemed to be to summon his Mother—never mind that she was already committed to Margaret and Paul—to come and help Shirley with her three young boys. He had also decided that for his family the new suburban wonder-town of Levittown, Long Island, New York would be a good place for them to live while he was in the Arctic.

The call to Mother from Bill did not come at a convenient time, either. Mathilda had only begun her new assignment with the

1949-50 school year and now was completing her second school year (1950-51) in Galesville. But when a worried son calls and wants help, it is difficult for a mother to do other than say yes.

It was a wild summer for all of them. He has recorded his own saga in the prologue to his book, *Plain Talk in an Arctic Chapel* (Augsburg 1954). There he graphically described the harrowing trip across the continent by car, pulling family belongings in a trailer, and finally, because of little two-month old John's condition, ". . . cried almost all the time, because he was starving"— Shirley had to fly from Indiana to New York with him in order to get medical attention, while Bill drove with David and Bobby non-stop the rest of the way with their household effects.

Mother arrived by train the next day (July 12, 1951) after Bill's reunion with Shirley and the boys. Coming through the train tunnel into Pennsylvania Station and experiencing New York City for the first time can provide culture shock for almost anyone. Mathilda had done her homework, however, and had in mind what it must be like. She expected to meet Bill at the station. But he wasn't there. He had instructed her to go to the lobby of the Pennsylvania Hotel across the street, in case he was delayed, and wait for him there. She proceeded to do that. When she asked a Red Cap how to get there, he pointed to a tunnel under 7th Avenue that would take her to the lower level of the hotel. So, with a suitcase in each hand, she started through the tunnel. And there, coming toward her as she trudged along among all those strangers, was her own son Bill with a smile, a hug and a welcome!

Mother wrote:

> We had to stop and inquire a few times about the way to Levittown, because Bill had just come the day before and that was at night. However, we made it. Arriving at the house, we were met by Shirley and the children. Everything was in a jumble, of course, because the trailer had just been unloaded. Shirley had put away some of the kitchen things and some of the things in the bathroom. By that time it was early afternoon. We had to get something to sleep on for the night, so Shirley and Bill went out to rustle up some beds. They bought some nice ones, and we all slept well that night.

Meanwhile, baby John, who had not gained much since his birth weight, was in Meadowbrook Hospital for observation. Bill was under pressure to get to Greenland. After a few days of tests, the doctor had said surgery was needed so the child could retain nourishment. Bill donated blood the evening before his departure. In his book, Bill wrote:

> From his bed in Meadowbrook Hospital, on Long Island, little John looked up at me and tried to smile. His operation had just been completed a few hours earlier, and I was supposed to leave that afternoon. I knew that he would get well if God wanted him to. It was a dirty trick on little John, and on the others for that matter, to pull out at a time like this, but . . .

Because Bill had to leave from Westover Air Force Base in Massachusetts and because John was being taken care of by the nurses in the hospital, they all got in their car and drove to Chicopee near Springfield, from which point the flight would go to Greenland. Then, in a fashion familiar to military personnel, after rushing to get there, he had to wait several days. Shirley and Mathilda couldn't wait, however, so they drove back to Levittown.

When little John had been home from the hospital a week, Mother wrote:

> We are happy about the baby. We can see he is gaining right along. Had gained 9 oz. when she brought him to the doctor the other day. He told her then what he said he hadn't wanted to tell her before—that the baby would have starved if he had not had the operation. So it is a good thing it is done.

Mother's letters from Levittown captured the suburban frontier development atmosphere of a burgeoning community sprawled out over former potato fields on Long Island. From the air one could see tiny boxes in circular patterns, a giant matrix formed of thousands of identical prefabricated houses placed almost overnight. There were few trees and no grass to begin with, but these would be brought in, assembly-line fashion. The Levitt brothers were making history—and making money!

Here are some of her observations of life in this pioneering new community:

- The housing project where we live is just completed and

looks somewhat bleak with no grass or trees except about five small evergreens. More trees will be planted and lawns seeded in August. Just now (July 15th) we are having a dry spell and we hear warnings over the radio about saving water.

- They like their house very much. The bedrooms are quite complete now with the exception of curtains. Drapes are ordered and will soon be here. Drapes are a necessity because one wall of the living room is all windows. The kitchen is equipped in a fine manner: all steel cabinets, a beautiful commodious sink, a GE refrigerator, Bendix de luxe washer, and a heating unit for radiant heat together with a hot water heater. Also a GE stove and cabinets above sink and refrigerator.

- We will be living under a handicap for some time to come, as there is no lawn as yet. Every home of this new subdivision is the same, so naturally there is a lot of dust. With small children running in and out it is difficult to keep the floors clean.

- The boys seem to like it out here and they seem right at home scraping up the dirt and throwing it around. Every night they are black as Africans and they're hard on clothes, the house and soap, but they enjoy it all. Bobby will soon be able to ride David's trike. Shirley and I have our hands full with them and the baby, but he's coming along pretty well too, so things are nicely under control.

- Shirley is lonely at times and restless; she misses Bill more, I think, than she expected. Expenses have been heavy and she has to learn to take care of the bills which has worried her, although she says she has wanted to manage the finances for a long time but Bill would never consent.

- We have nice neighbors. Several of the families are Jewish. Two men across the street have offered their help. One came down last night and brought his hose and watered our shrubs . . . Yesterday a tractor was around with a limer and scattered lime all over the lots. They plan to seed grass in a couple of weeks.

- Shirley came home from church quite pepped up. She met a lady married to an airline pilot whom she knew at Concordia. She had been a stewardess. Promised to pick her up next Thursday evening for a guild meeting to organize for next fall. I am glad she found someone she knew before.

- The mounds of dirt in the back have been removed. There is so much activity around all the time: cement mixers, bulldozers and dirt elevators. And planes overhead—they fly so low and make so much noise night and day.

- The two boys are quite a handful. They seem to have the energy of ten and can shout as loud as their father.

- We had callers one day this week. The first Sunday in church, Pastor (Herb) Hanson asked us to stand. After church a lady sitting ahead of us introduced herself, saying she was Mrs. Estrem, aunt of Norman and Erling. {Norman was my Luther College roommate and Erling taught in Spring Grove's parochial school.} Her daughter lives only about a mile from here and they came to call.

- There are so many peddlers and salesmen who constantly come around. Three bread wagons and I don't how many dairies and beer distributors, and the Good Humor and Howdy Doody ice cream wagons many times a day. At first David used to run out and say he wanted popsicles, but that had to be stopped. When David wants something he wants it.

- Rev. Hanson and family are on vacation in Pennsylvania. We miss them. He is a very fine man. They have a son in the Navy and a boy, nine.

The day of Mother's arrival by train into Manhattan, Bill had wanted to be sure she could get glimpses of some of the sights of the city she had read and heard about. He knew that she was always curious about new places and he loved the chance to be her tour guide. What with his getting ready to fly to the top of the world and having just made a difficult cross-country automobile-with-trailer trip, he likely found this quite a change of pace. Her travelogue sent to her family and friends indicates how much could be packed into a few hours:

> Bill thought this would be an opportune time for me to see some of the sights of New York as his car was available. We drove up Broadway right through the heart of Times Square, saw the New York Times building, the Astor Hotel, the traffic jams and the masses of humanity milling around. This was New York.
>
> We went from there "up town" past Radio City, Rockefeller Center, St. Patrick's Cathedral. We saw the outside of Rockefeller Center with the beautiful flowers which have often been pictured on the covers of *Post* and in *Life* magazine. We drove around and down Park Avenue through the building housing Grand Central Station. The street runs right through it and it's a skyscraper about fifty stories high.
>
> Then we went back down Park Avenue to the Waldorf Astoria Hotel. That's between Park Avenue and Lexington and between 50th and 51st Streets. Here Bill made me get out at the front entrance on Park Avenue, and walk through, up the stairs, and across the whole lobby of the Waldorf. I would have liked to linger, to look around and enjoy the many beautiful things I saw there, but Bill drove around the block and met me at the Lexington Ave. entrance.
>
> Then we headed up to the Cathedral of St. John the Divine. That's off Amsterdam Ave., near Columbia University. He let me out and I went in. It's the largest cathedral in America and the largest Gothic cathedral in the world. Chairs were used instead of pews. There were workmen in there repairing things. There was a group of school children being given a lecture on one of the stained glass windows. The rector was sitting in one of the front seats talking to a lady. Along the sides were niches in the wall containing gold vessels . . .
>
> We drove quickly through Central Park and saw the elaborate penthouses bordering it on all sides. Then Bill pointed out the different buildings of Columbia

University to me—Union Seminary, Julliard School of Music, Riverside Church and Grant's Tomb are all in the near vicinity. We at least had a good view of all of them. We went down Riverside Drive for a few blocks and could see the huge George Washington bridge and the New Jersey shore across the Hudson.

Then we swung back through Harlem. I've heard and read a lot about Harlem, but it seemed almost like any other town, only the people there were mostly all colored. It was quite closely packed together and the standards of living there are the lowest in the city. It's just below the hill called Morningside Heights on which the other above-mentioned places stand.

Then we headed for the expressway that follows the Hudson River down the west shore to lower Manhattan. This expressway was elevated, so looking back we could see the skyline of New York. The Empire State Building, over 100 stories high, loomed up among the other huge skyscrapers to our left. Below us to the right were the docks along the Hudson River where most of the shipping goes in and out. I was quite thrilled to see the docks, steamships and evidences of commerce. There were hundreds of piers and buildings, giving evidence of the extent of trade moving from New York to foreign shores. There were many huge liners. In the distance we saw one by far the largest. Bill said, "I bet that's the new huge ship, the United States." But when we came alongside we saw that it was the Queen Elizabeth, which actually is larger, over 1,000 feet.

I was hoping I would catch a glimpse of the Statue of Liberty, and sure enough, there it was! I saw it quite a few times in between the different docks, although it was far in the distance out in the harbor.

Long Island is laced with a network of parkways. They are fine systems for fast travel which is absolutely necessary with the mobs of people that go in and out of the city every day. Traffic races along them in both directions all day long.

One day Herb Hanson, pastor of the Good Shepherd Lutheran congregation in Levittown, was Mathilda's tour guide on a trip to the North Shore. They visited Mill Neck Manor, a former estate and mansion of the Dodge family, which is now a school called Lutheran Friends of the Deaf. It is owned and operated by a Lutheran Association, sponsored mainly by the Lutheran Church—Missouri Synod congregations. Mother was impressed by the formal gardens, the orchards, the barns, carriage house, caretaker's cottage and particularly the main house itself. "The approach to this vast three-storied home is a macadamized road winding through a lane of trees up to the top of a high hill," she wrote. "The house, perched on the crest of the hill, dominates the entire area. You can see the beautiful vista of shore and Long Island Sound with its sailboats and the dim outline of the Connecticut coastline off in the distance."

Because both Shirley and Mathilda were busy with young children while settling in to a new home, the time passed quickly. Shirley and Bill had agreed to try to write to each other every day. So there was mail—most of it, of course, for Shirley but Bill would send a letter now and then also to Mother. He, meanwhile, was in another world, in a strange, remote and inhospitable part of the planet. He preached, conducted worship services, baptized and confirmed construction workers, counseled worried and lonely men isolated in a compound with other men. Out of this difficult but rich pastoral experience came his book, a selection of his sermons to these men. At the same time he wrote a newspaper column, published weekly in the *Winona Republican Herald* back in Minnesota.

The arrangement in Levittown was not without its tensions. Mother-in-law and daughter-in-law relationships are often problematic and this one seemed to be also. Bill later described it to me as "traumatic." When I asked why he replied:

> Well, I had some guilt feelings about leaving my wife and kids there. I believed that I was doing the right thing in going. Shirley was young and it was a woeful burden on her. I know that I wanted to help out by having my mother come, which she did. I think after a period it got to be a little strained between Shirley and Mom. When she went back, it didn't really occur to me at the time that a little tension was a factor, but later on as Shirley and I chatted about it, some of this came to the surface. Mom had definite opinions about things and she always has had.

Meanwhile, in letters from her daughters, Mother was being urged to return. Margaret needed her. Naomi and Juliet were asking if someone else might be found to help Shirley. And then Mother wrote to me telling that Shirley's sister-in-law, Lou Ann (Ivan's wife) and son, Stevie, were coming and that this would permit Mathilda to go back to Spring Grove and, most likely, to Galesville. I had told her that I expected to come to New York for a meeting and maybe she would want to fly back with me.

She wrote, "I have decided to go back with you as Juliet suggested. Now if you can make a reservation for yourself for a return trip you could make one for me, too, could you not?"

I knew she had never flown before. I was so pleased to be able to escort her on her first experience in the skies. I was able to get a non-stop flight to Minneapolis in the big, bulky, but then luxurious, Northwest Airlines Stratoliner. Mathilda was converted to air travel from that time on, and during the remaining almost three decades of her life she would make numerous other air journeys to both coasts and Florida.

When she returned to Spring Grove it was already November of 1951. Before Christmas she would have checked in with her family in the area. First she would stop in Minneapolis with Elaine and me and our two—about to be three—children in our suburb of Richfield. Naomi and Niles now lived in Austin with their two sons, having just moved that fall from Rochester. Niles was beginning to climb the ladder of store management, at first in Minnesota—it was on to Fairbault, Virginia and Duluth in the 1950s. Later in New York City he would be dress marketing head of the Mercantile Corporation, parent company for a chain of department stores throughout the country.

Barbara and Archie were perhaps most eager to have Mother visit with them at their farm near Peterson, because Charlie had been born in September and needed to be introduced to his maternal grandmother. Sylvia and Fremont with a teen-ager and a first-grader, had missed the frequent visits from Mom which they had been used to.

In Galesville, Margaret and Paul were happy to learn that in January of 1952 Mother could resume where she had left off as a live-in helper in their home. Margaret was be relieved because, even though she was able to manage without help the first three months of the 1951-52 school year (she was now teaching in Galesville rather than at Centerville), it wasn't easy to be a full-time teacher and a full-time mother/housewife at the same time.

Paul explained that there were three bedrooms in the two-story house they lived in. Mother shared the largest bedroom with Mary while Jack had his own room and Margaret and Paul were in the third bedroom. In later years, Mary and her Grandmother each had a bedroom and Jack slept on a cot in an alcove.

"We got along very well all those years when she was with us in Galesville. We never had an argument about anything. That's quite a thing because it was over many years," Paul said.

Margaret echoed that, saying:

> I heard her say more than once to someone else, not to me but in my presence, that she thought a lot of Paul. She said, "In all the years that I was there he never said an unkind word to me." And the fact that I heard her say it more than once, I am sure she meant it. And I think Paul appreciated very much what she was doing, that she was there with the children and all. There was never any mother-in-law problem, that's for sure! But I do think that we were all real busy, we were doing our work and we were going our own ways. And the best part of all is that she had her job. That was what she wanted, she asked for it, and I paid her.

Paul said:

> She would fix most of the meals. She would make out a list of things needed and I would buy them and bring them home. Her cooking was good and practical—nothing fancy. She had had good experience with her own family.

She got up and made breakfast for the family. Margaret got up before anybody to get ready for her day at school and sometimes stayed late:

> Every week night I put on my housecoat, as we called it in those days, and sat in the breakfast room with my books and my basket and my grade plans . . . She baked cookies a lot and the kids loved that. And Jack would come home from school and call, "Grandma!" It didn't matter much what she was doing or what he was going to do, he just liked the feeling of someone being there. And it was reassuring to me to hear that, too.

Jack, who was in grade school at the time, remembers that "Grandma" was the one who held the household down:

> She did a lot of the cooking and she did the cleaning and the chores. Both my sister and I had our own chores and she made sure we did them . . . I know she had to keep after us on our weekend cleaning assignment. One of mine was to clean the blinds. We had the big wooden blinds and we had the attachment for that and I had to go from top to bottom and do all the blinds in the house and suck the dust off them. I don't think you find that anymore these days. That was one of my chores. And there were other chores. Probably the biggest one we faced the most was doing the dishes. And to this day I am probably better at cleanup than I am at fixing meals. She always took care of the meals but it was up to my sister and me to get the dishes done.

Mary, who was almost 11 when her Grandmother came back to Galesville from Levittown, explained it this way:

> She was the one at home when we would come from school. Without her assistance as housekeeper, cook and child supervisor, my Mom could never have taught school and continued her education. But Grandma was our companion then, and she would hear all our news, complaints, or excitement when we returned home after school.

Jack: "She was a member of our family. And she was there, not because she was needing a place. It was because we needed her as a member of the family. If you could have a choice of two mothers, she was like a second mother to me."

Mary: "We learned to respect her ways and attitudes. We were usually careful not to give flip statements for answers, since she didn't like that much. During her relaxation at home, she read a lot, always had knitting handiwork, and after we got TV, we all laughed at some of the family shows like *The Honeymooners*, *Father Knows Best*, and later the *Lucy* shows. Some episodes were so silly she laughed as hard as we did."

Paul agreed that she liked television and said that he had one of the first TV sets in town. He remembers it was a Satchel Carlson. At first they could just receive Minneapolis and Rochester stations. Mother also enjoyed listening to radio soap operas, he said. The family enjoyed movies and always got in free at the local theater. Paul had rescued the Johnsons, the owners of the theater, when, during the Depression and the Bank Holiday in the early 1930s, they couldn't afford to pay a projectionist. He was single then and could handle any mechanical challenge. He also needed a place to stay. So, in return for room and board, he operated the projector. They were so grateful, he said, that forever after they gave free entry to Paul's family, including "Grandma."

Mathilda was known for her knitting—sweaters, socks, mittens, capes, and even dresses. It was one of the ways she could relax and still feel she was producing something useful.

Margaret recounted, "She always went to church with us. She was well known by everybody at church and by people around town, too. I don't know that she went down town a great deal. But they knew me and they knew Paul and so they knew Mother, too. And the people in the community and at church and the neighbors liked her and they would have enjoyed having her lead a little social life in the afternoons, but she declined because she thought that the chance for a nap, lying down for a few hours in the afternoon, was far more valuable."

Paul added: "She never missed church and almost always walked. She was prim and would walk straight and tall off to church. And her personality was like that also, not deviating from the straight and narrow. She wasn't really caustic, but was a bit sharp around the edges."

Jack commented, "I am sure there were some times when there was some friction by her being around but I think it worked out pretty good. I was probably immune from witnessing any of that. But she was always one who was pretty stalwart and stuck to her side of things and she made us do what we knew we were supposed to do . . . I think that probably at times within the family that may have gotten on my parents' nerves maybe—I don't know. But I don't remember any strong issues or disagreements . . . When she would become upset, I guess she would become a recluse, or hold it within herself. She would sort of tighten up her chin and nod and go off and hibernate somewhere. I don't think she was one who would share her burdens with anyone else. She was one who would carry them herself."

Mary: "Teenagers are usually a challenge to any family, and I will always remember a phrase she said to me after I probably had spouted off with some teenage statement she thought needed to be addressed. She said, 'Remember, Mary, it is better to remain silent and be thought a fool than to open your mouth and remove all doubt.' I *have* remembered that one, Grandma!"

Margaret recalled that everyone thought Mother was remarkable—"She liked to dress well and, with the help of some of her daughters, and her own tastes, she always looked nice and had lovely clothes and all of her family seemed to give her jewelry."

Mary said, "She had extraordinary eyesight that enabled her to read and knit so much," adding that "she once knit two children's Norwegian sweaters for me after merely 'copying' two adult-size sweaters for the pattern. Just imagine the skill involved!"

While Mother lived at Galesville with the Thies family her responsibilities spanned the school year, September to June. In the summers, Paul and Margaret would often travel and add more photos to their tour albums. During June, July and August, Mother would re-establish her headquarters in Spring Grove.

Bill and Shirley moved to Decorah in June of 1953 when Bill joined the religion faculty of Luther College. This made it possible for Mathilda to have additional family close. As if playing continental "musical chairs," Elaine and I and our family moved to New

York from Minnesota a year later when I began a new job with Lutheran Film Associates.

We tried to make an annual visit to the Midwest from our Long Island home and we usually would head for Decorah. There on Center Street near the college we would enjoy the hospitality of Erling and Sally Naeseth on one side of the street and Bill and Shirley Lee just across from them on the other side. And our children and theirs could have cousin-type fun together. Being in Decorah, of course, meant that Mother was just a half hour away by car and we made the trip often during our vacations.

Our being in New York gave Mother another incentive to return to the place that earlier she had found so fascinating. Margaret, who had visited us almost immediately after our move in July of 1954 (there were still packing boxes around at the time), encouraged Mother to go to Baldwin for a visit during the Easter break in 1955. She went with granddaughter, Mary, who was then a 14-year-old eighth-grader. Mathilda was so stimulated by that experience that she determined she would chronicle the trip for the rest of the family. What she wrote about then to "family and friends" reveals facets of her personality, interests, tastes, historical knowledge and capacity for fun:

> Baldwin, L.I., New York
> April 15, 1955
>
> This is the last evening of a two weeks' stay at Baldwin, Long Island and other places in the East. Maybe I'd better start at the beginning and relate the different things we have seen and the places we have been since we left home.
>
> About 9:30 a.m. Saturday, April 2nd, Mary Lee Thies and I departed for LaCrosse where we boarded a train for Milwaukee; arriving there we took a taxi to the airport where we had a wait of approximately two and one half hours. We then boarded a Northwest Airlines plane for the International Airport at Idlewild (New York). It was my second flight and Mary's first. She seemed to enjoy it immensely and didn't mind it a bit. We made a very brief landing at Detroit and arrived at Idlewild at 8:40 p.m. Bob met us there and took us to his house. We were amazed at the traffic congestion on that Saturday night. It delayed us considerably but at about 10:15 we arrived at Bob's house.

Elaine was up to welcome us but said she had had a nap previously. We had some rolls and coffee and a nice visit . . . also some good music by Bob and Elaine, and Mary also tried out their new acquisition—a grand piano. They have a very comfortable and roomy home here, which they enjoy very much. One of the interesting things about it is the "patio" which is built along one entire side of the house. There are five steps leading down to it from the dining room above. The ceiling is beamed and covered with translucent fibre-glass; the window arrangement is interesting—it has a rose colored panel of the same fibre-glass in the center with tall windows on either side. The outside of the house is brick which also provides two of the walls of the patio interior . . .

As the next morning was Palm Sunday we attended church in shifts. Bob brought Elaine and the children over for first service at 9:30 and he and I and Sigrid attended the 11 o'clock service. Richard had to stay home as he is too noisy. They have a very fine church here, spacious and beautifully appointed . . . a fine choir and the assistant pastor is also the organist. There seems to be a large congregation as the church was filled at both services. We spent the rest of the day quietly at home as we were a little bit tired after our trip. On our way home from the airport Bob said, "Do you know where we are going on Monday?" And of course we said we didn't. He said, "We are going to Washington, D.C. I have to make a trip and I'm taking you and Mary along. I'm driving down and we will stay overnight and come back the next day."

We left here at 9:30. Bob had to make a stop at his office before leaving to check on his mail and different other things and we agreed that perhaps the Public Library would be a good place to spend some time until he was ready to leave the city. So we browsed around there for almost two hours and saw quite a lot of interesting things. One thing that was interesting about it was that they had a children's library in the basement and at that particular time they were featuring the works of Hans Christian Anderson; they had many of his original works there and I also saw a book that had been given to him by Charles Dickens. In one room of the library the whole room was given up to the works of Walt Whitman;

there was a fascinating display—many, many showcases full of manuscripts, documents, etc. One upper corridor was devoted to Negro literature, about them and by Negro authors.

On the way into the city that morning we passed one of the very old cemeteries on Long Island. It was so immense and the stones were so old and worn and close together—one could hardly imagine such a sight. On a later trip we passed another part of the same cemetery which was kept in a much better condition. On entering the city, Mary had another first experience . . . we went through the Queens Midtown Tunnel which goes under the East River connecting Long Island with Manhattan Island. On entering Manhattan we could see the UN building which was not very far away . . . we also crossed the famous Third Avenue over which runs the old elevated railroad, which had its last day today! On leaving for Washington, D.C. we crossed Manhattan about midtown and left it by way of the Lincoln Tunnel and entered the State of New Jersey. Then we went on the New Jersey Turnpike, which extends southerly for 120 miles. The joy of this is that there are no stop lights and the only stops are for fuel and food. One of the unique things we noticed while driving here in the East is the system of toll stations, which seemed to occur quite frequently!

On our way down we passed through the city of Baltimore which was a very tedious operation because the traffic was so congested and the streets narrow and the city so large that it slows one up considerably. We arrived in Washington about 7 p.m.

Before going to our hotel we drove around the city to see some of the buildings. Many of the public buildings are easily seen as you enter, as the Washington Monument, the Capitol building, and many of the other office buildings are so tall and stately that they can be seen from afar. We viewed the Lincoln Memorial after it was dark and the lights were on. Near the memorial is a rectangular pool which at night reflects the Washington Monument in its clear water. Behind the Washington Monument could be seen the dome of the Capitol, which was also lit. Going up the steps of the Lincoln Memorial, entering, and viewing that sad, impressive figure sitting in his chair in deep reflection and reading the inscribed Gettysburg Address on one side and his Second Inaugural Address on the other make in the minds of so many people, myself included, the most impressive sight in Washington.

Bob had rooms reserved for us at the Statler Hotel. After leaving the Lincoln Memorial we checked into the hotel and retired to our rooms. Bob had an appointment with the lawyer for Lutheran Church Productions; Mary and I went out and had something to eat, after which we wrote some letters and retired. In the hotel room there was a TV set which had the same program on—it happened to be *I Love Lucy*—which we watch at home.

The next morning we arranged for a tour which took us first to the Bureau of Engraving, second to the Pan American building then to the White House and from there to the Smithsonian Institution, and after this to the Capitol. The crowds were so thick in Washington, it being vacation week and so many organizations and families and scouts and high school students were there that we had to stand in line for a very long time at each place and we didn't get back to the hotel until 3 p.m. We noticed especially at the White House that we were hurried through. There were guards standing here and there all over saying, "Step lively, stay close together . . . and keep moving." Mary took some pictures of the White House grounds. They told us no pictures allowed inside. We saw the pictures that have been mentioned in the newspapers about Washington and Lincoln's picture being placed in the Foyer instead of Truman's The rooms were very beautiful and I think we saw the pictures of most of the presidents.

At the Capitol the congestion was so great that while the guides took their parties through—especially in the rotunda—we could hardly hear the explanations they made. They dwelt quite a bit on the paintings on the ceilings, all of which I can't take time to talk about here. There were many historical paintings and busts of the great Americans here and there. We had tickets for a session of the Senate which unfortunately had recessed the day before. But we were taken into the Senate chambers and one of the guides explained about the desks in the chamber, they were not very modern or good looking, but as a matter of sentiment, they wished to keep their same old desks when the building was modernized a few years ago. There were many famous names carved on them . . . they mentioned Daniel Webster's. The front seats were occupied by the senior members.

The Union Depot in Washington is very close to the Capitol. It's fancy. We checked out from the hotel about 4:50 p.m. and made our way home, which, considering the time of the day and the length it takes (approximately seven hours I would say) was a bit wearying. Another first for Mary was the trip across on the Staten Island Ferry and a view of the harbor of New York by night with the millions of lights aglow. We arrived home about midnight. Mary, however, slept quite a bit of the way.

That week, being Holy Week, we did not do any more sight-seeing, also partly due to the fact that Bob had many business appointments and our feeling we would be much better off under his guidance rather than trying to make our way through the big city. We did, however, attend church services on Good Friday afternoon. I had the pleasure of hearing Pastor Russell Helgeson, who I knew on my previous stay at Long Island.

Sunday morning we attended Easter services which were very impressive with a service at 11 o'clock for Bob and me, and a children's service earlier for Elaine and the girls. They had more special music than we are accustomed to at home. Easter Sunday started our second week here. On leaving Galesville, we had fully intended to return home Tuesday the 12th of April, but Bob and Elaine prevailed on us to stay until Saturday the 16th.

On Monday morning, Bob and Elaine proposed that we all go in to the city and see the sights. However, I thought it would be better for me to remain here with the two youngest children and let Elaine take the girls in, which they proceeded to do. They stood in line for a long time to get in to Radio City Music Hall, where they saw the movie The Glass Slipper, and the special Easter stage show which included the famous Rockettes. They picnicked in Central park and took a trip to the top of the RCA Building's observation roof. This outing gave Mary, as well as the Lee children, a first subway ride.

On Tuesday morning Mary and I went into the city with Bob. We had decided before hand that we were to spend the forenoon in the Metropolitan Museum of Art, which is located on 82nd Street and Fifth Avenue bordering on Central Park. When I told Mary we were going to an art museum, she said, "Oh . . . art . . ." just as if to say, "Who cares about art?" But to her surprise, I think, she found it really wonderful. There are more beautiful things there to see than one can ever imagine. She found the Egyptian division to be very comprehensive—it covers everything, what they ate and drank and wore . . . their homes, even their coffins and their mummies. They even had models of different tombs of some of the ancient kings and they had a reproduction of a tomb on one wall of one of the rooms. In it were some of the things they brought in for the dead—different articles such as food. Mary spent quite a bit of time there and I'm sure she'll be able to tell you much more about it than I can. I was more interested in the art exhibits. There were so many original paintings done by famous painters, most of them around the 14th and 15th centuries. Many millionaires, such as J. P. Morgan and Governor Lehman, had donated so many things. There were also many wonderful tapestries and chinaware and clocks and canopied beds from the Louis XIV era.

Bob picked us up at almost one o'clock and took us to lunch. He had secured tickets for us to see *Cinerama Holiday*, which, by the way, was produced by Louis de Rochemont, the same producer whose company did *Martin Luther*. The president of the company, Borden Mace, was with us at lunch. He explained quite a bit about it in advance as he was the assistant producer. *Cinerama* is so marvelous and can hardly be described, but I shall attempt to mention a few things about it. They took a couple of ordinary young people from Kansas City, Mo. to Switzerland to see the sights there and from Switzerland to Paris. At the same time they brought over a young couple from Switzerland to America to see the sights in America. The point of the picture is to show the reaction of the different couples to what they saw. The strange part of it is that you seem to be going along with them as, for instance, in Switzerland they were skiing on the mountains and the audience would just scream as we would be tearing along a corridor between huge snow drifts. In another part of the show there were jet fighter planes which seemed to fly right over us and the noise was so loud you might think they were real. And before we knew it, it seemed that we were out over the ocean and finally landed on the huge deck of an aircraft carrier. There we saw planes take off, and could even see how they were caught by the hook in landing. It seemed that the audience participates in the things that are being shown on the screen.

According to this narrative it would seem that our main purpose in coming east was to see the sights. This is not the case, you know, as we really came to make a good visit and that is what we have had a chance to do. Mary has had a good time with the little girls. She is very adaptable, she can enjoy herself with girls her own age and she can also enjoy herself with younger ones. For instance, today, the first sunny day in several days as we have had quite a bit of rain here, they have spent most of the day down by the brook and also making mud pies. After this they all had to leave their shoes and socks and spend considerable time getting all of them cleaned up. This being my last day here, Bob thought that he would take me to Levittown to call on some of the friends and neighbors that I knew there. We were fortunate in finding every one at home that we wanted to see. First we called on the Caulfields. Mr. and Mrs. were both there and they said they were very glad to see me and asked about Bill and Shirley and wondered about Shirley's baby, and wondered if it was a boy. From there we crossed the street to the Anchins. Mrs. Anchin was at home with her children and she seemed very pleased to see us and invited Bob to come and see them sometime. She also asked about Bill and Shirley and the baby. From there we went to Braufmans. Jean and the children were home. When Bill wrote I really didn't know who he meant by the Braufmans, but when I got there I recognized who they were. Louise was the little girl David used to go and play with and Mrs. B. recognized me right away. She also asked about Shirley and Bill and the children. I had asked about the Schlingheides and heard that Mr. S. had been ill during the winter. He had had a bad heart attack, but now was all right and back at work.

Elaine is kept mighty busy here and especially so now with two extra to feed and we have been well fed. One can imagine that taking care of a husband and family of four and two visitors is enough or too much for anyone. The children surely are intelligent, both Barbara and Peggy for their age read remarkably well. Even Sigrid knows all the songs and often when singing tries to outdo the others. The two older girls have had vacation since last Thursday so they have had a chance to play with Mary. They have friends coming to play with them and, as it has been rainy this week, they have been underfoot quite a bit of the time. The piano is kept busy much of the time. Elaine hasn't started them on regular lessons yet but she intends to. Richard is very lively. He doesn't talk but makes himself heard and understood when there is something he wants.

It is now 11:15—time to hit the sack, as the boys would say, and get ready for our trip home in the morning. We leave at 9:40 from LaGuardia airport via United Airlines with a stop at Cleveland on the way to Milwaukee. We plan to arrive home at 5 p.m. Saturday, April 16. We have had a trip which I hope we will long remember.

(Thank you, Bob, for being my secretary and Elaine for the coffee which she has served us while we were doing this.)

Our family enjoyed their visit too and we have replayed it a number of times in a home movie I took as we were getting ready to depart for LaGuardia that morning. We have often enjoyed the sight of an impatient and anxious grandmother, looking at her watch and pacing back and forth on the sidewalk in front of our small 1950 two-door Ford. She didn't want to miss that flight. But with our whole family coming along to see them off, the final trips to the bathroom and putting on coats and jackets—it was mid-April—took time. At the airport we also got a shot of their plane lifting off from the runway. They were on their way home to Wisconsin.

Back in Galesville they must have been enthusiastic in reporting to the Thies family about their trip and about the wonders of New York because the next summer of 1956, Jack was enabled to come for a three week visit with the Lee family in Baldwin.

In the spring of 1958, Mathilda was sad to learn from her brother, Willie, that he was selling the family farm in Black Hammer. She wrote to Bill:

> That surely was a big surprise. I am going down this week for his sale on Thursday. Maybe you will want to be there, too. Guess it will be the last chance for me to see the place, inside anyhow. I have always had a sentimental feeling for the old farm. It has been in the family for 85 years. I had a letter from Lillie and she said he was too tired to think of starting up again. She asked if they could rent my apartment till they found a house. This happened quickly I guess and they haven't had time to plan. I told them they were welcome to stay there but I couldn't accept any rent. He has done so much work around the house that he deserved a favor in return.

In June of 1958, Mother was visiting with Naomi and Niles and family in Duluth at the time that I was attending a church convention in Minneapolis. So, after making my report there on my work with Lutheran Film Associates, I flew up to join them briefly. Mother was getting acquainted with Naomi's fourth son, Tom, who was then just seven months old and her other older boys—all growing rapidly—Bill three, Jon eight and Nick 12. Then, inasmuch as I was flying back to the Twin Cities, Mother decided she would fly back with me. Naturally, it reminded me of our first flight together seven years before. On our arrival at the airport, she and I were able to rendezvous with Margaret and Paul, who were enroute to a wedding somewhere in the Minneapolis area.

She learned from Bill that he had been given a sabbatical from Luther College so that he could gain more graduate study credits toward a doctor's degree. Bill went alone to New York on Memorial Day weekend of 1958 to start classes at Teacher's College of Columbia University. He stayed with us in Baldwin and helped me build a retaining wall in our back yard. Shirley and the boys followed in three weeks. They were able to rent their house for the entire year. He was asked to supply the pulpit for the summer months at the same church in Glen Head where he had been interim pastor after his return from Greenland. And, beginning in November, he was supply pastor at Our Savior's Lutheran Church in Brooklyn. His family had quarters in the old parish house which was due for demolition before the new church would be built on the site. Meanwhile Shirley used her nurses training by working nights at Lutheran Medical Center first during the inter-session period between the summer and fall terms at Columbia and continuing at other periods in the following months.

Mother was enticed back to New York for that Christmas of 1958 in order to share the holidays with her two sons and their families. Both Bill and I had work commitments which this time prevented our taking our Mother on visits to museums and theaters. Our wives had commitments also—Shirley was on duty part of the time at the Lutheran Medical Center and Elaine at the time of the visit had only a month to wait before our sixth child, Paul, was born. Yet, it was wonderful for us and, we think, for her to spend Christmas Eve with the Baldwin Lees and Christmas Day with the Brooklyn Lees. Her flight back was a bit harried at the outset. She had her ticket on American Airlines and then, just as the new year of 1959 dawned, AA flights were cancelled because of a strike. We had to scramble to find a substitute flight and couldn't confirm one until 7 a.m. on her day of departure, January 4th. But she didn't seem to worry, probably because by now she was a seasoned air traveler.

Back in Galesville, Paul Thies recalls that Mathilda's health seemed good to him when she lived with them. "Oh, perhaps some rheumatism and some pains and aches once in a while, but nothing big was wrong," he told me. "She was in good shape."

Margaret mentioned that one time, "probably when she was lonely or maybe it was in the winter when she had not been able to see the rest of her family often enough, I told her, 'You almost sound like you have self pity' and she didn't like that. 'I do not feel sorry for myself! I have never felt sorry for myself.' I said it kind of sounded that way to me. And I added, 'After all, you have a big family and they are good to you and they are all doing things.' I suppose she was just down in the dumps and we can all get that way. I didn't pursue it and it wasn't long before she just forgot it."

Actually Mother tended to be a bit stoical about any physical problems or illnesses. But in the fall of 1959 she suffered some spells in Galesville which seemed to frighten her. Margaret knew the full story, of course, and Barbara seemed to be aware. She wrote to Juliet and Naomi and Sylvia and asked if Sylvia would forward the letter on to Bill so "I will have to tell it one less time." Here in her words is the story:

You probably have not heard that I was sort of sick Saturday, October 21. While I was resting Friday afternoon, I felt what I thought was a charley horse in my left leg. I got up and went downstairs and finished my work in the kitchen and back room, going over woodwork and washing both floors. Also getting supper. I had an ache in the leg, not bad. After sitting down in the evening my foot started to ache quite badly and was swelling up a little. After going to bed at the usual time, I couldn't sleep on account of the aching. Some time after midnight, perhaps one a.m., I went to the bathroom and got an aspirin. After a while I went to sleep.

At 9:30 a.m. Margaret came into the room and awakened me. She said, "Are you asleep?" So I got up and went downstairs and after getting down I felt queer, sort of faint. I took some juice but no breakfast. I lay down in the dining room a little while but felt the same. So I started up the stairs and got just as far as the landing and sort of lay there. Margaret, I believe, was working with the hall curtain. She took it down and I guess was putting up a new one. She kept at me to put my head down. She was scared I would fall and hit against the book case or some thing. I did not quite go under but was pretty close and awfully sick to my stomach. I wanted to get to the bathroom and after a little I did. Then it started to recede and I went to bed.

Margaret right away called Dr. Rhode's house and he was home and he came up at noon and checked my blood pressure and heart. He said both were all right. Said to stay in bed that day but could go down for supper and also to slow down! I got two kinds of medicine. Said he wanted to see me soon but he was going to Chicago to a convention the following week. I felt groggy while I was taking the medicine but Sunday morning I was back at church and you saw me at the wedding the following Saturday. On Monday morning I made an appointment to see the doctor on Wednesday (11/11). It is not too easy to get in. And I went down at 4 o'clock. He examined my blood pressure then too and said that it was O.K. Then he started to tell me to lay off work. He also told me that the first time, but this time he laid it on the line and said just to do very light work. You are to do no laundry, no cleaning of floors, and I don't want you to stoop. So I asked if this had anything

> to do with my leg and he said, yes. We call it a warning, a very, very mild seizure. Be lazy. Said to act normal. But it is not very normal when one has been so active. He said not to take to the rocking chair.
>
> I did not feel a bit sick when I went down, but it gave me quite a jolt. I am getting used to it now. The only thing he said about diet was that I could have two cups of coffee a day and I am adhering to that. Oh yes, my blood count is down—he said ten and it should be twelve. So I am taking iron. I guess the faint spell came from that. He said you may never have another one, but said for a while to take it easy and slow down, which I am doing now. He said I could read, watch television and also knit. I have been getting supper and lunch at noon for Paul and myself.
>
> I won't be knowing what my plans will be from now on. It is very comfortable to be here, if they don't mind having me around. I will be going down to Sigrid's for a few days, maybe towards the last of the week. She called up because she had heard it through Inga Olson who teaches in Barbara's school. I have not written [yet] to any of the girls.

She must have recovered well since she lived for almost two more decades and she spent a busy summer of 1960 in Spring Grove again. About the time of her 77th birthday on July 20th her family came together—all except me and my family. I was in Europe working on the production of the movie, *Question 7* and Elaine joined me for a few weeks. Mother wrote us there and told us that she had her grandson, Charlie Gilbertson, visiting her for 10 days. He was then almost nine and it was perhaps the beginning of a special bonding with him that he felt continued into his teenage and young adult years.

That same month she had a most welcome visit from her first cousin, Selma Fredrikson. She had never married and had retired in Los Angeles where she had been a salesperson in a large department store for many years. Selma was five years younger than Mathilda and the two cousins had not been together often as adults. Mother enjoyed her company and they visited about their various travels. Selma had some interesting stories about her trips abroad. (I remember hearing some of them when I invited her out to dinner one time when I was in Los Angeles.)

Nixon was nominated that summer as the Republican party's

candidate for president of the United States to run in November against John F. Kennedy. I remember hearing the nomination on my car radio in Germany. At the same moment Mother was watching it on television in Caledonia with two of her daughters, Sylvia and Barbara, according to her letter of July 28, 1960.

Christian, her oldest brother, died on August 16th in LaCrosse. He was ten years older than Mathilda and she had looked to him both as an elder brother and as a kind of surrogate father, since she had been fatherless from the age of nine. There was a very large funeral in Spring Grove, with the family's LaCrosse pastor, the Rev. George Ulvilden, officiating.

Our Uncle Christ's six daughters and two sons and their families were there—most of the 22 grandchildren and 23 great grandchildren. Mathilda was again able to be together with her surviving brothers—Duffy, Edwin, Arthur and Willie—and their wives. Now with the death of Christian, another chapter of the Glasrud legend was concluded.

Mother wrote from Spring Grove that the Skustads and the Thieses went on a trip together to Florida early in August:

> I think Paul and Margaret have made a down payment on the lots that are for sale . . . they are seriously considering moving to Florida. Paul plans to go down this winter and investigate the work situation. They would sell the house here and keep the cottage. I don't think it would be wise to break all ties with the north. There is a possibility that they might not like it there.

Their decision to move to Florida was made. And as it turned out, they did like it there. Very much! For Mathilda it would be the end of one chapter and the beginning of a new phase of her life. She would return to live year around in Spring Grove and from there she would experience, with the rest of the world, the turbulent 1960s. She would be free to come and go as she wished. And that's just what she did.

CHAPTER TWELVE

North to South, East to West

Mathilda was, it seemed, determined to spend as much time as possible during the rest of her life with her children and their children. Her home base would be her apartment in Spring Grove, where she was still renting the downstairs and living upstairs. Sylvia was less than 10 miles away in Caledonia, Barbara less than 60 miles away in Winona and Juliet less than 90 miles away in Grand Meadow.

The rest of her family were scattered. Margaret and family were moving to Florida. Mother had never been there but, like most of us, had dreamed of it. And now she saw that she would want to spend some weeks or months where it was warm in the winter. Bill and Shirley would shortly transfer from Decorah, less than 25 miles away, when his teaching would take him from Luther College to Pacific Lutheran and they would live in the state of Washington, first in Parkland, then in Tacoma, and finally in Issaquah. Elaine and I had been living on New York's Long Island since 1954 and in 1961 Naomi and Niles would move to Merrick, which was a neighboring town to our Baldwin.

"She loved to travel, She absolutely loved to fly!"her grandson, Charles Gilbertson, remarked, adding, "She also thought it wonderful that people in town would wag their tongues and say, 'There she goes again. Where is she off to this week?' I think she enjoyed that."

Doubtless air travel appealed to her. But she was never one to carry anything to excess. She personified practicality. She saw flying as a convenient and efficient way to accomplish her purpose of giving attention to her children and allowing them to give attention to her.

Clearly, however, she hadn't yet settled into a regimen of full retreat from helping others if she could. She could write letters, knowing well how important it is to receive them. So she wrote. She could lead a Bible class at church and she did. She could find opportunities to relate supportively to her grandchildren, at least those nearby and others when she could travel to their homes at a distance.

"Late in my grade school and junior high school days I looked forward to spending time with Grandma during summer months for a few weeks,"Charles told me. "It seemed mostly a way for me to have a change and for her once again to have under her rein and control another human being." Charles said that they would do things together every day—take walks, go for rides with Uncle Willie, watch television. They talked. But she would not allow him to talk while she was watching her soap operas. He recalled she watched *The Edge of Night*.

"I needed her. It's difficult to explain. At the time I was growing up, I needed a grandmother such as she in my life and she fulfilled that one hundred percent. She showed me an awful lot of love and a lot of private concern. She would let me know that concern through certain things she would do, not so much by what she would say regarding my family life, but things she would do for me. Things she would say to me were like Christian talk but without any Bible type of fanaticism at all—Christianity in the sense of forgive and forget."

Charlie continued, "I was in awe of her. I was never afraid of her but I didn't want to cross her either. But it seemed there was some untapped or undiscovered wrath in her that I've never seen but have only heard about. She was stately. If she had been born at a different time in a different country—and with money!—I could picture her as royalty. And in her own way she was royalty. She was a class act—with a twist!"

She never seemed to be able to get that close to her first grandchild, Robert Deters. She felt he was having some difficulties but there were not many times when she could reach him. It seemed that his mother, Sylvia, did not open herself to talking about any problems in the family. Mathilda was happy for her grandson when he and the woman he wanted to marry, Marie Schwartzhoff, resolved their Lutheran—Roman Catholic dilemma which had divided her family from his. They were married in 1957 after Marie decided to become a Lutheran. But there was a price to pay. Her own family, in effect, disowned her. That pre-Vatican II period was a time of intense hostility, suspicion and mistrust between Catholics and Protestants, particularly Lutherans. Today the religious climate is much more cooperative and ecumenical. And Marie and her family later restored their relationship.

"I was surprised at the warmth she showed me as a granddaughter-in-law," Marie wrote. "At that time I worked at the Spring Grove office of our law firm three afternoons a week. Mathilda invited me several times to (coffee) parties she had at her home, always serving a wonderful lunch. I would come at about 5 p.m. as the party was about over."

Robert's grandmother was delighted when a great grandchild was on the way. Scott was born on the third of October, 1960. Less than a month later, Marie was faced with a baffling crisis: her husband disappeared! Vanished! His car was found abandoned down by the Mississippi River. The Sheriff's Department of Houston County had search parties looking for him.

All Marie knew was that, after he had put on two pair of jeans and took an extra shirt, he told her he was going down to the river to look for something he had left there while deer hunting. A day later a young man from the community came to her with a message from her husband: "Don't apply for any life insurance!" The messenger said Robert had told him that he was running away.

"I think the second message really knocked me for a loop," Marie said. "It was then that Mathilda came to stay with me. She was there for a week or so. I remember how calm she was. I also remember that Scott was not sleeping through the night. He would waken often to be fed. Grandma Lee said that he needed some cereal. My doctor had said that Scott should not have solid food for several months. I naturally felt the doctor must be right. But she put a little cereal in my evening feeding—took a needle and enlarged the hole in the nipple. Scott slept the entire evening. Of course, she was right. I'm sure she had more background in feeding children than the doctor did."

About six weeks later Robert reappeared. But not at the farm where his wife and baby boy were or where he had milking cows that someone else had to tend to while he was gone. He surfaced in Grand Meadow and came to Juliet and Marvin's farm. Juliet alerted Marie and Sylvia and Fremont and they came over. Apparently they learned then that he had taken his boat across to the Wisconsin side of the Mississippi and abandoned it there and then had hitchhiked away. Juliet recalls that Marie, Robert and his parents had some sessions of difficult talking among themselves to determine what should be done. They decided he needed professional help.

Juliet said she was surprised he chose to surface at their place because earlier she had scolded him for what she felt was improper behavior. Perhaps he interpreted her stern talk as honest concern for him, which is what she surely intended.

Marie was especially grateful to Robert's "Grandma Lee" and said, "Even after I decided to separate from Robert, I always felt welcome and a sense of warmth from her. She was a remarkable lady. She was very open-minded and would have been great as a community leader in today's world."

Regardless of what she may have thought privately, Mathilda refused to openly criticize any member of the family who may have strayed from the straight and narrow as she might define it. And none of us would get by "casting aspersions" about someone in the family. She modeled for us a kind of tolerance for human frailty that was rare. Somehow it doesn't seem to fit her often stern facade which many might interpret as a judgmental attitude. Naomi reports that Mathilda counselled her daughters not to be critical of their sisters-in-law. "Don't gang up on them, "Naomi quoted her as saying, adding that Mother had a strong sense of loyalty: "Keep things within the family that belong within the family. Don't peddle dirt. Don't pick it up from others. Tend to your own business. Keep things private."

Early in 1961, Paul Thies had gone ahead to Florida to rent a home near Brooksville and make plans for building a house. Margaret and her family would follow, probably when her school term was over in late spring. In mid-February I was able to join Mother, Margaret and her family in Galesville. I wanted them—particularly Mother—to see the new theatrical movie I had produced in Germany, *Question 7*. We were able to have a private screening at the local theater whose owners, the Johnsons, were close friends of the Thieses. And we invited a dozen other family members and friends.

A follow-up letter from Mother to me reveals what concerns and changes were occupying her mind on March 3, 1961:

> Dear Bob, Elaine and family,
>
> . . . Due to Bob's visit we had lots of news about the family and himself. We surely packed in a lot of things during his short visit as he must have told you. The following weekend after Bob was here we had quite a snow storm—about 10 inches. Since then we have had lovely weather. The snow is almost gone except where it was piled up.
>
> Two weeks ago today I had a short note from Ida saying that Duffy was ill at St. Joseph's Hospital in St. Paul. She gave no particulars about his ailment. She had also written to Willie in the same manner. The following Wednesday Willie and Lillie came up here and we called Lyla (Lyla Fisher, daughter of Mathilda and Willie's brother, Peter, who had died in 1926) as Ida said she had been staying with her. Lyla said Ida did not want anyone to know what was wrong with him but she (Lyla) had called his doctor who told her he had cancer of the tongue in an advanced stage. He was getting treatment.
>
> Last Sunday Art, Edwin, Willie, Sigrid Vaaler and I went up to see him . . . He seemed very thin and drowsy, but seemed to enjoy seeing us . . . He had been ailing since October and evidently had received no help until, as he said, the pain became almost unbearable . . . We did not get to see Ida. Lyla and Sam (her husband) had insisted she notify his folks, otherwise I guess we wouldn't have known. I understand she has had a Christian Science practitioner work on him. I don't see how they allow that at a Catholic hospital. I told him Bob had been here and brought his film for a private viewing and he said, "He has been working on that a long time."
>
> Last Sunday afternoon Margaret talked to Paul for

about 45 minutes on a short wave set. She was at Cog Hogden's in Ettrick. He has a ham set. Margaret is flying down during Easter vacation.

Tell Sylvia [our daughter, then six years old] that Grandma did not knit for a long time after Christmas but has started again. Naomi sent yarn and instructions for sweaters for Billy and Tommy. Marie wanted a pair of booties for Scott, so I hurriedly made them and sent them. Maybe by next fall, if I know what is needed, I could make something to send to N.Y. too.

Barbara has enrolled for the spring quarter at Teacher's College at Winona. She has a leave of absence from teaching. If she attends the quarter and the first term of summer school, she could get her degree in July. She has never been able to get the things required during summer sessions.

I am enclosing a write up in the paper about the showing of the film. Mrs. Ellison called up and asked for it. So Margaret and I wrote it up.

Love,

Mother

Duffy died later that year of 1961, on November 22. Margaret remembers that when Mother first came down to Florida after they had moved there that year, she talked about Duffy. Margaret told me, "She felt so sad about Uncle Duffy, his having died of tongue cancer, cancer of the mouth. It's one of the cancers that is considered easily curable or more easily curable. And because of the Christian Science part of his living, and on the part of Ida, his wife, he didn't see a doctor and didn't get any help and she felt sad about that. But I remember her saying, after she came back from the funeral, that people from their Christian Science Church were just wonderful, nice people. They had been so kind and so good. For Mother I thought this was pretty good. She did mellow and she was more tolerant. I thought it was nice of her to say that, knowing that she had wished that both of them had stayed with their regular religion that they had been brought up in, you know. And I remember the first time I saw Mother cry. That was when her brother, Peter, had died (in 1926). That was Lyla Glasrud's father in North Dakota. And I believe it was the first of her brothers to die. And I'm sure she felt close to him. I am sure she cared a lot about her brothers."

Her brother Ted died in 1948, Christian in 1960 and Willie in

1971, while Arthur passed away earlier the same year, 1978, that Mathilda herself died. Edwin survived her by just a year.

In March of 1962, Willie and Lillie invited her to ride along with them to Florida. They had decided it would be good to escape Minnesota winter at long last, now that he had fully retired. She may have preferred to fly but who can pass up a free trip? It turned out to be an emotionally expensive journey. While they were guests at the house Paul and Margaret were still renting (they were building their own home in that same development) at Hill 'n Dale near Brooksville, Lillie died in her sleep. In the morning when Willie tried to rouse her he discovered she was indeed dead. Paul remembers that Margaret hurried over to where Paul was working on the new house to tell him. Willie was desperate to leave for home right away, Paul said, and of course Mathilda would ride back with him. She later said it was a wild ride. He drove straight through and very fast without stopping for overnights.

Our Dad's only sister, our aunt, Maria Peterson, also died in 1962. Sylvia and Juliet went to Decorah to assist when she had suffered a stroke and was in the hospital. When it seemed that there might be a protracted comatose condition, they arranged to have her transferred to a nursing home. But the next day, before she could be moved, she died. So then my sisters had to make the funeral arrangements and dispose of her household belongings. If Bill and family had still been living in Decorah, they likely would have handled things. Aunt Maria had felt almost a part of their family and saw them as the only local family she ever had.

"It just plain broke her heart, "Bill said when he had told her they were leaving Decorah for the Pacific Northwest. He even tried to coax her into coming out with them but she couldn't leave the only place she had ever lived in her whole life. "She didn't live long after that. She was incredulous. Uncle Charlie had died four or five years prior to that and she was totally crestfallen."

The service for Aunt Maria in Decorah was another funeral for Mathilda to attend. Almost every letter included a report on someone's death. She once told me, later when she was in her 90s, how strange it was to realize that almost all her contemporaries were gone and that everyone within her circle of relatives and friends was younger. "Never in my life did I believe I would live so long," she remarked.

The summer of 1963 marked Mathilda's 80th birthday. I couldn't be there on July 20th for her party because I was in Berlin doing research for my novel, *Behind the Wall.* I was also on my way to the Lutheran World Federation Assembly in Helsinki, Finland, that summer. I was able to send her a garnet pin from Berlin and I was delighted and relieved to learn that it had arrived on the day of her birthday. She sent me almost immediately an air-mail report of her party:

> The girls and nieces had planned a party for me at Scandinavia (restaurant and motel) so there was no fuss for me. I couldn't have had much of a party here because Juliet came over on Friday and Sylvia too and they papered and painted floor and woodwork in the vacant bedroom. Now all I need is a bed to make an extra bed-room again . . .
>
> There were 22 in all at the party on Saturday. Gudrun Muller is back again running it (Scandinavia). Barbara came back from Florida Wednesday and she came over. Sigrid Vaaler from LaCrosse, Olga and Orrel's wife and step-daughter, Sigrid M., Borghild, Eldora, Mathilda Solum, Inga Solum, Minnie Ellingson, Rhoda Stenehjem (Onstad) from Plentywood. Bill called in the afternoon. Also sent a card which Juliet read and embellished like she can. Elsie, Edwin and Gunhild, Uncle Willie and Clarence gave me an electric percolator which I have long wanted but was surprised to get. Elaine sent an original card which Peggy had made, which I treasured and numerous other cards . . . I think you know about the dress the Hysells sent. The pin is just right for it. We passed it around at the party, also the note that came with it.

Marie said, "I remember wondering if I should attend her 80th birthday party. Joe and Carol came to Caledonia and went with Scott and me. I well remember how happy she was to see us and how much a part of the family I felt."

Mother later wrote me that she had tried to hear my news reports on the radio from Finland but was unsuccessful. But she did say that a friend of ours, Chuck Anderson, had told her he had caught my broadcast on his car radio while driving from Spring Grove to LaCrosse.

Florida was on her mind during the Minnesota cold of early 1964 and when Mother learned that Sylvia and Barbara were plan-ning to drive to visit Margaret, and that Naomi planned to fly down from New York, she rather insisted she would want to go along, according to Margaret. What could they do? They really had hoped to have a kind of free-for-all sisters confab where they could let down their hair and enjoy what used to be called a "hen party," But Mother did go with them. She wanted some fun, too. Margaret also reported that Sylvia was a bit testy and annoyed about this. Margaret thought it might have been exacerbated by Mother's tendency to be a back-seat driver and Sylvia, who wanted to do all the driving in her car, would not appreciate Mother wanting to "help."

Sylvia Deters, Mathilda's first-born, was also the first to die. She succumbed to cancer in May of 1965, leaving her husband Fremont and two sons, Robert and Joseph.

Later that year, when Sylvia did want help with something that needed to be done, she discovered that Mom, somehow, wasn't available. And this bothered Sylvia and, according to Margaret, led to some tension and resentment on Sylvia's part. But it happened almost simultaneously with Sylvia's discovering that she had inoperable cancer. She hadn't told Mother nor anyone else at the time, apparently. Julie found out from her son, Mark, who was almost daily with Sylvia's son Joe at Winona State. Finally toward the end of 1964 the letters from Sylvia to her brothers and sisters came with the bad news.

It hit us all hard, but certainly, beyond her husband, Fremont, and sons Robert and Joe, it must have been hardest for our Mother. Margaret saw an opportunity, after talking with both Sylvia and Mother. Mother had felt the coolness and was bothered by it. She told Margaret that now, while she was ill, Sylvia seemed to spurn her offers to help. "I was able to tell Sylvia that," Margaret told me, "and I just think it helped to make a little peace between them and for that I was grateful."

Sylvia was working at the time at the court house where Fremont was the County Treasurer. She and Fremont might commute in together from their farm near the hamlet of Eitzen, south of Caledonia, or they might drive separate cars. I remember wanting to visit her several months before she died, on one of my trips back to Minnesota because I had learned that the cancer had progressed dangerously. I rented a car and drove to Caledonia to meet her, having telephoned first. When I got to her office I discovered she had left for home. As I drove through the village, I saw her there putting some things in her own car and I parked. She didn't seem to recognize me—or maybe didn't want to greet me there on Main Street. So I waited and she drove off. I had been warned that their driveway from the highway to their house on the farm was treacherous from the mud and when I got there I should sound the horn and someone would come with a tractor or pickup truck and take me the rest of the way.

The visit was very strange. I felt a barrier in communicating with her unlike any I have ever experienced before or since—she was lying on the couch and probably was in pain. There was a coolness, a distance that I could not bridge. It was the last time I saw her alive. I could only sense that, at least in part, she was too consumed by her illness and perhaps too self-conscious of her condition to be conversationally responsive.

Sylvia desperately wanted to make one more trip to Florida.

She had told Margaret, "I am just living to get to Florida."And she did. In spite of the difficulty of travel, she and Fremont flew down at Easter time in 1965 and stayed for two weeks. Margaret said that at on Good Friday they had to take her into Brooksville to a doctor to have accumulated fluid "tapped" from her body.

A few weeks after their return Sylvia was again hospitalized in LaCrosse. Juliet, who had been at home with her for a week together with Mother, has written, "I will always remember her courage and our sadness when the ambulance took her for the final trip to St. Francis Hospital. I cried on my way home to Grand Meadow."

Mother maintained a hospital vigil for the final week. Marie said that she herself came every day to see Sylvia, and Mathilda was always there. "I remember one of the nurses thinking that Grandma Lee was a sister," Marie told me. Sylvia died on May 18th.

Her funeral in Caledonia brought Mathilda's family together again. Funerals have a way of doing that and in Mathilda's long life she had survived many funerals but this was the first of her children to die. And Sylvia, who had almost reached the age of 58, was Mathilda's first-born.

Sylvia's husband, Fremont, survived Sylvia for only eight years. He died from a heart attack in 1972, while he was still County Treasurer. Even though Robert had been divorced by Marie, Fremont had sustained a close friendship with her and even, she said, introduced her to Donald Ellestad, whose wife she became and with whom she has been happy for many years.

Loneliness—being alone in her Spring Grove apartment—doubtless prompted Mathilda to spend time in the homes of her children. "She was a good visitor," Naomi said. "She was a good example for me and I have tried to follow that when possible as I visit in my children's homes. She kept herself well entertained with reading, handiwork, and knitting of course. She was rather quiet. She watched TV shows, especially a soap opera, *As the World Turns*. She always took a rest."

Naomi noted especially her effect on her grandchildren. "She was grandmother to the children. She related to the boys quite well when they were in junior high and high school rather than when they were toddlers. She didn't like little kids who ran around. She would like them out of the house and out from under foot. But when they got to their high school years and would talk about American history or civics or literature, she would be in there with them. I recall at different times when she and the boys would have discussions about what they were writing themes on.

They always felt a kind of kinship with her that I didn't have when I was that age.

"Jon said it 'blew my mind' when his grandmother said to him, 'Jon, there's something I want to ask you.' He wondered what might have upset her. But he responded, 'Okay, what?' and she asked, 'What do you think John Lennon is going to do? Are he and Yoko Ono going to get married or what?' It tickled him that she was keeping up with things like that."

It was Naomi's view that Mother liked it when Niles teased her. She remembered that it was what our Dad used to do. "She liked it but didn't want to let on that she liked it," Naomi said.

Almost always when Mother was visiting at the Hysells, either in Merrick or in Allendale, New Jersey, where they moved in the mid-1960s, she would spend a few days also at our home in Baldwin. She was always ready to go to a movie or a concert. I have the memory of her laughter while enjoying a fast boat ride out in Freeport Bay with Bob Busche, a pastor friend of ours and of Naomi and Niles.

When she was with us in the New York—New Jersey area near the end of 1965 she agreed to let me interview her again on tape. (My first oral history session with her was in 1959—Bill did his own recorded interview with her in 1971.) We talked about reading. I asked her what kind of reading she enjoyed most.

"Well, I used to enjoy fiction. But I don't enjoy it so much anymore." Why? Was it because fiction has changed or because she had changed? "Well, I have changed and the fiction has changed. I think that would be true to say that."

She mentioned she had read *War and Peace* and *Gone With the Wind* and books by Sigrid Undset and Ole Rolvaag. We had a discussion about *Giants in the Earth*; she said some of Rolvaag's books "weren't very real." She was more critical, however, of newspapers and magazines.

"Now that I'm here I have been looking through the *New York Times* and I have a hard time to find the news for all the ads that clutter up the pages. The ads bring in the money and the *Spring Grove Herald* likes ads, too, so the news has to suffer. I don't say that the *New York Times* doesn't print all the news, because I am sure they do—and some that isn't very important news, too. So it's the money part of it. Well, you know what happened to the *Saturday Evening Post* and the *Ladies Home Journal*. For all the years I read the *Post* there never was a liquor ad. And of course they changed to advertise liquor. I used to love to read the fiction in the

Saturday Evening Post because it was clean. Now there is hardly a story you can find unless there is adultery in it. And it seems that is important. And I hate it. I really do."

I remember walking arm-in-arm down Fifth Avenue with her one time. She told me then, and I have never forgotten it, that she felt then like she did when she was out strolling on a city street arm-in-arm with my Dad.

She and Naomi took me to lunch in Manhattan on my birthday in November of 1965. They gave me a box of chocolates to take home for the children. Little did they know that on my homeward journey on the Long Island Railroad at 5:35 that afternoon, the entire East Coast region would experience the worst electrical blackout in its history! They made it back to Allendale before the power failure. I, however, was trapped for seven hours in the tunnel under the East River. The candy came in handy. After a couple of hours, when all of us were already missing our dinners, I decided it would be a good gesture to share the box of chocolates with my fellow passengers. It was a catalyst and helped to get conversations going. Under normal circumstances commuter protocol would not include talking to strangers.

Naomi remembers taking her into Manhattan to enjoy a flower show at the Colosseum. And they would eat at a restaurant, but not at a "fancy place," according to Naomi. "But she enjoyed fancy restaurants, too. "One time we took her to dinner at the Marriott in New Jersey and she had two or three glasses of wine and I thought she got a bit tipsy!"

Mathilda loved to knit. It was a hobby, almost an avocation, that she could work on almost anywhere. Give her an armchair in a comfortable room and, with her yarn and knitting needles, she could be occupied and absorbed in her own world, but with an ear and eye open to what was going on also in the world around her. She might do some knitting almost daily, but never on Sunday! This was brought home to our Sylvia and Sigrid when they wanted her to teach them to knit. They made the mistake of asking her on a Sunday. At the time she was still trying to perpetuate the pious strictures of her own youth when "Remember the Sabbath Day to Keep it Holy" meant no work on the Day of Rest. To our kids, knitting could never be considered work but only relaxation and pleasure. And, if pushed, their grandmother would most likely have to agree.

One time at our house in Baldwin I proposed that we send an audio letter by tape recording to Bill's family in Tacoma. Mother had experienced some difficulties with tape recorders—Paul and

Margaret had given her one for Christmas one year and it never worked well and they had it exchanged for a different model. But when we were playing back what we had recorded the sound at first was fast like a high-pitched and rapid Donald Duck patter and then became so drunkenly slow and sluggish sounding that Mother couldn't contain her laughter and we all were hooting and hollering almost hysterically. Then, when we got it operating normally, Mathilda took the microphone:

> I want to say something to Shirley. You know, the suit I made from the yarn that you all sent to me—I got an idea just a week before I left. I had a lot of the yarn left and I decided I would make a little shell, sleeveless, with a little red collar and so I knitted it and think it's very, very nice and I'm very pleased with it myself. As you know, the suit jacket is very bulky and this way, wearing the knitted sleeveless shell with it makes it very comfortable. And I never really did like the neck of it because it was a little bit low and it was difficult to get a blouse that was satisfactory and now I like it ever so much better and I have had many favorable comments on it. And I just wanted to say that to you, Shirley, because you were the one who maneuvered toward getting the yarn for me.

Shirley told us later, when all of Mathilda's children and spouses were together in Rochester at Julie's place, that Bill had played that tape for her. She then explained how the yarn purchase came about:

> She and I had been shopping in Tacoma and she stopped in front of a mannequin that had a beautiful knit dress on it and said to me, "Oh my! Isn't that lovely? I could do that." It was during a Christmas season she was spending with Shirley and Bill and family. I went and bought the pattern that she wanted, because she liked it so much, and got the whole box full of yarn. She knew nothing about it and when she opened it up, she said, "Oh, my!" She was very pleased with it. It was a gift the others in the family were able to contribute to. They remembered that it was green and wondered how long it took her to do it. Well, the next time we came to see her, she wore it to the airport. She had it ready!

Barbara added:

> I still have the dress, and I have an extra ball or two of the yarn. She gave me the dress at one time and said, "Maybe you could rip this and make something for yourself out of it."

Margaret added:

> She knit three dresses for me. When I had been sick that year, she made one in brown with a kind of pinkish collar. It was a two-piece. Then, later on, she knit a dark green one with wooden buttons. Then she made one with a white material with a gold fleck in it. I bought the yarn for that. But, three dresses!

Shirley had another Mathilda story from that same visit to Tacoma:

> One Sunday morning as we were all going to church—we were all dressed and were hustled out the front door. It was wintertime, and although we usually don't have ice around, this Sunday there was a little streak of ice on the sidewalk. She had just turned the corner and—*Whhhht!*—your Mother went out and landed flat on her back. And I thought, "Oh my stars!" I panicked. But she said, "I'm fine, I'm fine. Everything's just fine. I don't hurt or anything." And we marched off to church. She had landed absolutely, perfectly flat.

That reminded Margaret of the time in Galesville when they also were on their way to church:

> Paul had Sunday school so he went ahead. And then Mother and I came. And then, turning around, oh, about two blocks away, she fell down. We were kind of late so I just got her up and walked her right away. Instead of my saying, "Oh, Mother, goodness sakes! Do you want to go home?" all I did was get her up and keep going. She told me later—and I laughed—she couldn't believe that I would do that. But she was fine. Of course, she didn't

land on her head!

And Naomi was reminded of the time she fell down by the Calvary Free Church, then on Main Street in Spring Grove. "She broke her glasses that time. And somebody came along and gave her a helping hand, and she told us about it. None of us ever saw this or were there when it happened." Barbara elaborated, "She was black and blue all over her legs. I came over on a Friday night and she had no glasses; they had been broken."

Shirley remembered something else: "Now that we've mentioned all this falling business, here's a story she told on herself. When she was carrying one of you—you hadn't been born, I don't remember which one it was—and there had been a big snow and she was going downtown. It was real deep snow and she fell straight forward into the snow. So one of you was buried in snow before you were born!"

Two of her grandchildren were students at Luther College during the second half of the 1960s—our daughter Peg (Margaret) and Bill and Shirley's son David. Decorah was very close so each of them would get up to see their grandmother on occasion when they got rides with a classmate from Spring Grove who would be going home for the weekend. Sometimes they would come together. On one such trip Peg, an art student, sketched a portrait of her grandmother. It was an excellent likeness and I had it copied and shared it with all my siblings.

Mother was included one Thanksgiving during those same years when Barbara and Juliet got the cousins together from Luther, St. Olaf and Winona State at Grand Meadow. Along with Peg and Dave it must have included Jane, Mark, Joe and Nick together with Kip and Joanne.

Kip on that occasion may have worn the white turtleneck sweater his Grandmother had knit to his measurements. He explained that, a few years after he and Joanne were married, they drove over to Spring Grove one Sunday afternoon to visit her. Quite innocently he had mentioned that he had been looking for such a sweater to wear with a sport coat. He quoted her as responding, "That's no problem. I'll make you one." He really hadn't expected that. "She told me to stand up and she went to get her tape measure and measured me on the spot, making some notes for future reference. A short while later, maybe only two or three weeks. she called up and said, 'Come over and get your sweater.' It fit perfectly. I still cherish it as a memento of her. I am awed by someone who has the skills to create something like that without a blueprint."

At age 88, Mathilda was still actively traveling from coast to coast. This photo was taken in Tacoma in 1971 at Bill and Shirley's 25th wedding anniversary.

Mother was present at Luther when Peg was honored at October Homecoming time in 1967. That was the year that I had been invited to be the speaker at the alumni dinner and there among the listeners, along with Elaine and Mother, were Juliet and Marvin, Barbara, and even Paul Thies. He happened to be visiting in Caledonia with his father and brother at the time. At the coronation ceremony that night for the Homecoming Queen at the C.K. Preus Gymnasium, Mother was sitting next to me. An announcement came after a trumpet fanfare and then the "royal" parade entered from the rear and proceeded to the stage. Mother leaned over to whisper to me, "Did he say 'Queen Margaret'?" We knew she was a finalist, together with two of her roommates among others, but until that moment we hadn't known which of them was chosen. Seeing her crowned as Queen was a delicious surprise for both parents and grandparent.

A year later, at different times, Mathilda would attend weddings at Decorah for these Luther students—Peg to Frank Barth and Dave to Kay Bradley. The occasions brought our family from the East Coast in May and Bill and Shirley's family from the West Coast in December. And it meant another opportunity for a reunion with Mother.

David, who said he had always had as a child an impression of his grandmother as "an austere woman," came to know her during his college days as "a special and complex person." This was confirmed for him at Peg's wedding at Decorah Lutheran Church when his grandmother was sitting a few rows ahead of David and he observed how moved she was during the ceremony. "I glanced ahead and noticed Grandma dabbing a tear on her cheek."

Some of us were able to come to Spring Grove for Mathilda's 86th birthday on June 20, 1969. We will always remember that date because it coincided with the historic walk on the moon. Whenever the video footage is replayed of Neil Armstrong coming down the steps of the Lunar Module and then speaking the now-legendary words, "One small step for man, one giant leap for mankind," I recall the setting in Mother's living room where we watched it as it happened "live" on her TV.

I am amused when I think of her watching television in her apartment, often lounging on her couch and dozing off as she got sleepier and sleepier in an afternoon. I smile at the thought because one afternoon I was on the national TV show, *To Tell the Truth*, and she was watching it. The idea of the show is that there are three participants who pretend to be the person the emcee is describing and only one of us was the actual individual. A press agent for one of my films had arranged my appearance. Only at the end of the episode—after each of us had been doing his best to field the panel's questions and two of us were finally unmasked as imposters—were we allowed to say who we were and what our work was. Mother never noticed that it was I speaking during the times that the camera was on me. But suddenly, when it was time "to tell the truth," she heard a voice—it was my voice—say, "My name is Robert E. A. Lee" and she immediately sat up to check the screen. Sure enough, it was her baby!

In November 1968 the word quickly spread among her children that she was in the Spring Grove Hospital. Questions flew by phone around the country: What's the trouble? What happened? Why? Naomi didn't wait for reassurance. She flew out from New Jersey and came to Mathilda's hospital bed. "Oh, I'm not sick," Mother told her. "You didn't need to come. I am not that sick." Well, Naomi and Barbara said she did have pneumonia and for a person 85 years of age that would justify hospitalization.

A few years later Bill drew out Mother's own version of the hospitalization story her in his 1971 recorded interview with her. He had been probing into her past and she was beginning to object, saying "I don't like to be torn back into those days. They are past and gone. Let the dead bury its dead." To which Bill replied, "But you're not dead, Mother, you're still alive!" And that triggered a narrative flow and the recording machine heard every word:

> I'm going to tell you about something now. You know, I told you that I had the flu before Thanksgiving. And this time I made up my mind. We don't have any doctors available you might say. There's two old, elderly doctors there. And I'm not really satisfied with either of them. Two years ago when I had the flu, I happened to take my temperature after I thought I was over the flu and here I had nearly a hundred fever. So I called Uncle Bill and asked if he would see the doctor because he goes down for his mail every day. And I guess he had seen Dr. Rogne and he said, "Bring her over to the hospital" because they don't make house calls, you know. So I went over to the hospital and they undressed me right away and put me to bed to wait for the doctor. And there I stayed for twelve days. I didn't think I was sick enough, you know. I thought I would have recovered. If I had got some medicine, I would have been all right.
>
> *But they never gave you treatment or care or anything?*
>
> Yes, they did. Because when you get to the hospital you get the works.
>
> *But your convalescence was very tedious and slow?*
>
> It seemed so. I wasn't released for about twelve days. I did have a pain here (pointing to her stomach) but I

thought it was from the strong medicines because I thought it was down in my esophagus but they checked that and it was nothing.

Pastor came to see you, didn't he?

Yes, but I wasn't deathly sick or anything. and they knew that anybody like me was . . .

Ready to meet the Lord anyway?

Well, I hope so. And so I thought, well, I'm not going to see a doctor here because I don't want to be sent to the hospital. So Juliet and Marvin came down and I went back with them because they have a good doctor there, a Japanese fellow. Very sharp and so thorough. And I told him about my fall and he kept on about that—I suppose he was digging, like you're digging—and he kind of intimated that, seeing that I fell and I said I had a little shakiness in my hands, a little palsied, he thought I may have had Parkinson's Disease. But I said, "No, I am sure it isn't." Well, so then, next time he said, "I want to give you a blood test. So he examined me all over in every possible way and probed and asked questions and everything. So then they took that blood test. And first he tried a vein here and couldn't find it and then he took—oh, a half a cup of blood. He had three different bottles, you know, that he put it into. And then I think I went home and I went back again and he had the diagnosis. And I went in to see him—I had an appointment—and I was put in a chair in another room and I sat there and when he came he said, "Put your hands out like that." Yes, I said, but just a minute! I had that done to me maybe twenty-five years ago at the LaCrosse Lutheran Hospital and he said, "What did they do for you?" I said I got some iodine. "Well," he said, "that was all they knew at that time." That's what it is, you know, it's a lack of iodine. So we talked for a bit and I said, "What's the result of the diagnosis?" "Overactive thyroid," he said.

Really? That's all it was?

Isn't that something? And he wanted me to stay. "I have treated a woman, she came to me, and she was much worse off than you are," he said. And he had treated her and got her over it. And he wanted me to stay and take those treatments. But he thought it could take a year or two. Well, I said, at my age, how do you know that I

> would be around for a year? And he said, "You're living now and you are my patient. And I want to get you well." But I said I am going to go to Florida after Christmas. And he said, "I am going to talk you out of it." And I said I think you'll have a hard time talking me out of it. And he said, "I suppose they have doctors there, too." But I will never go to a doctor here (in Florida) when I know what they charge Margaret for her . . . It runs into $50 for two or three calls, you know.

Jack Thies remembers that when his Grandmother was with them in Florida—and he at the time was a college student at Tampa—her style of "back-seat driving" seemed to reverse itself. When he was first driving back in Wisconsin, he remembers her giving him instructions from the back seat about his speed. "Finally I dimmed the dash lights down at night so that she couldn't see the speedometer so that I could do what I wanted to do." But in Florida, it seemed to him that she was more apt to ask, "What's taking so long?"

"One of the first times we were on the plane together coming back to New York," Naomi recalls, "it was an early trip and I was very fearful. When we started our descent, I just kept my eyes shut. But she kept saying, "Oh, look! There's the Statue of Liberty! And on and on. She was chipper."

Usually, even when travelling alone, she didn't seem fazed by turbulence in the air or transfers within airports on the ground. Naomi also recalls one time when Mother was scheduled to take a direct flight from New York to Minneapolis. They took her to Kennedy airport only to learn that the Northwest Airlines flight had been cancelled because of icing in the Twin Cities. She was booked on a later flight, however, and got assurances from the agent that someone would be at the Minneapolis gate to help her so that she could continue on to Rochester, where Juliet and Marvin were expecting to meet her.

There was no airline agent at the arrival gate in Minneapolis. So she tagged along with another passenger to the main desk of Northwest Airlines. It was late and there were no more flights to Rochester that night. The only person there said he had no information and, besides, he had to leave to go home. Another person she asked told her "It's not my job." Finally one of the other passengers in a similar predicament recognized her difficulty and told her the airline would put them up in a hotel in St. Paul and they could travel in the morning by bus to Rochester. So that's what they did. But Mathilda did not think to leave a wake-up call at the hotel and she was awake most of the night, worrying about oversleeping. Juliet and Marvin had no information until the next morning when they got a phone call from the hotel advising them as to where and when the bus would arrive.

"Her arrival in Rochester was delayed almost 24 hours," Naomi said. "You'd expect she would have been discouraged after an experience like that, but she took it in stride. She was a good traveler."

It was too bad that Joe hadn't been on duty that night. Her own grandson, Joe Deters, a Northwest ticket agent, had seen duty at the Minneapolis airport and had done stints also in Rochester and Madison, Wisconsin as well. He had helped her on several occasions as he had helped us. When Jack Thies wanted his grandmother to fly to North Carolina for his wedding to Joyce Flake in 1970, he sent her a choice of itineraries she might use and suggested that Joe could help her with making the arrangements.

In those days I had a heavy travel schedule and it allowed me to get to the Upper Midwest somewhat frequently. That often allowed me, when on Lutheran Council business at the Minneapolis headquarters of the American Lutheran Church, for example, also to get down to LaCrosse or Rochester with the chance to visit with Mother and my sisters and their families in Winona or Grand Meadow. One such visit in September of 1972 led to a coincidental meeting of Mother and me at the LaCrosse airport. She was coming and I was going—on the same plane. We had about 10 minutes to chat between her arrival and my departure. She had flown to Tacoma for the wedding of my namesake, Bob Lee, and his bride, Rebecca Jacobson and was returning home via LaCrosse. I had been doing some filming at Luther College. Barbara and Sigrid Vaaler took me to the airport where they were due to meet Mother. I expected her but she was surprised to see me!

Again a funeral provided us with the opportunity of a family reunion. When Mathilda's youngest brother, Willie, died in November 1971, I was asked to sing at the funeral in Black Hammer. I suppose I shall always remember the scene that greeted me on my arrival: a church basement full of Glasrud relatives—uncles, aunts, and cousins galore, many of whom I had not seen for a dozen or twenty years. After the funeral, Genevieve, Willie's widow, was gracious in receiving into the Glasrud home the several dozens of us relatives who had come from afar. She and Willie (but she always called him Bill) were married in 1966. She was the mother of Niles Hysell and was thus doubly related to our family—Naomi could know her as both mother-in-law and aunt.

Mathilda's own extended family, and many relatives and friends from far and near celebrated her 90th birthday in July of 1973. The occasion demanded a party. Mother herself wrote that an "open house" was decided as a way to involve many relatives and friends. Because she had been one of the founders and early leaders establishing the released-time parochial school operated by Trinity Lutheran Church, the party planners thought it most appropriate to have the affair in Trinity Center, just a stone's throw across the alley from her own house and across the street from the public school.

She didn't want any gifts for herself, but if people wanted to give something, she suggested it be in the form of donations to the parochial school. It gave her great satisfaction to turn over $400 for that cause she held so dear.

Relatives and friends gathered in Spring Grove in July 1973 to honor Mathilda on her 90th birthday. With daughter Barbara happily looking on, Mathilda chatted with niece Lillian Stenehjem.

Some of the family argued for no program but Mother insisted that there be one. And she selected Juliet to be the mistress of ceremonies. It was scheduled for Sunday, July 22, even though her actual birthday was the previous Friday, July 20. On that evening all of Mathilda's living children and their spouses were together at what she herself termed "a festive dinner party" in Rushford.

Trinity Center became crowded early that Sunday afternoon. While some came and went, most were there for the entire time because they didn't want to miss greeting one another. Mathilda was surely the star of the show and her children were the supporting cast. Long dresses for the women were de rigueur. Mother herself looked regal in an elegant dress provided by the Hysells and reflecting Niles' professionalism in the New York fashion world.

In welcoming everybody, Juliet was blunt about explaining her own hesitance at assuming that role. "Mother wanted a little program and she told me a couple of months ago that I would have to announce that program," she confessed. "And I said, 'Why me? I have two brothers who are public speakers.' But we learned long ago that we don't say 'no' to my mother."

Juliet had each of her siblings stand and tell about our families and introduce any of them who were present. It turned out to be a very informal process accompanied by side remarks and friendly kibitzing. When, after proudly listing his four sons and their occupations, Bill forgot to mention his wife Shirley. Our sister Barbara at that point interrupted him to ask, "Do they have a mother?" and that brought laughter. And when Juliet almost forgot to introduce me, I was able to mention that she had taken care of me for my first decade and perhaps she wanted to forget. But she made up for it in her lavish introduction of me as she called on me to sing. With Elaine's very supporting piano accompaniment, I offered two of Mother's favorite songs, "The Lost Chord" and "The Holy City."

Mikky—the Rev. Oscar Mikkelson—came from his retirement in Red Wing, Minnesota , to honor her. "We had Mathilda on the board of the parochial school," he said, "and I was a teacher there one year and I was scared stiff of her!" He added, "She has been a doer, not just a hearer of God's Word. She always found time to do her labor for the Lord in the church. She did a little writing for us and the records of the church are worn because she had been paging through them in order to produce several histories." He concluded by saying, "I can't say how much this family has meant to me."

Sigrid Vaaler, who had been like a sister to Mathilda, came prepared with her own tribute which she was pleased to share:

> I would like to pay this tribute to my aunt, whom I remember as far back as my memory goes. She has always been an integral part of my life. Growing up, I sometimes stood in awe of her, but I also loved her, and knew that she gave strength and direction. You'd better tread the straight and narrow path if you knew what was good for you!
>
> She has lived in nine-tenths of a century of great change; she has seen the greatest changes the world has ever known; she could write a great book about those ninety years, beginning with her childhood, when the mode of transportation was horse and buggy. Anyway, that's the transportation Uncle Knute had when he courted her. Then of course the automobile became popular, but these days Mathilda has been traveling by plane from north to south, and east to west.
>
> As I think of her greatest attribute, it has been the background and nurture she has given her family—she used the Bible and common sense. The goal she taught was not success for success' sake, nor acquiring material things. She motivated her family to develop their natural bents and careers with hard work and perseverance. It was peppered with admonition for living within the Christian structure. Nor did it end there. Her philosophy and interests touched all of us, both relatives and friends. For these I wish to thank our Lord. And her crusade isn't over yet!

In her response to all of this adulation, Mathilda, was brief. She felt moved simply to make this confession:

> I regret that I haven't had as much love of people as I should have had. I think I have failed. I have tried to do what's right, but . . .
>
> I give credit to all the good people who have been so kind to me, and especially to my children. I can't tell you how much I think of all of them and how good they have been to me. I have been blessed with fair health and have

been able to get around by myself. And I don't think anyone who gets to be 90 years old can expect much more.

Thank you so much, every one of you.

A few days later an article appeared in the *Winona Republican Herald*:

SPRING GROVE WOMAN
CELEBRATES 90 YEARS

SPRING GROVE, Minn. (Special)—Mrs. Mathilda Lee, Spring Grove, an attractive, well-groomed woman busy with church activities, crocheting and knitting, happily admitted to being 90 years of age as she celebrated her birthday Sunday with an open house at Trinity Lutheran Church parlors.

The open house was hosted by her six children: Mrs. Archie (Barbara) Gilbertson, Winona; Mrs. Marvin (Juliette) Skustad, Grand Meadow, Minn.; Mrs. Paul (Margaret) Thies, Brooksville, Fla.; Dr. Knute Lee, Tacoma, Wash.; Mrs. Niles (Naomi) Hysell, Allendale, N.J.; and Robert E. A. Lee, Baldwin, N.Y. One daughter had died.

Mrs. Lee has 23 grandchildren and 12 great-grandchildren . . .

Active in community, civic and church affairs throughout her life, she is a charter member of the local PTA, served as chairman of the Houston Country Red Cross, and the chairman of the Republican party in the county. She also served on the committee when the parochial school was organized in 1924. She also assisted the Rev. Oscar Mikkelson in writing the history of Trinity Church and the Spring Grove Ladies' Aid for the Centennial of the church.

Mrs. Lee is a veteran air traveler, flying to various parts of the country to visit her family, and when she is not busy with church activities and her needlework, she enjoys watching television.

CHAPTER THIRTEEN

Toward Thanatopsis

Two days after Christmas in 1974 I had the chance to spend an afternoon alone with Mother in her Spring Grove apartment. Our East Coast family—at that time with three of our children in colleges in the Midwest—had decided this was a year when we would gather for Christmas in Decorah and we were able to use two apartments in married student housing at Luther College. (Thanks to the college business manager, Erling Naeseth, Elaine's brother!) We went to church in Spring Grove with Mother at an early candlelight service Christmas Eve and, in addition, Elaine and I returned for additional visits.

She showed me her little diary. Actually it was just a very few entries from the momentous year in her life, 1939, when her husband Knute, our father, died. She had written in a little notebook she had saved since 1935. It had a pocket in the back in which she had some receipts, a recipe, and notes for a PTA committee she chaired which was planning a carnival at school. It was the right size for a diary but, alas, she didn't keep it up. The last entry was on a Sunday morning, the 19th of November, 1939:

> Just four weeks ago yesterday since Dad passed away. I shall have to go to church alone this morning. Almost the first time no one else in the family has been there. Indeed things change.

She asked me to write down in that diary for her some additional things from that current year then drawing to a close, 1974. Clearly, she had wished she had kept a journal of sorts and now she might have been thinking that perhaps it wasn't too late. So I wrote more or less what she wanted me to write. First she summarized what she obviously felt was one of the great events in her life, her 90th Birthday party in the summer of 1973 (cf. previous chapter), Then I wrote down (in third person) the additional items she wanted recorded. Among them the following:

- Mother has had continuing good health following her 90th birthday. She has been able to maintain her own household in Spring Grove and take care of her own business affairs.

- She has traveled also, spending five to six weeks in Florida with Margaret and Paul Thies and then went to New Jersey to stay two and a half weeks with Naomi and Niles Hysell. She wanted to be back in Spring Grove by April 1 because her house insurance was due then.

- In the fall of 1974 she paid $165.75 to the City of Spring Grove as water assessment tax.

- She wants to note that her son-in-law, Marvin Skustad, (Juliet's husband) died in May. He had been ailing for several years. He had had surgery on his hip and had suffered a a heart attack.

- Mrs. Rose Storlie had occupied the downstairs apartment for eight years. She had not felt well in the fall. In

October it was discovered that she had cancer and needed surgery. On the 21st of November she was brought back to the Spring Grove hospital where she died. A kidney had been removed in Rochester. Mother had been very attached to her as a dear friend and almost as a member of the family. This loss was very upsetting.

- Christmas of 1974 was special to Bob and his family who joined Mother on Christmas Eve for a candlelight service in church and a supper at Mother's apartment. Juliet came the next day and Elaine and Bob returned from Decorah for a few additional hours.

After her death, I found the diary in her apartment and I claimed it, without objection from my siblings. I noted that she had continued it briefly with summary entries written for three different dates. Here's what she wrote:

December 31, 1974

Bob came back from Decorah and spent much of last Friday with me. I could not help but think how fortunate people are who have sons living near them. Especially since I have gotten so old, I feel more helpless and it seems to be much harder to make decisions. In October I believe of 1974 Barbara and Archie and Charles Gilbertson went to Florida to live for the winter. They rented their house in Winona to a lady who teaches at St. Theresa's. I miss Barbara's weekly or semi-weekly visits. Juliet is the only one around here. She is good about coming home also and bringing me to her house for a visit. However, she has two new grandsons and with her job at school and baby sitting and with a roomer, she is a very busy person.

My brother Edwin has been in the local hospital for several weeks now. He is bed-ridden and very weak. It doesn't look very good. He is two years younger than I am. Gunhild [his wife] is not very well either. His sons Paul and Bill live in town and change off staying with their mother nights.

We have had lots of cold weather and snow at the end of December. Mildred Kjome called on me last week. She was staying at Andy's for a few days.

Bill and Shirley wanted me to come out to Seattle for John's wedding to Patricia Bodin but I didn't think I could make it. They [Margaret and Paul] have wanted me to come to Florida, too, but I can't plan anything ahead.

My eyes are getting weaker all the time. I can still knit and read if I can hold the book close up to my face.

After Uncle Bill died, Genevieve sold the house and went to Cannon Falls to live. She has two sisters living in the area and several nieces and a nephew. Naomi came for Marvin's funeral in May. She has not been here since.

Saturday, January 4, 1975

My new renter, Charlotte Strow, arrived. Her brother was with her. They had a U-Haul behind their car. She is a speech therapist for the school here and also Mabel and Canton schools. I think I will like her. She had me down for supper tonight.

Maurice Knutson, who is married to Borghild Glasrud, had surgery a week ago at St. Francis Hospital. He had a malignancy and they removed an eye and part of his cheekbone.

We have quite a bit of snow and more is predicted. At 9 a.m. today I went to circle. I am in a new morning circle. There were eight of us. A very good group.

Bill called me again yesterday thinking I should get together with Juliet and come to the reception for them [John and Pat Lee] in Minneapolis the 18th of this month.

October 26, 1975

We did not get together at John's wedding reception. Weather bitterly cold.

Juliet and I had a trip together. Started by plane from Rochester, July 21, and went out to Bill's at Issaquah, Washington. We stayed a day over a week and we had a wonderful time. It is beautiful out there with the woods and the mountains.

October 2, 3, 4 and 5 we had a wonderful get-together, mostly at Juliet's. Bill and Bob, Niles and Naomi were here at my house and at Juliet's. Then they decided that since they were all here except Margaret in Florida, that they would call her and urge her to come, which she did and left [again] for home Sunday afternoon. By plane both ways. I sent each family a copy which I wrote for the Spring Grove Herald which they were gracious enough to print. The very hardest thing about writing is getting started . . . [Ed. Note: How true, Mother, how true!]

Mathilda's delightful first-person account of that weekend did indeed appear at the top of page one of the October 23, 1975 issue of the *Spring Grove Herald*. In another era, she might have been, with the opportunity for experience and training, a first-class journalist. As it is, she has left us with a lot of clear and direct information about her life and her thinking during almost a full century of living.

Letters To The Editor

MATHILDA LEE FAMILY HAS GET TOGETHER

The weekend of 3rd, 4th and 5th of October 1975 was a memorable one for me and my family through several coincidences, not birthdays or anniversaries. It was possible for me and all my children to be together at the home of my daughter, Juliet Skustad, at Grand Meadow, Minn. It happened this way:

My two sons, Knute, (Bill to us and former friends) and Bob each had a meeting in the Midwest—Bill at St. Peter, Minn., and Bob at St. Louis, Mo.; and they planned to meet here in Spring Grove. This happened as planned, so both with a tape recorder, started out in the morning of October 4th, aiming to circle the town to find the old haunts they used to know during their childhood before leaving home and hoping to meet several friends which they did, but hearing later, missed some good friends. Norman Foss had been here and had asked for Bill. He also missed his good friend Mervin Dvergsten. They found the remaining walls of an old brewery which I knew about but they had never heard of. They walked until nearly one p.m. when Bob had enough but Bill wanted to finish. He makes a practice when at home, almost every morning, to jog or really running at least half a mile but often as much as a mile and sometimes even two miles. He says it keeps him in good health and condition.

Another coincidence was that Archie and Barbara Gilbertson were here. Archie had serious surgery and was recuperating. They have since returned to Florida.

Niles and Naomi Hysell were also here, visiting Niles' mother and myself. His mother, Genevieve

> Glasrud was with them . . . Late Friday afternoon and evening was spent at my daughter, Juliet Skustad's home. My family is fond of music and soon someone, I think it was Bob, was at the organ. Soon everyone was singing old popular songs and some favorite hymns.
>
> About 9:30 p.m. someone shouted, "Everyone to the Airport!" Margaret was coming on a 9:30 plane. So everyone went and Margaret came. This was Friday, Oct. 3rd and she had been at school that day.
>
> It was a happy time for everyone. We had not all been together since July 1973, and it will be long remembered.
>
> I have not written anything for the paper since I wrote my husband's obituary in 1939 and, since no one else has submitted anything, it seemed that it was up to me to do so.
>
> While Bill was here he visited at the hospital with Edwin Glasrud, his uncle. Bill said he closed the door and spoke as loud as he could because the men in there were very deaf. He read scriptures and prayed with them. When Mike Horgen saw Bill he said, "If I live to be 150 years old, I would never forget when I saw you going down the street riding your motorcycle with your hands high over your head. I wondered what in the world happened to that guy."
>
> My children's names are as follows:
>
> Barbara Gilbertson, Brooksville, Florida. Juliet Skustad, (widow), Grand Meadow, Mn. Margaret, Mrs. Paul Thies, Brooksville, Florida. Dr. Knute Lee, Issaquah, Washington. Naomi Hysell, Allendale, New Jersey. Robert E. A. Lee, Baldwin, New York.
>
> Mathilda Lee

On the fly leaf of her diary, Mother had scrawled a note about paying up the mortgage on the house and itemized what she had paid out for some repairs and taxes. Then she added this line: "My family has been very good to me and have helped out with trips, etc."

Mother flew to New York in March for a visit with the Hysells in Allendale, New Jersey and with us in Baldwin on Long Island. Naomi remembers that Mother especially enjoyed being at a coffee party at the home of Pastor and Mrs. C. O. Peterson—he had been a legendary church leader of Brooklyn's Norwegian Lutheran community for many years prior to their retirement to the same Bergen

County suburbs where the Hysells lived. Naomi especially remembers how Mother responded to their hosts while saying goodbye. Mrs. Peterson, at the door, said "We'll see you when you come next year" and Mathilda replied, "Yes . . . if I live!"

On a visit to her daughter Juliet in Grand Meadow, Minn. in 1977, Mathilda reviews her life's journey and looks to the future while holding her great-grandson, Benjamin Skustad.

Naomi became aware of the numerous spells Mother was having. She felt that they were small strokes, commonly called TIAs. Mother's only medication for these episodes of dizziness or blackouts was blackberry brandy and Naomi kept a bottle of it handy. She placed some at Mother's bedside because sometimes these spells came at night. She remembers one night hearing the sound of a bump or a thump from the bathroom and discovered that Mother was "out of it" and Naomi had some difficulty getting her to lie down on a couch. She thought this may have happened more than a half dozen times.

Back in Spring Grove, Mother wrote to Bill in September 1976:

> Got your letter when I got home from Barb and Archie's last Friday. I had spent a week with them at 1058 West King [in Winona]. They will be going to Florida the early part of October. I have not felt like doing any letter writing all summer. For one thing my hand is too shaky. My trouble is over-active thyroid. I am feeling much better now than I did a while back. My two teachers are back again. I have no plans for the winter, but will stay here as long as I am able. It is nice to be with the family but home is best. One cannot make plans far ahead at my age.

Margaret shared a story about our Mother's health that had both a frightening aspect to it and one of Mathilda's classic punchlines:

> When she came down to Florida to visit us in the winters, why, Pat and Ellen and Paul and I were going to Lakeland, we had concert tickets for a couple of years there. She was really very choked up, sort of, and coughing. I hated to leave her. But I did go to a drugstore and ask what would be good for getting phlegm up because I didn't want her to get pneumonia or something like that. So I came home with it and I think it must have been about twenty-percent alcohol or whatever! And she didn't know the difference. I was really worried. But she said, 'Oh, Margaret, I think you're just afraid I'm going to die at your house!'

Juliet recalled one very cold winter when Mother was staying with her in Grand Meadow and their furnace was out and they had to sit around with coats and sweaters on until their heating unit was fixed. It was likely that same cold winter when, before Mother left for Florida, she needed to get down to the bank in Spring Grove.

Juliet wrote:

> So I was going to take her down there, which I did, and we got to the bank, and by that time she was very shaky, you know, and had quite a time getting her check-book out, and getting her deposits and everything. She was going to make out a check to the bank or something and finally I said to Mother, "Shall I write out this check for you and you can sign it?" Her reply was, "Don't you think I've ever been to the bank before?"

Juliet added that Mother finally got the checks deposited and the business completed. "She realized she had been curt and became apologetic. Another time when she received a letter from Sigrid Vaaler, I asked, 'What was in Sigrid's letter?' She retorted, 'None of your business.' But about an hour later she said, 'Sigrid sent me some money.' Sometimes she blurted out things she didn't mean."

Julie also told of receiving a call from Mother one day about five o'clock in the afternoon:

> It was just before she went to Florida for the last time. I know I was making vegetable soup. And she said, "Can you come down here? I'm real sick." So I turned the soup off, and it was in the fall, I think October. And I didn't want to drive down there alone. So I called my friend and I said, "Would you go with me down to Spring Grove? I have to go and see my mother." So then, when we got there, she said, "I want to come back with you." I figured she would want to, so I remember we cleaned out her refrigerator—this friend of mine helped me—and we packed her bag, and she came back with me. And the next morning I said, "Well, I think we'll take you up to Dr. Mori." She liked him so well. And she said, "No, I'm all right now." She said, "I was just lone-some. I missed Barbara so much." Barbara had already gone to Florida.

From Florida in March 1978, she wrote a birthday letter to Bill:

> I have been taking care of most of the Lee family birth-days so I must not forget yours. Paul and Margaret are back

from their trip to the Holy Land. He bought a package of slides which were on tape which I enjoyed very much. Also they read in the paper about the robbery at Tel Aviv. They had been there the day before that happened . . .

Barbara had word from her daughter in Louisville, Kentucky and will be leaving for there on Wednesday. Then I will go back to Margaret's. I expect to go home some time in April. The green grass is growing by the road sides and the azaleas are blooming. But the weather has been below freezing many times. Paul has been covering his plants by the pool many times. Florida seems to be full of people . . .

She also wrote to Elaine for her birthday that same month. I was in Europe at the time filming our Bach television movie. Elaine's note to me on the envelope said, "You may want to keep this. There may not be many more."

Dear Elaine,

This will have to be an Easter card and birthday card combined as I have neither and I have done so little letter writing since I have been in Florida. Margaret plans to write and so does Barbara but they are so busy and I guess if I try I can get something out. There have been in the past so many March birthdays but many who had them are not here any more. My oldest brother Christian's was also the 29th.

I have been quite well since I came here but you can see by my hand writing that my hand is shaky. I am still doing a lot of knitting. Margaret started an afghan for herself but has not too much time to spare so I have started on that now. I think perhaps you have seen the one I made for Naomi.

Barbara is back from a trip to Louisville, Ken., because they, the Andersons (Naomi), are transferring to Indianapolis, so Naomi had to go there house hunting and Barbara had to stay with the children. I went with Archie to the airport to pick her up. The airport at Tampa is about as complicated as the one at Kennedy.

The weather has been cold here too this winter, but of course we have not had any snow.

I have met many people I knew from other times I

have been here and many new ones. We have such a lovely church and a very good pastor but I think perhaps Bob has been to church since the new one was built. Margaret and Paul are back from the Holy Land . . . Barbara and Archie will be going home around the first of May but I will not be going home with them because they will be driving and stopping over at Indianapolis and I will go by plane to Rochester and Juliet will meet me. Juliet and Sylvia Meitrodt had a week's visit to Hawaii, which they enjoyed very much.

There have been a lot of deaths in Spring Grove since I left. I did not have the *S.G. Herald* sent down but have had letters from Nora and Inga Solum. I am enclosing a gift of five dollars, which amounts to about one dollar or less now. How long is this inflation going on?

I hope that some time I shall have the privilege of seeing Bob's creation of *The Joy of Bach.* Have a pleasant birthday, Elaine. I have not had anything personal from Bob lately which I plainly can understand.

Love,

Mother

Mathilda had flown to Florida on November 22, 1977 and returned to Minnesota on April 1, 1978. Barbara and Archie lived in the Hill 'n Dale development near Brooksville just a few hundred yards from the home Paul and Margaret had built there and Mother stayed a couple of months with each daughter and son-in-law. Margaret has described her leaving Florida for the last time:

We went to the airport. Barbara went with me and I drove. And on the way we stopped to pick up some fruit. Mother was flying up to Julie's and Barbara wanted to send some fruit. In Florida they love to have you take fruit and it's very simple—you just buy bags of it and they check them through for you. And we leisurely took our time. We had started out early. And then we got going again and when we got to the airport and parked, just as we got out of the car, Mother said to me, "Margaret, I didn't even have to tell you once to slow down!" Even though she had come almost every winter and I was no longer her youngster, she definitely was in charge of me. She never stopped being my mother. I believe I never

> quite outgrew the fact that Mother did intimidate me a bit. I let her, maybe. What do you think?

She was glad to be back with Juliet even though she enjoyed being with her Florida daughters too. She had once told Julie, "I won't ever go to a nursing home. When the time comes, I'd like to live with you."

In this last photo taken before her death in 1978, Mathilda in Florida still models the correct posture she preached all her life: "Stand up straight, stand tall! Shoulders back! Don't slouch!"

Naomi had noticed that Mother's mental acuity had eroded somewhat. For several years she sometimes might withdraw, inwardly at least, from a group she was a part of, or perhaps even sit off by herself and not participate. Naomi also became aware that Mother had suffered some memory loss.

This proved to be rather personal for Naomi that 1978 June at the time of Genevieve Glasrud's 80th birthday party in Cannon Falls, Minnesota. Niles and Naomi had come out from New Jersey for the event plus some days of vacation and when they arrived at the luncheon, Mother was there already sitting with Juliet and Barbara. Naomi greeted her effusively as usual and then moved on to others. Mother then turned to Barbara and asked, "Who was that?"

Just a few days later, we were all shocked to learn of Mother's accident. Juliet has written her recollection of and reflections on this in several of her memoirs:

> Mother was living with me that summer of 1978. We had shopped in Rochester that day for a wedding gift for one of her young friends. One night in June she got out of bed to go to the bathroom. She probably was disoriented because she accidentally opened the door to the basement and plunged to the bottom. I was awakened by a loud crash. I thought, "Oh, no!" Yes, she had fallen down the basement stairs. With a fast-beating heart I quickly ran down, covered her with a blanket and called 911. I was so relieved when the emergency group arrived almost immediately. She was taken to St. Mary's Hospital in Rochester. That was a terrible night and I've been haunted by it ever since. After calling the family, I went to Rochester to await the X-ray results. She had a broken neck.

Naomi got the news just before she and Niles were to return home. Niles had to get back to his job but Naomi came right down from Cannon Falls to Rochester to join Barbara and Julie for their vigil at St. Mary's. Ironically, this was the very time of the devastating flood that inundated some sections of Rochester and highways leading in and out of the city. Naomi phoned me. She told me she had talked to the doctor who wanted to take some "heroic measures"—surgery or brace or body cast—and told him there was no way they could permit that at her age. She survived for a week.

She was just 15 days short of achieving the age of 95 when she died on July 5, 1978.

"I doubt if anyone realizes how shattered I was by my mother's fatal fall," Juliet wrote in her 1992 *Reflections*. "I blamed myself. I should have heard her get up. Had I remembered to shut the basement door? Had I left it open? I will never know."

Certainly no one else ascribed blame to her. But we all understood how we would have felt if it had happened at our house. We could also recall Mother's own prophetic words earlier when we had worried about her going up and down those outside stairs at her Spring Grove apartment: "I haven't fallen so far and I probably won't but if I do, it's not your fault!"

* * * * *

This is the end of Mathilda's "journey"—the life story of Clara Mathilda Glasrud Lee. I wish she were here to read her own biography. I think she would approve. She had enough pride and ego to enjoy all of the attention. She would appreciate the love we all had for her. But, as a good Norwegian Lutheran, she wouldn't be able to think of herself as a worthy subject for a whole book. She took a dim view of this form of modern literature: she's on record (in her oral history interview of 1971) as saying, "You know, these biographies are often more fiction than fact."

Who could invent the story of Mathilda? It had to be lived. Throughout this narrative, the final stanza of William Cullen Bryant's poem *Thanatopsis*, a musing on death, has seemed to float above the surface of these lines like a propelling current of spiritual energy. Tillie first memorized it a century ago under the tutelage of Professor Breckenridge at his Decorah Institute. The indelible exhortation "So live . . . " followed Mathilda on her remarkable journey through life.

So live that when thy summons comes to join
The innumerable caravan that moves
To that mysterious realm, where each shall take
His chamber in the silent halls of death,
Thou go not, like the quarry-slave at night,
Scourged to his dungeon, but, sustained and soothed
By an unfaltering trust, approach thy grave
Like one who wraps the drapery of his couch
About him, and lies down to pleasant dreams.

ABOUT THE AUTHOR

Robert E. A. Lee has his roots in the environs of Spring Grove, Minnesota, the primary locale of *Mathilda's Journey*. He knew when he had first recorded an oral history interview with his mother in 1959. that someday he would have to write her story. "Suddenly, when she started describing events of her childhood and youth that I had known nothing about before, I realized that I had a rare opportunity to share this, outside the family as well as within it. She made history come alive and it was fascinating," Lee said.

After an active career as a musician, broadcaster, film and TV producer, writer and communication executive, Lee established REALWorld Communications in 1987. He continued to write for others, produce educational and religious videos, train church executives and pastors for media presentations and offer consultation services.

He has published five earlier books: *Question 7* (a novelization of the movie for which he was executive producer), *Behind the Wall* (a novel), *Martin Luther: The Reformation Years* (a visualized edition of Allan Sloane's screenplay for the movie, *Martin Luther*), *Popcorn and Parable* (a film guide co-authored with Roger Kahle) and *The Joy of Bach* (companion to his TV production, a Christmas special on PBS four years in a row.)

The radio program, *Children's Chapel*, which he originated in 1947, dramatized his scripts of Bible stories and grew to several hundred stations and continued for six years. He was a movie critic on a national radio broadcast, *Cinema Sound* during the 1970s, was film reviewer for *The Lutheran* magazine in the early 1980s and was host-producer of the cable television program *VISN on Film* for three years. He taught a course in Religion and Contemporary Cinema at Adelphi University, Garden City, NY, for three years.

Lee served as executive director of Lutheran Film Associates for 33 years and for 20 of those years was also head of communication for the Lutheran Council in the USA.

Susquehanna University honored him with a Doctor of Fine Arts degree in 1979 and he received his Bachelor of Arts from Luther College in 1942.

During World War II, Lee saw combat in the Pacific war with Japan as a patrol bomber seaplane pilot for the U.S. Navy and earned the Distinguished Flying Cross and Air Medal with three clusters.

He and his wife, Elaine, live in Baldwin, Long Island, New York. They have six adult children—Margaret Lee Yu, a designer; Barbara Greenfeldt, a teacher of French; Sigrid Lee, a musician and record producer; Richard Lee, a philosophy professor; Sylvia Lee-Thompson, a social service administrator; and Paul Lee, an electronics engineer.